Death of a "Jewish Science"

Death of a "Jewish Science"

Psychoanalysis in the Third Reich

James E. Goggin
and
Eileen Brockman Goggin

Purdue University Press

West Lafayette, Indiana

05   04   03   02   01   5   4   3   2   1

⊖   The paper used in this book meets the minimum requirements of American National Standard
for Information Sciences—Permanence of Paper for Printed Library Materials, ANSI Z39.48-1992.

Printed in the United States of America

Library of Congress Cataloging-in-Publication Data

Goggin, James E., 1940-
Death of a "Jewish science" : psychoanalysis in the Third Reich /
James E.Goggin and Eileen Brockman Goggin.
p.   cm.
Includes bibliographical references and index.
ISBN 1-55753-193-5 (alk. paper)
1. Psychoanalysis—Germany—History.   2. Psychoanalysis—Political aspects—
Germany—History.   3. National socialism.   4. Deutsche Psychoanalytische Gesellschaft—
History.   I. Goggin, Eileen Brockman, 1941-   II. Title.
RC503.G63   2000
616.89'17'0943—dc21   99-050840

Designed and composed by inari in Bloomington, Indiana.

Dedication

The quintessential values of love, truth, work, and democracy were the most significant motivating forces behind this project. Those values were taught to us by our parents whose day-to-day lives characterized these beliefs and values. We humbly dedicate this book to the memories of Elizabeth Huber Goggin, Gertrude Greenstein Brockman, Mark Brockman, and James A. Goggin. Their lives continue to serve as a beacon to the meaning of commitment.

Dedication

CONTENTS

ACKNOWLEDGMENTS

This book took twelve years from its inspiration and initial conceptualization to publication. The authors are neither psychoanalysts nor historians.
We are psychologists who practice psychoanalytically informed psychotherapy. When we decided that we wanted to write a book about the fate of
psychoanalysis during the Third Reich, we realized we would need to con-
sult a variety of professional historians and psychoanalysts. We also found it
necessary to acquire the help of a translator, and at one point we needed
our own editor. It is with humility and respect that we express our gratitude
to the long list of talented people who have encouraged and helped us, and
made this book possible.

Early on we were given access to a veritable treasure trove of correspondence among Ernest Jones, Anna Freud, and Sigmund Freud at the
Archives of the British Psycho-Analytical Society in London. Jill Duncan
ably showed us how to find the then recently computerized correspondence
and made the search easier. We quote from this correspondence with the
kind permission of Riccardo Steiner, the present Honorary Archivist of the
Archives of the British Psycho-Analytical Society. Permission to cite the
Rickman Report and include the entire Rickman Report in the appendix
was generously given by John Rickman's daughter, Lucy Rickman Baruch
and Pearl King, former Honorary Archivist of the Archives of the British
Psycho-Analytical Society. We are particularly grateful to Lucy Rickman
Baruch for correcting some misconceptions we had, and to Pearl King for
sending us additional material.

It was our great fortune to have contacted Judith Kestenberg, an
internationally renowned scholar and psychoanalyst. She had all the basic
qualifications needed to help us initiate our project. Judith Kestenberg
had completed her medical education and neurological training in Vienna
during the 1930s. She was well aware of the political forces within the city
and was a member of a party committed to a democratic and humanitarian form of government. She completed her psychoanalytic training after
immigrating to the United States in 1937. She was an acknowledged
leader and the inspirational force for an ongoing study of how the trauma
of Holocaust victims was transmitted from one generation to the next.
Her involvement in studies of children of the Nazi perpetrators kept her

in touch with the German psychoanalytic community. During the early phases of our study she gave freely of her time providing us with information relevant to plan our project and also reviewed the initial drafts of our manuscript. Dr. Kestenberg then provided us with an invaluable introduction to one of the leading psychoanalysts in Berlin. Her encouragement has been a vital influence in our completing the project. We felt a profound sense of loss when we learned of Judith Kestenberg's passing in January 1999.

Ludger Hermanns is a distinguished German psychoanalyst who practices in Berlin. When we contacted him in 1991 he generously sent us a copy of a fundamental book on our topic, referred to in English as *The Catalog*. He also set up an interview for us with Regine Lockot, who he described as the "outstanding researcher" on the fate of psychoanalysis during the Third Reich. Regine Lockot has been an invaluable source of help to us. Many of our formulations were influenced by Regine Lockot's work in this area, particularly her books and articles. She also graciously gave us two interviews and took the time to respond to our correspondence over the years. Regine Lockot also provided us with the kind of perspective necessary to understand how the German psychoanalysts experienced life during the Third Reich on a day-to-day basis. That kind of empathetic stance is a necessary prerequisite if we are to avoid allowing our knowledge of how things turned out to overly bias our judgment and understanding of events during that period.

We had the experience of spending many hours discussing our work with two exceptional historians. Paul Roazen is a world-class historian whose special area of study is psychoanalysis. He provided us with a basic overview of the essential sources we needed to understand the history of the earliest two psychoanalytic institutes, in Vienna and Berlin respectively. He also helped us to conceptualize how to present our findings. Otto Nelson was our consulting historian on the period of the Third Reich. He carefully reviewed our later manuscripts and provided us with an essential awareness of the basic historical facts and sources of information that were relevant to our study of the Göring Institute. Otto Nelson helped us understand German history in the kind of depth and scope that was essential for our project. He was generous with his help and guidance and became a good friend in the process. We are in his debt.

Martin Wangh, M.D., is a psychoanalytic scholar who was born in Germany, trained in the United States, and now lives in Jerusalem. Our correspondence with him provided us a unique overview of the painful events surrounding the first international psychoanalytic meeting to be held in Germany since World War II. Martin Wangh has been involved in the very painful process of working through the intense problems existing between German and Jewish psychoanalysts. His critical review and comments about our manuscript corrected misconceptions and provided useful insights.

Michael Gorkin became involved in our project in the spring of 1997 when it became clear that our manuscript had expanded to an inordinate length and had started to lose its essential focus. Michael Gorkin is a psychoanalyst turned writer who has unique editing skills that enabled us to prune the manuscript to a workable size. We are thankful to both Martin Nass, who teaches at the N.Y.U. post-doctoral psychoanalytic program and Michael Moskowitz for helping us find Michael Gorkin.

It was clear at the start of our project that we would need a translator to help us with the large number of documents, articles, and books we needed to review that were written in German. Jürgen Heise was the right person for the job. He was born and raised in Germany. He has a good understanding of technical terms and teaches in the English department at Texas Tech University. He was another invaluable expert who was connected to our project.

Geoffrey Cocks's diligent research resulting in his 1985 book inspired our interest in the subject, and he has generously commented on the final version of the manuscript. We also owe a debt of gratitude to Hannah S. Decker whose participation as a discussant in a symposium at the Texas Psychological Association's annual convention on November 14, 1998, made a significant contribution to our book. She helped clarify for us a more nuanced conception of the difference between our interpretation and that of Geoffrey Cocks. In 1991, David G. Marwell, director of the Berlin Document Center (BDC), gave us access to the archival information, answered our questions, and continued to respond to our requests after we returned to the United States. We would like to express our appreciation to Peter Gay, who took the time to read an early and unsolicited draft of our manuscript in 1994. His encouragement and comments were helpful.

It is with sincere pleasure that we have the opportunity to thank the various members of the Purdue University Press for taking an interest in our manuscript and for deciding to publish it. Thomas Bacher, director, and Suzanne Wilson, acquisitions editor, helped guide us through the initial stages of the process. It is hard to overestimate the importance of the contribution of a good editor to a book. Margaret Hunt, our editor at Purdue University Press, was patient with the many questions of two neophyte writers. Her enthusiasm, insightful guidance and good cheer are greatly appreciated. We are also thankful to John McGuigan of Inari Information Services for the way he copyedited our manuscript. His careful reading of the manuscript, and his insightful suggestions regarding style and structure helped us achieve a more readable end product.

Zvi Lothane has been a steady source of support, useful references, intellectual stimulation, and sage advice. Our remarkable chance encounter with Peter Happel, dubbed the "Congress Baby" of the VIII International Psychoanalytical Congress by Sigmund Freud (Brecht et al. 1985, 90–91), would prove most enlightening. As the son of the émigré psychoanalyst, Clara Happel, he helped us better understand the difficult circumstances related to the émigrés' departure from Germany and the subtleties of their perspective as they looked back on Germany. Another chance meeting, this time with Leigh McCullough-Vaillant on an airplane, led to numerous contacts with publishers. We greatly appreciate her enthusiastic support.

Alain de Mijolla, president of the International Association for the History of Psychoanalysis, provided us with useful references and put us in contact with Elisabeth Roudinesco. We are grateful to both of these individuals who took the time to review our project and provided us important feedback.

Sanford Gifford has made useful comments, provided rare sources of information and has been most generous with his time. Verena Michels, Richard Sterba's daughter, was kind enough to help us understand a letter written to her father from Müller-Braunschweig.

In the early phases of our project Michael Molnar read our manuscript and gave us his time and valuable advise.

The senior author's old friends from Muhlenberg College—Ted Wachs, Bob Karp and Robert Levine—all provided very useful comments and other valuable help. Ted Wachs, who teaches at Purdue University, made the effort to take our manuscript to the Purdue University Press. Cliff and Syliva Ashby, friends and both experienced authors, spent many nights offering us invaluable suggestions and encouragement at various phases during the project. We are in their debt.

The members of the Southwest Psychotherapy Study Group in Lubbock heard numerous presentations on the topics of our manuscript and made several suggestions that were incorporated in the book. We would like to thank the students that helped us over the long years of this project who acted as research assistants. They are Cathy York, Brett Jacobson, Lindsey Walker, Kristy Parsons, Amanda Summers, and especially Mark Trittipo. The access we were given to the Texas Tech University Library and the Texas

Tech University Health Science Center Library was crucial to the carrying out of our research. Their staffs were always ready to lend assistance.

We would like to thank our typist, Lois Tanner, who has typed the innumerable drafts of this manuscript. Her efficiency and skill were indispensable. She has traveled this long road with us and has been there when we needed her.

Finally, we wish to thank the friends, too numerous to mention, who have offered support and encouragement along the way. Despite all the advice and generous help we received, the responsibility for all interpretations and any errors are entirely ours.

ABBREVIATIONS

AÄGP   *Allgemeine Ärztliche Gesellschaft für Psychotherapie* (General Medical Society for Psychotherapy)

BDC   Berlin Document Center. An archive in Berlin-Zehlendorf established after the end of World War II under the auspices of the U.S. Army, turned over to the German government on July 1, 1994.

BPI   *Berliner Psychoanalytisches Institut* (Berlin Psychoanalytic Institute)

DAÄGP   *Deutsche Allgemeine Ärztliche Gesellschaft für Psychotherapie* (German General Medical Society for Psychotherapy)

DAF   *Deutsche Arbeitsfront* (German Labour Front)

DPG   *Deutsche Psychoanalytische Gesellschaft* (German Psychoanalytical Society)

DPO   *Diplom Prüfungsordnung.* A diploma marking psychology as an independent profession created on June 16, 1941.

DPV   *Deutsche Psychoanalytische Vereinigung* (German Psychoanalytical Association)

GPRB   German Personnel Research Branch of the Control Committee. Established by Allied powers after the defeat of Germany for the purpose of finding Germans who did not approve of Hitler's regime and thus could be employed in rebuilding postwar Germany.

IPA   International Psychoanalytic Association

KGB   Soviet State security organization, founded as the Cheka in 1917. The Cheka was supplanted by the OGPU in 1923. The OGPU was absorbed into the NKVD in 1934 and renamed the KGB in 1954.

KPD   *Kommunistische Partei Deutschlands* (Communist Party of Germany). Formed in 1918. Had direct links to Moscow and promoted revolutionary change (violent overthrow of the Weimar Republic).

NS   *Nationalsozialismus* (National Socialism)

NSDAP   *Nationalsozialistische Deutsche Arbeiterpartei* (German National Socialist Party)

NSV   *Nationalsozialistische Volkswohlfahrt* (National Socialist People's Welfare Organization)

OKW   *Oberkommando der Wehrmacht* (High Command of the German Armed Forces)

RAF   Royal Air Force of Great Britain

SA   *Sturmabteilung.* An organization of storm troopers known as "brownshirts," formed prior to Hitler's being named chancellor. Their purpose was to take on and defeat communists.

SD   *Sicherheitsdienst.* An intelligence service of the SS, headed by Reinhard Heydrich. Used terror tactics, thought-control, and in general served as an instrument of totalitarian control.

SPD   *Sozialdemokratische Partei Deutschlands* (Social Democrat Party of Germany). A moderate Marxist party promoting more gradual change within Germany.

SS   *Schutzstaffel.* An elite paramilitary organization, formed in 1923, known as "blackshirts." Started as the personal bodyguard for Adolf Hitler, but under Heinrich Himmler grew into a huge organization that incorporated a major part of the German army, a vast secret police network, and the government agencies responsible for planning and implementing the "Final Solution."

USSR   Union of Soviet Socialist Republics. Major communist power beginning in 1917 with the Bolshevik Revolution in Russia, officially constituted in 1923 and disbanded in 1991.

WPV   *Wiener Psychoanalytische Vereinigung* (Vienna Psychoanalytical Association)

Death
of a
"Jewish
Science"

Introduction

DURING THE LAST TWENTY YEARS, some twenty professional articles and four books have been published on the history of the Berlin Psychoanalytic Institute (BPI) during the Third Reich. The great majority of these publications have been written in the last twelve years. An American historian, Geoffrey Cocks, and a German psychoanalyst, Regine Lockot, have each published two authoritative books on the subject, and an American, Edith Kurzweil, has written a comparative review of psychoanalysis which also examines this Institute. Perhaps the outstanding historical evaluation and description of the events affecting the BPI during the Third Reich is a compilation of original documents pertaining to the Nazi rise to power and impact on the BPI and psychoanalysis during the Third Reich. This document has been nicknamed *The Catalog*, and its five editors were K. Brecht, V. Friedrich, L. M. Hermanns, I. J. Kaminer, and D. H. Juelich. It was published both in English and German. Its purpose was to provide information requested by the International Psychoanalytical Association (IPA) in 1977 regarding the German Psychoanalytic Institute's collaboration with the Nazis during the Third Reich. A conference in Hamburg was held in 1985 in response to that same mandate during which seminars, conferences and presentations explored the Nazi impact on psychoanalysis. The conference included an exhibition of documents and pictures, and *The Catalog* was a companion to this exhibition. Another project with great promise was started by four psychoanalysts connected to the William Alanson White Institute. They published several articles between 1975 and 1985 in American psychoanalytic journals. The German journal *Psyche* has consistently published articles debating this topic and devoted one whole issue to it. In addition, various authors publishing biographies on Freud have made judgments about the continuity of psychoanalysis during the Third Reich.

What was so special about the Berlin Psychoanalytical Institute before and during the Third Reich that it would generate so much literature following the war and would provoke such an emotional debate? Since Freud was the dominant architect in designing and establishing the theory and practice of psychoanalysis, and he was centered in Vienna, how important could the BPI be? What was there about the BPI that differentiated it from the Vienna Institute? What accounts for the inordinate research on the BPI? To start to answer these important questions, a larger perspective is needed.

One of the unending difficulties in understanding the individual psychoanalyst's personal response to the events that transformed the Berlin Psychoanalytic Institute (BPI) into the Göring Institute is assessing the role of the continual trauma that the Third Reich had on each psychoanalyst. The initial problems evaluating these individual reactions during that period have become increasingly more complex, particularly since the people are no longer alive, and there are no clinical data in the traditional sense in which that term is used. Hampering efforts to study an individual psychoanalyst's attempt to work within the totalitarian nature of the Third Reich has been the lack of availability of his or her free associations, dreams, transference reactions, resistance, and the relatively unstructured nature of the psychoanalytic situations from which valid interpretations could emerge. Thus, the very core of psychoanalytic techniques are unavailable to study any individual psychoanalyst of that period.

What we need to establish at the outset of our study is that none of the individuals we will discuss were major perpetrators of the Nazi horrors. As we researched the individual German gentile psychoanalysts at the Göring Institute to assess their degree of collaboration with the Third Reich, we found that none of these individuals could be characterized as perpetrators of atrocities on the level of Adolf Hitler, Adolf Eichmann, Hermann Göring, Heinrich Himmler, or Josef Mengele. In our reading of Regine Lockot's books and articles on the biographical data of the most significant gentile psychoanalysts who chose to stay and practice in Berlin after Hitler came to power, the pictures that emerge are of individuals with ordinary backgrounds and lifestyles. The more we learned, the more we saw a complex picture of varying degrees of collaboration and resistance, degrees of cowardice, betrayal, and attempts to stand one's ground, degrees of pragmatic ambition, careerism, and misplaced idealism.

The purpose of this investigation is to determine whether or not psychoanalysis survived during the Third Reich at the Göring Institute, as has been proposed in the historical and psychoanalytical literature during the past twenty-five years. The question of a profession's survival is one of great complexity and has been examined using various methodologies. What methods are available to study the transformation of the BPI into the Göring Institute during the Third Reich? How did some come to conclude psychoanalysis survived? There is the method of institutional and structural analysis that Geoffrey Cocks (1983; 1985) has used, and which led him to the conclusion that the Third Reich witnessed the professional and institutional development of psychotherapy (Cocks 1985, 4). Cocks makes the case that the profession of psychoanalysis survived by becoming integrated with other forms of psychotherapy which continued to be practiced, and made gains in professional development from 1933 to 1945 (Cocks 1985, 252). In proposing that psychoanalysis survived, the essential criterion for verification rests upon a structural analysis of the institution that demonstrated its continuity of function as an organization over time. The point is made that the psychoanalysts and psychotherapists made their successful survival "within, and often against, the medical establishment in Germany between 1933 and 1945." (Cocks 1985, 5). However, the bottom line of using this institutional analysis method has been its reliance on overarching sociological explanations of events to demonstrate survival, and therefore it does not adequately examine individual personality factors and human motivation. Perhaps it could be stated that a structural analysis of social conditions represents a necessary condition upon which individual motivation and decisions must be evaluated, but it is not a sufficient condition. An institutional analysis never deals adequately with the matter of personal responsibility for decisions.

From our perspective any means that explains institutional functions in a way that marginalizes individual responsibility, however informative, is inadequate and incomplete. If the period of the Third Reich has demonstrated nothing else, it has clearly documented that its organizations were led by individuals who were responsible for the decisions and the actions that followed. In Germany, the idea of individual responsibility for the crimes committed by the Nazis was never lost. After eleven years of whitewashing murder, the Nazis had not destroyed the idea of responsibility. Studying the behavior of the German citizenry during the Third Reich's rule reveals more conformity than any widespread willingness to sacrifice one's life. This characterization may differ from other societies at other times only in degree. Those individuals who dared defy Hitler are worthy of remembrance. Among those exceptional people who had clung to the civilized belief of individual responsibility for murder of innocents and other war crimes committed by Nazis in the name of the German people were the conspirators of the July 20, 1944, plot to kill Hitler. If one reads the small details of the officers' plot of July 20, many of the principles upon which they justified their intention to kill Hitler were based upon the doctrine of natural law and laws generally accepted by the community of nations. It was their intention that all those guilty of murder, with the exception of only those whose very lives were threatened, would be tried for their actions. Following orders from supervisors would not suffice to justify or alleviate anyone of personal responsibility in such acts (Hoffman 1977). If this small minority of the German military and civilian members of the resistance could cling to the rule of law and the belief in individual responsibility during the horrors of the Third Reich, how could we do less?

Since the end of World War II, it has become obvious that for civilization to continue to exist the lessons of both the loss of individual rights and the general failure of individual responsibility during the Third Reich must be understood in order to prevent such a catastrophe from being repeated. It is our major assumption that institutions are organized and operated by human beings who are responsible for the decisions that are made and carried out. The psychological theories we believe that can best begin to explain the depth and range of human behavior are the various models of psychoanalysis. Yet, even a sophisticated understanding of drive, classical, ego, object relations, and the "self" school of psychoanalytic thought can provide only a relatively limited way to assess psychological responsibility.

When we turn to Sigmund Freud for his perspective on using psychoanalysis to understand human behavior from a historical vantage point, we are immediately confronted with the limitations he placed on psychoanalytic reconstruction. Freud spoke of this in a letter to the English biographer Lytton Strachey. The 1928 letter compliments Strachey:

> You recognize what historians are otherwise apt to ignore, that it is impossible to understand the past with any certainty, because we cannot guess at men's motives and their mental processes, and so cannot interpret their actions. . . . So the people of times past are to us like dreams for which we are given no associations, and only laymen can expect us to interpret dreams like that. Thus you show yourself to be a historian imbued with the spirit of psychoanalysis. (Freud to Strachey, December 25, 1928, in Freud, E., Freud, L., and Grubrich-Simitis 1985, 1:244)

Freud was more adamant when he warned Arnold Zweig regarding the pitfalls in application of psychoanalytic principles in the service of biography. In the letter to Zweig, Freud indicated:

> [Y]ou who have so many more attractive and important things to do, who can appoint kings and survey the brutal folly of mankind from the height of a watch-tower! No, I am far too fond of you to allow such a thing to happen. Anyone turning biographer commits himself to lies, to concealment, to hypocrisy, to flattery, and even to hiding his own lack of understanding for biographical truth is not to be had, and even if it were it couldn't be used. (Freud to Arnold Zweig, May 31, 1936, in E. Freud 1960, 460)

In pointing out these limitations, Freud was also protecting his own privacy. Zweig had suggested that he become Freud's biographer, and the founder of psychoanalysis had responded in horror. However, it is important to realize that at times Freud was the master of the principle "do what I say, not what I do." His collaboration with W. C. Bullitt on the personality of Woodrow Wilson (Freud and Bullitt 1967) is the prime example of what poor psychohistory is all about. On the other hand, his brilliance in *Civilization and Its Discontents* (1930) in warning the world of the awesome destruction that human beings are capable of is the other side of the coin. Psychoanalysis used with restraint and with a full appreciation of the subject matter can be a very powerful and constructive tool in understanding a wide variety of phenomena.

There is a literature generated by several prominent psychoanalysts who have demonstrated the ways in which psychoanalytic theory could be coupled with accurate historical evidence to yield productive and significant research studies. Erik Erikson's study of Gandhi is a remarkable example of psychoanalysis being used to explore how a great religious leader would find creative solutions to complex ethical problems. In his biographical research, Erikson used historical facts, the interview method, as well as his own variation of psychoanalytically informed theory to understand the individuals he was studying (Erikson 1963; 1964; 1975).

Saul Friedländer has pointed out that Erikson did not always use facts to guide how he came to conclusions. In Erikson's study of Martin Luther (1958), Friedländer indicates that "Erikson literally invents little Martin's relation to his mother, using as a basis (as a 'document') the behavior of Luther the man." By reconstructing Luther's early interactions with his mother from a presumed characteristic of Luther "is enough to make the most well-disposed historians shudder" (Friedländer 1993, 27). We agree that this kind of elaboration of a family interaction from an initial theoretical construct can hardly be considered history. We also concur with Hannah S. Decker, who pointed to the trouble historians have in trusting the reliability of interview data where the questions touch upon the individual's feelings of "personal shame, sorrow, or defiance" (Decker 1998).

Despite the kind of unacceptable reconstructions identified above we have utilized many of Erikson's principles to serve this study. To use psychoanalytic theory to understand history, it is crucial to accept that each individual's action within a culture is an interaction that is part of a particular historical moment. It must be assumed that each age develops its own form of interplay between individuals, leaders, institutions, and the given political actuality within a nation. We have used an approach similar to Erikson's in combining the interview method, the psychoanalytic theory of personality, and reviews of known factual information to provide answers that neither history nor psychology alone could provide. Furthermore, as Erikson noted, to study history from a psychoanalytic perspective requires an acute awareness of one's irrational attitudes and emotions—that is, countertransference—about the period under study. And perhaps, no other historical period evokes more countertransference than that of the Third Reich.

A prime example of the influence of such countertransference is the 1994 book *Ein Jahrhundert Psychoanalytische Bewegung in Deutschland: Die Psychotherapie unter dem Einfluß Freuds* by Annemarie Dührssen (Dührssen 1994). Annemarie Dührssen is an important German psychoanalyst who was trained during WWII at the Göring Institute. She was a student of Harald Schultz-Hencke, whose "neo-analysis" represented a departure from Freudian psychoanalysis. Dührssen has been considered one of Germany's best psychoanalysts after the war, and was one of the leaders who enabled psychoanalysis to be designated as a medical specialty and, therefore, be covered under the medical insurance plan. That this book was published by a reputable scientific press in Germany augments the controversy that has followed its publication. The view she presents of the last century of psychoanalysis and the influence of Freud can arguably be seen as a reenactment of the Nazi attacks against the Jews. In his review essay of the book, Lars Rensmann, a political psychology instructor at the Free University of Berlin, described it as a revisionist history in which

> the reader is confronted with a subjective concoction: an idiosyncratically inspired down playing of National Socialism combined with particularly anti-Semitic stereotypes that go far beyond subtle prejudices in their openness and shamelessness. (Rensmann 1996, 197-206)

Dührssen asks if early psychoanalysis under the influence of Freud was a "Jewish science" (Dührssen 1994, 184–98), a phrase used by the National Socialists themselves. Her claim is that by eliminating the Jewish psychoanalysts from practicing in Germany, the Nazis stripped the psychoanalytic movement of the "elite, conspiratorial" sect (i.e., the Jews) that was dominating it. Furthermore, the removal of the Jewish analysts allowed the remaining German gentile analysts to defend the principles of the Enlightenment against the irrational, mystical Jungians. She claims that after the war the émigré psychoanalysts were enraged that psychoanalysis survived and flourished without them and their special group dynamic, and that through the International Psychoanalytic Association (IPA) they tried to take hold of the former German "colony" in 1951. Rensmann concludes that Dührssen's account "outdoes most revisionists and their publications on the extreme right, such as Ernst Nolte" (Rensmann 1996, 205). Her portrayal gives us a small taste of what intellectual life must have been like at the Göring Institute.

In Cocks's even-handed and scholarly review of Dührssen's book (Cocks 1994, 207–15), he also comments on the presence of prejudiced stereotypes and lack of sensitivity. But he suggests that some attempts to assess Dührssen's motives are "hard to document convincingly and has at least the whiff of the ad hominem about it" (p. 212). He finds that what is valuable about her account is the placement of psychoanalysis "within a larger context of developments in the realm of medical psychology in the twentieth century" (Cocks 1994, 213). He concludes that

> while Dührssen's book does offer some general historical context as well
> as some illuminating discussion of the politics of postwar public policy
> regarding psychoanalysis and psychotherapy, a much better source . . .
> can be found in Lockot's two books. (Cocks 1994, 215)

That Dührssen's book and its vision has found an audience in the last decade of the twentieth century is a testament to the difficulties involved in understanding that period. The obstacles to a reasonably objective understanding, be they countertransference to the period or the impact of "shame, horror or defiance" (Decker 1998) on memory, are hard to overcome. It is with considerable trepidation that we now enter into the debate.

Throughout this book we attempt to be as objective as possible, at the same time making clear our own political and moral values. In assessing the transformations—and continuities—within the psychoanalytic community in Germany during the Third Reich, we have arrived at one central conclusion: namely, the major ideas and world view represented by the psychoanalytic movement did not, and could not, survive in Nazi Germany. As we hope to make evident, the very nature of totalitarianism during the Third Reich renders it highly unlikely, if not impossible, for psychoanalysis to be permitted and practiced. While Nazi Germany was never a perfect totalitarian state, the fact that psychoanalysis was considered a "Jewish science" and drew the attention of the Nazi leadership (Cocks 1997, 199–200) meant it fell under the regime's harshest racial policies that were systematically enforced. Despite the heroic attempts of a few individuals in Nazi Germany to keep psychoanalysis alive, the psychoanalytic movement did not survive during those years. In examining how and why this was so, we hope to shed further light on that darkness that was the Third Reich; and above all, we hope to clarify the ways and means by which the profession of psychoanalysis, as we know it, was extinguished in that darkness.

Part 1
The Background

1

The Way They Were

The Berlin Psychoanalytical Institute (BPI) Emerges as a Role Model for the Profession

ON NOVEMBER 22, 1909, C. G. JUNG wrote an important letter to Freud after having participated in a Swiss psychiatry conference held in Zürich. In that letter, Jung announced, "[Y]our, that is, our cause is winning all along the line, so that we had the last word, in fact we're on top of the world." He further elaborated that "[T]he psychiatrists' society is ours." In this professional battleground over theory, there exists only "Freud and Antifreud." Apparently, with Switzerland now conquered, Jung concluded, "Now it's Germany's turn" (McGuire 1988, 268). While this letter reveals Jung's own intensely competitive nature, he correctly identified the next important country in which the psychoanalytic movement was to spread. Freud accepted the challenge. He answered Jung's letter by stating, "So Germany is coming along! Aren't we (justifiably) childish to get so much pleasure out of every least bit of recognition, when in reality it matters so little and our ultimate conquest of the world still lies so far ahead?" (McGuire 1988, 272). After Jung had turned away from psychoanalysis in 1913, Freud hoped he could be replaced by the Berlin Psychoanalytic Society (Lockot 1985, 40).

During the 1920s and early 1930s the BPI became the most highly developed psychoanalytic center in the world; even though Vienna had its own fine institute (Roazen 1992a, 183-84), Berlin had the unique combination of funds, clinical expertise, and administrative leadership that brought together from all over Europe a talented group of intellectuals who were interested in psychoanalysis. The organizational structure of the BPI helped it become the role model for all future psychoanalytic training centers.

The reason that the BPI attracted some of the most gifted students during the 1920s was due, in large part, to Karl Abraham's exceptional ability as a clinician and organizer. In 1907, Abraham had come to Freud and asked for his advice and help in establishing a psychoanalytic career in Berlin. Freud was pleased to support the idea of a Berlin branch of psychoanalysis and encouraged Abraham to follow through with his plans. Hannah Decker (1977) considers the date Abraham set up his practice of psychoanalysis in Berlin in December 1907 as a significant landmark in the history of psychoanalysis in Germany: "Before that year Freud had a small number of supporters, admirers, and imitators in Germany, but he had no disciple who had received his official approval" (Decker 1977, 19). Yet, Freud's appreciation of Abraham was always more restrained than for some of his more colorful followers. When one compares the correspondence between Freud and Jung with that of Freud and Abraham on the issue of establishing psychoanalysis in Germany, it is obvious that Jung's more assertive style and higher degree of self-confidence elicited a livelier and more favorable response from the founder of psychoanalysis. Freud not only supported Jung's dreams of conquest, but he seemed to join him in spirit, albeit with a greater sense of irony and distance.

Two years earlier, Freud had responded to an older and more mature Abraham in a cautious way. Nonetheless, it was Abraham who would bring psychoanalysis into the establishment in Germany in a remarkably short period of time. Abraham's success was achieved by inviting his medical colleagues who were interested in psychoanalysis into his home for challenging intellectual discussions, and he went so far as to have a lively debate on Freud's theories. Abraham also set up courses for doctors to keep them informed of Freud's latest work (Kurzweil 1989).

When Abraham took on the medical establishment, he was actually going against Freud's advice. Although Freud thought Abraham could not convince the German physicians of the psychoanalytic cause and that he should appeal directly to the public to win acceptance, Abraham was able to win sufficient support from the medical community to attract young physicians. One of Abraham's greatest strengths was his capacity to trust his own judgment rather than rely solely on Freud's. The ultimate success of psychoanalysis in Berlin was, ironically, Freud's underestimation of Abraham and his idealization of Jung. In Jung's correspondence with Freud,

Jung's description of conquering Germany for psychoanalysis was premature. He would follow up on his own advice only in the 1930s, but then only for his own cause. Jung's description of his conquest of Swiss psychiatrists at Zürich and his future campaign plans to conquer Germany were noteworthy for their bluster and bravado.

During the 1920s the major challenge facing psychoanalysis was coming to terms with Freud's increasing age and the fact that he would no longer be able to personally guide the growth of the profession he developed as he had done in the past. Therefore, the major task would be to determine the nature of training that would be required for future psychoanalysts and how that training would be conducted. There was the problem with "wild analysis" and eclectic training centers starting up all over Europe and the United States—for example, London's Tavistock. Psychoanalysis was faced with establishing the organizational framework to cope with the growth of the movement. These issues were faced at an IPA congress in 1918, just before the end of World War I. The congress was held in Budapest in September, and Freud set a quietly optimistic mood during his remarks about the movement's future. Freud stated his belief that psychoanalysis would eventually be available to individuals of all social classes in private and government supported programs. In 1918, Freud considered the obligation of the state urgent and revealed the liberal side of his political philosophy in regard to the state's responsibility to provide medical care for indigent patients when he argued, "[A]t some point this must occur" (Gifford 1994, 650). With Freud's increasing age and limitations in directing the growth of psychoanalytic institutes, the fifth IPA Congress recognized the need to organize systematic training approaches for analysts. The basic training standards would require that every analyst have a training analysis and that local institutes and societies should be established to teach courses and conduct seminars for analysts in training, and ensure that all future analysts have supervised control analysis. (Control analysis is the analysis of a patient made by a trainee under supervision.)

In 1920, Max Eitingon, along with Karl Abraham, became the prime movers in establishing the Berlin Psychoanalytic Institute. Just as the independently wealthy Hungarian analyst Lajos Levy had been an early financial benefactor for the Vienna Society, so would Max Eitingon provide financial backing for the Berlin Institute (Roazen 1993, 109). Eitingon was building on the work of Abraham, who had established the Berlin Psychoanalytic Society on August 21, 1908, and had singlehandedly advanced the interest of psychoanalysis at medical meeting after medical meeting in which he faced fierce and bitter opposition; but his intellectual integrity and determination won increasingly greater respect among his medical colleagues. And, ultimately, it was under his and Eitingon's stewardship that the BPI became *the* leading training center for psychoanalysis in Europe.

In order to understand the difficulties involved in the BPI's establishment during this particular era, the turmoil of the national government and the chaos in the streets of Berlin have to be appreciated. To grow and prosper, the BPI required a sophisticated organizational structure, but most important, a stable milieu was needed. The stability was to come from the unique group of individuals who had been drawn to the BPI. The national government and the climate of Berlin from 1918 to 1933 was anything but stable.

What were Berlin and Germany like from 1918 to 1933? In the first place the emergence of the Weimar Republic, a real democracy, would only follow Germany's defeat in World War I. From the start, the Republic was on shaky footing, and until it collapsed in 1933, it never steadied itself. Political threats—putsches and revolutions—from both the Right and Left were an ever-looming menace. Contributing to this political instability were the financial crises that beset the Weimar Republic.

Two economic crises occurred during the fourteen years of the Weimar Republic's existence. The first one was the inflation of the early 1920s leading to the hyperinflation of 1923, a time when people literally brought suitcases of money to banks, and people were paid not by the week or by the day, but by the half-day because money was being devalued so quickly. By using a combination of dramatic financial reforms, the hyperinflation was brought under control within a relatively short period of time, but the social problems that emerged would also create a great degree of political instability. With life savings gone, and no jobs for a large portion of older German men, an increasing bitterness and rage affected many individuals and families. What was gained in financial stability probably created an even greater degree of social and political instability. Of course, there lay ahead the Great Depression, which would doubly hurt because it would be the second time in less than ten years that a major economic disaster would befall the German people. It was this crisis that provided Hitler the political instability enabling National Socialism to rise from what was considered a crackpot party in 1928 to become the largest political party in 1932.

Nonetheless, within this unstable political economic framework, there was a flourishing cultural life. The period of the 1920s was called the "Golden Twenties," and the city of Berlin was referred to as the "Babylon-on-the-Spree." In 1919, a major invasion of foreigners arrived in Berlin.

These were White Russians fleeing the civil war that was being lost to the Bolsheviks. Some fifty thousand Russians came to Berlin that year. They brought not only their own lost cause, but the lost cause of the czar, and with them came the message of the impending demise of all European royalty. But some White Russians also brought with them hopes of a better future, including people like Konstantin W. Stanislavski with his Moscow Arts Theater, the film director Sergei Eisenstein, the painter Vasili Kandinski, and the pianist Vladimir Horowitz.

At this time Berlin started to be called a "cultural supernova" (Read and Fisher 1994, 171). The arts and sciences were bursting all over the city. The theater of Berlin flourished with thirty-five packed houses operating every night. Bertolt Brecht's great hit of 1928, *The Three Penny Opera,* would become world-renowned. Berlin was the center of German film, with *The Cabinet of Dr. Caligari* and *The Blue Angel* being competitive with the best of Hollywood's output. There were three major opera companies in Berlin, and the sciences were represented by Albert Einstein and Max Planck, who worked in Berlin on their scientific and academic research. A new school of architectural style, the "Bauhaus Movement," also emerged in Berlin. When Otto Friedrich wrote his book on Berlin, *Before the Deluge* (1972), he interviewed many of the celebrated Jews who had been forced to become émigrés and flee to the United States when Hitler came to power. Many of the émigrés described Berlin as if it were a "moveable feast" (Friedrich 1972, 11). "It was a Renaissance," said Sol Hurok, "the greatest Renaissance in this century" (Friedrich 1972, 11). When Friedrich interviewed Rabbi Joachim Prinz, the president of the American Jewish Congress, Prinz said, "[I]f I could choose a time to live, any time, any place, I'd choose the 1920s in Berlin" (Friedrich 1972, 11).

It was within this atmosphere of cultural ferment and political upheaval that the BPI established itself. The cultural openness contributed to attracting some of the finest people to Berlin, but in the end it was the intellectual stimulation and the organization's strength that would put the final stamp on the BPI's development. As if to underline the continual instability surrounding the development of the BPI, on its very first day operating as an Institute in March 1920, with Karl Abraham giving his first lecture, the famous Kapp Putsch began. A general strike by the socialists was called and the former Freikorps were sent to crush it. These ultraconservative forces marched on Berlin in perfect parade ground order with their banners flowing and their nationalist symbols in full view. As the attack on the city continued, and the strike was on, Abraham gave his lecture. The strike continued for six days, during which Berlin was occupied by the Freikorps. For six days no municipal services were available; nothing worked or moved. After six days, with Berlin paralyzed, the Freikorps marched out as if they had won (Read and Fisher 1994, 166–67).

In 1920, Max Eitingon donated the first public psychoanalytic poly-clinic and teaching facility in the world. This generous gift set the stage for what would follow (Lockot 1985, 41). The BPI began to acquire the very best young candidates, who were attracted by the free expression of ideas and avant-garde atmosphere.

One of the primary motives in establishing the BPI was to provide some form of psychoanalytically informed treatment to everyone who was willing to come. While the BPI was excluded from medical insurance in Germany at that time, the clinic was financed by Eitingon, and each of the analysts, and the analysts in training, had to pledge 10 percent of their time and 4 percent of their income for these humanitarian purposes. The humanitarian nature of the BPI was established by the priority of the functions it would serve. Its priorities were to

> 1) make our therapy accessible to the great numbers of people who do not suffer from their neurosis any less than the rich people, but who are not able to pay for the cost of their treatment; 2) develop a place in which analysis will be taught theoretically and where the experiences of older analysts can be transferred to students who are eager to learn and finally to make our knowledge of the neurotic diseases and our thera-peutic techniques more complete by applying and testing them in new circumstances. (Freud 1930, quoted in Lockot 1985, 41)

Thus Freud gave his complete support to a set of priorities that have the spirit of a very different attitude about financial relations with patients than that which is typically taught in the United States.

The classical pattern of psychoanalytical training had evolved by 1927, when it was expected that all participating students would have a training analysis, would provide treatment of clinic patients under supervision, and attend case seminars and lectures. The lectures were not only medical and psychoanalytic, but tended to be broadly humanistic and related to religion and education. Most of the people who were trained there found it to be an exhilarating experience.

All kinds of innovation in treatment were encouraged, including family therapy, friendship-type therapy, and short-term psychotherapy in addition to psychoanalysis. During these ten years, there were about 2,000 consultations, 721 cases that were treated, including 127 cases of compulsion neurosis, 95 cases of neurotic inhibitions, 129 cases of hysteria, 32 cases of schizophrenia, 15 manic depressive disorders, and 13 perversion cases. The patients included laborers, craftsmen, clerks, teachers, doctors, and artists. Of the 363 fully completed analyses, the length of treatment ran from six months to about three years, with the mode (108) averaging one year. Among 721 cases, 116 were reported improved, 89 as substantially improved and 11 as "cured." All in all this was a tremendous accomplishment for the first ten years (Gifford 1994, 652). Peter Gay has described the Berlin Institute as "the most spectacular of the centers in which psychoanalysis ensured its future" (Gay 1988, 464). Indeed, it is not too much to say that by 1930 the BPI had established itself as a role model for the profession. In 1970, Anna Freud acknowledged that the BPI established the traditional way the psychoanalytic movement would be organized and perpetuated. She wrote:

> The psychoanalytical world should not forget that the close ties
> between treatment, teaching and research which nowadays characterise
> the existence of every analytical institute, found their first development
> 50 years ago in Berlin. (Brecht et al. 1985, 36)

Yet, three years after the Institute's first ten-year report had been written, this auspicious beginning would be fundamentally undermined with the rise of the Third Reich.

2

The Role of the Göring Institute in the Endurance and Modification of the Psychoanalytic Continuum in Germany

IN THIS CHAPTER, WE SHALL SUMMARIZE the positions of two principle investigators whose research has led to conclusions at variance with our own. Indeed, it was their work that provided a major impetus for our own wish to explore the data. Using different methods, psychoanalyst Rose Spiegel (and her colleagues), and the historian Geoffrey Cocks in 1985 came to the conclusion that the psychoanalytic movement survived during the Third Reich. We will examine the 1985 findings of both Spiegel and Cocks regarding the role of the Göring Institute in the development of psychoanalysis in Germany and review Cocks's (1994, 1997, 1998) revised conclusions about the impact of the Göring Institute on psychoanalysis. Let us take a brief look now at their major formulations.

Rose Spiegel: A Psychoanalytic Inquiry into the Third Reich and the Berlin Psychoanalytic Institute

The first series of articles written in English about psychoanalysis during the Third Reich appeared in the *Journal of Contemporary Psychoanalysis* in 1975 (Spiegel, Chrazanowski and Feiner 1975, 479). Rose Spiegel, Gerard Chrazanowski, and Arthur F. Feiner, psychoanalysts associated with the William Alanson White Institute, decided to study the question of the survival of psychoanalysis in Berlin during the Third Reich after they had attended a conference in Mexico during which they met a number of German analysts who affirmed that the profession did, indeed, survive under Hitler. They conducted their study by interviewing 1) former psychoanalysts who had knowledge of the Göring Institute, 2) an analyst who survived in Berlin during that period, and 3) the family members of the psychiatrist M. H. Göring, who was the director of the Institute. Spiegel's two publications (1975 and 1985) emanating from that research dealt in particular with the issue of the survival of psychoanalysis.

Much time and effort was spent in interviewing over forty individuals and families in the course of this study. The project took over a decade to complete. However, we contend that Spiegel's sole reliance on interview data without historical corroboration undermined the validity of her conclusions. Moreover, in Spiegel's introduction to the section of her publication on M. H. Göring's contribution toward the Institute's survival, she states, "[O]ur search had begun, not only with inquiry into the fate of psychoanalysis, but with a wish that in the vortex of Nazism, somehow human decency had somewhere, somehow survived" (Spiegel 1985, 525). Is it not possible that this wish, however noble, led her to interpret data one way, when another interpretation would be more consistent with the pattern of facts?

In the initial introduction to the series of articles, Spiegel states, "These papers gave the lie to Ernest Jones' final judgment, in his biography of Freud (1962), that psychoanalysis had died in Europe during the Third Reich" (Spiegel 1985, 525). In fact, Jones's earlier comments in his letters to Anna Freud often contained such claims as "Boehm saved psychoanalysis" (Jones to A. Freud, letter of October 2, 1933. All unpublished letters referred to in this manuscript are from the archives of the British Psycho-Analytical Society, with their permission). Knowing how supportive Jones was of the abilities of gentile psychoanalysts to rescue psychoanalysis in the early to mid-1930s leads us to raise the question why he later changed his mind. A review of the correspondence among Jones and the other analysts in the archives of the British Psychoanalytic Society revealed that Jones worked very hard, not only to save many Jewish analysts, but to preserve the integrity of the BPI and those gentile analysts who remained in Germany. One could argue that he would be predisposed to see his efforts as successful, if the evidence could at all support such a conclusion.

Some of the facts in Spiegel's articles are inconsistent with other evidence and/or documents in archival material (for example, the Berlin Document Center), other publications in the field, other informants such as secretaries, or other interviews of the same person. The following are examples of this discrepancy. In describing the building that the Göring Institute had taken from the BPI, Spiegel states, "The building was 'leased' from the owners with payments to be made to them. However, in effect the lease was terminated with the destruction of the building by Allied bombing late in the war" (Spiegel 1975, 488). The facts are quite different. The building was taken from the BPI without remuneration (Brecht et al. 1985, 146; Cocks 1985, 144), and the building was destroyed by Soviet troops after M. H. Göring allowed SS troops to enter it, perhaps as a refuge in their final defense of Berlin. When Soviet troops entered the Institute, they were fired on from above (Brecht et al. 1985, 153; Lockot, 1985, 86; Lockot 1994c). Apparently Spiegel was incorrectly informed by Werner Kemper (a German psychoanalyst who worked at the BPI during the Third Reich) about the fate of the building. She was also incorrectly informed that M. H. Göring made "zealous efforts" to save the life of John Rittmeister, a Freudian psychoanalyst who was executed by the Nazis (Spiegel 1975, 489). Once again, this information was supplied by Werner Kemper, but other evidence strongly contradicts his claim (Brecht et al. 1985, 186–90). Interviews with M. H. Göring's own son, Ernst (Cocks 1985, 167), refute this notion. Regine Lockot also contradicts the idea that M. H. Göring tried to save Rittmeister (Lockot 1985, 86).

At one point in Spiegel's 1985 article she quotes M. H. Göring's son, Ernst, as saying, "[F]or a member of the Institut [*sic*], it was an absolute necessity to belong to the Party; if not, the hunt was on and it was soon over with for that individual" (Spiegel 1985, 527–28). The statement made to Spiegel by Ernst Göring is incorrect. Only the leader of the group had to be a member of the Nazi Party. However, the percentage of Nazi members at the Göring Institute was far greater than that indicated in the report of her colleague, Arthur Feiner, who determined that "only 5% of the Institute's members joined the party." Feiner's source is an interview and personal communication with Kemper in 1972 (Feiner 1985, 543).

Spiegel and her colleagues should not be faulted for the distortions reported to them. Yet, what she and her colleagues were told can now be verified against more reliable historical data. The question of why Werner Kemper reported such obvious distortions of the facts needs to be raised (and we do so in chapter 16). The question must be raised whether Kemper's factual distortion was a conscious evasion of the truth for the purpose of escaping the consequences of retribution, or rather the result of unconscious conflicts that color the memory of emotionally charged events of the past, or some combination of both.

It is our distinct impression that the Spiegel article initially raised the central issues that needed to be explored and then never followed up on answering these questions; nor did it deal with their relevance. For example, the questions of how psychoanalytic training was done and the need in psychoanalysis for open discussion and freedom were raised but never examined. It appears that M. H. Göring's behavior is always interpreted in the most positive light.

The most recent available evidence reveals that Spiegel's conclusion about M. H. Göring's personal integrity and her claims of the survival of psychoanalysis at the Göring Institute were a naïve acceptance of the interview data from individuals whose perceptions of reality after the war were vulnerable to defensive distortion, if not outright coverup.

The records at the Berlin Document Center (BDC) on M. H. Göring reveal the organizations to which he belonged on May 1, 1933. Only Party membership was necessary to lead an organization, but M. H. Göring belonged to the Sturmabteilung (SA) and the Dozentenbund, which were both ideologically extreme "right wing" elements of the Nazi movement. The Dozentenbund was the Nazi organization responsible for identifying those professionals whose personal ideology was "politically incorrect." This could suggest that he went further in his enthusiasm than would have been required to be "politically correct" and that he demonstrated a tendency to identify with the principles, goals, and spirit of Nazi ideology.

As we shall demonstrate, M. H. Göring's support of National Socialism was more than a superficial cosmetic attempt to assure the government of the Institute's loyalty and therefore keep the Nazis at bay. Göring required all members of the Göring Institute to read *Mein Kampf* and make its philosophy central to the way they practiced. It can be argued that Göring recommended it rather than required it, that the reading of it wasn't enforced, or that it was not an official part of the course curriculum. Such arguments in interpretation are legitimate. However, they are difficult to resolve definitely due to insufficient or conflicting evidence. Yet we are persuaded by the preponderance of evidence that Göring's identification with National Socialist ideology was sincere. He believed in the racial ideology and the anti-Semitism it espoused. It can also be argued that Göring was more of a German nationalist than a Nazi. There is merit to this distinction, and there is support for the idea that M. H. Göring was initially a rather conservative German nationalist. However, by 1944 the policies and the direction of the government were clearly veering off from the path of conservative German nationalism. Therefore, to have supported the regime towards the end of the war suggests Göring became an enthusiastic Nazi. Despite the massive and devastating destruction of the people and city of Berlin, there is evidence that Göring willingly carried out Hitler's fanatical last orders for Berliners to fight to the death. M. H. Göring, we maintain, had bought into the ideology of National Socialism and Hitler's authority. He cooperated with the regime willingly.

In the last paragraph of her 1985 article, Spiegel proclaims that psychoanalysis did survive the Third Reich at the Göring Institute, and she praises in the same breath M. H. Göring and the executed psychoanalyst John Rittmeister. She states: "[B]oth accepted the destruction of their bodily selves in honor of one's self-hood and integrity against the torrential force of totalitarian passionately violent society which we still seek to understand" (Spiegel 1985, 535). This conclusion more than anything else reveals how the generous but naïve assumption that guided her through more than ten years of research was bound to slant her research effort from the start. The "wish that in the vortex of Nazism, somehow human decency had somewhere, somehow survived" (Spiegel 1985, 535) is a kind of optimism that is out of place when studying the Third Reich. For a psychoanalyst, whose training prepared her to face and understand the most painful truths of the human condition, to arrive at such a conclusion is hard to grasp, but once that wish is proclaimed, it is predictable that the conclusions reached could only reflect the nature of that idealized distortion of reality.

A Historical Examination of the Status of the Berlin Psychoanalytical Institute during the Third Reich

In the early 1970s, Geoffrey Cocks became the first historian to have discovered that the subject of psychotherapy and psychoanalysis during the Third Reich was not the dead issue that it previously had been considered. He was a graduate student in German history searching for a dissertation topic when he discovered that a group of psychotherapeutic clinicians had practiced their profession throughout the period of the Third Reich within the organizational framework that has become known as the Göring Institute. Cocks's historical analysis of the Third Reich has continued over the years to become increasingly nuanced and attuned to the recently published reports of the younger psychoanalysts in Germany. In comparing Cocks's perspective with our own work, there is one area of complete agreement. In reviewing a book by another author in 1996, Cocks (1996) describes the importance of Regine Lockot's two previous books to his own 1997 work. He praises her diligent attention to historical facts and documents, in contrast with "stereotypical" arguments. Similarly, her publications have provided the cornerstone for much of our work, and we have particularly found her objective behavioral description of the individual psychoanalysts to be invaluable.

For over ten years, Cocks's original 1985 publication was the only extensive historical account in English about psychoanalysis during the Third Reich. He deduced that psychoanalysis survived as an institutional structure. Cocks's (1985) conclusion that psychoanalysis did in fact survive the Third Reich in Berlin remained unchallenged apart from the few critical book reviews at the time it was published. As Hannah Decker has indicated:

> Cocks startles us by finding something worthwhile in the Third Reich, i.e., the creation of a lay, state-certified group of psychotherapists who competed successfully with established psychotherapy. (Decker 1998)

Cocks not only startled us, but he also dismayed us by insisting that psychoanalysis not only survived, but it experienced professional growth during the Third Reich. It was this claim that led us to investigate the particular issue of whether or not psychoanalysis survived.

In Cocks's (1997) latest publication, he has significantly altered his conclusions about what happened to psychotherapy during the Third Reich. He states,

> While the Nazis may have atomized German society by dissolving traditional social groupings, a competitive "hierarchical continuum of achievement" also allowed groups such as psychotherapists to advance their ongoing culturally shaped and encouraged corporate interests in both service and sacrifice to the state. The Nazi system was one that, as we have seen, cultivated the self-serving aspirations of both individuals and groups in the name of national and racial solidarity. The war cut both ways, creating an environment both of individual "survivalism" and of shared purpose and misery. (Cocks 1997, 413)

This part of his conclusion is one with which we agree. Cocks continues:

> While the Göring Institute itself would not survive Hitler's Reich and Hitler's war, it had, as a result of all these historical circumstances, served as a vital component of the continuous professional development of psychotherapy in modern Germany before 1933 and after 1945. (Cocks 1997, 413)

Thus, Cocks maintains a consistent position—that the Göring Institute

served to provide for various schools of psychotherapy, including psychoanalysis, the means to not only endure the Third Reich but to maintain
their status as a profession. Thus, the history of psychotherapy became for
Cocks a part of a larger picture of the development in modern Germany
and the West of the "professionalization of doctors, the 'medicalization' of
society, the role of the state in medical professionalization, health, and public hygiene" (Cocks 1997, 405). It is through this lens that Cocks finds the
continuities in psychoanalysis before, during, and after the Third Reich.
After sorting through the complex data presented by Cocks (1985 and
1997) and reviewing other relevant documents and evidence, we have
come to the conclusion that for psychoanalysis the Third Reich represented
a major fault line or a historical discontinuity. In a recent communication
from Cocks, he responds to our views by further differentiating his position on what represents a continuity and what does not. He states:

> I agree there was significant discontinuity in terms of psychoanalysis as
> an autonomous scientific and cultural movement stemming primarily
> from the rich Jewish intellectual tradition in Central Europe. However
> impressive the reconstruction of psychoanalysis in Western Germany
> after the war, Jewish culture, including Freud's psychoanalysis, in Cen-
> tral Europe is of course gone forever. (Cocks 1999)

The discrepancy between our respective positions regarding this aspect of
the discontinuity issue has been diminished significantly.

Our understanding of Cocks's approach is that he considers institutional continuity as primary evidence for psychoanalysis's endurance. We
intend to examine the issue of psychoanalysis's survival from frameworks
requiring both political context and psychoanalytical explorations. As such,
we go beyond the structural analysis of the profession to consideration of
questions such as What are the defining qualities of the psychoanalytic
endeavor? What are the defining qualities that did survive during the
period of the Göring Institute? What do we mean by survival? And how do
we put together the evidence of "institutional analysis" with evidence of the
behavior of various individuals involved?

In terms of the defining qualities of psychoanalysis, we consider the
possibilities of free association and exploration of transference in a safe setting to be professional requirements or demand characteristics inherent in
the practice of psychoanalysis. We also examine how the nature of political
systems and ideological goals influence the practice of psychoanalysis. One
of the problems with Cocks's 1985 and 1997 works is that he studied both

psychoanalysis and psychotherapy and at times used the terms in ways that could be confusing. The present venture will deal only with what happened to Freudian psychoanalysis. We will use as a definition of psychoanalysis the one accepted by the Copenhagen Congress for the International Psychoanalytic Association in 1967. It is as follows:

> The term "psychoanalysis" refers to a theory of personality structure and function, application of this theory to other branches of knowledge, and, finally, to a specific psychotherapeutic technique. This body of knowledge is based on and derived from the fundamental psychological discoveries made by Sigmund Freud. (*International Journal of Psycho-Analysis* 1968, 151)

Our specific aim is to determine whether psychoanalysis as a profession with a distinct philosophy and world view survived in the Third Reich. While we have established different priorities than those of Cocks, we realize that our work would have been impossible without his enormous contribution to the history of psychoanalysis during the Third Reich. Without Cocks's meticulous accumulation of the facts, there would be no thorough history in English for that period. Furthermore, we agree with Edith Kurzweil's assessment of Cocks's 1985 work even though we have come to different conclusions:

> If Cocks has been too soft on these German psychotherapists, this may well be because he was the first person to dig into the available historical documents and to inspire confidence in the surviving protagonists—and because so many of them have died. Indeed, he has performed an enormous service: long before this book was published, his original dissertation inspired a number of Germans to reexamine the history of psychotherapy during the Nazi period. It was he who turned a taboo subject into a hot topic. (Kurzweil 1985, 144–49)

We would add "a hot topic in Germany, maybe, but not in the United States or Britain." The first step will be to summarize the major conclusion Cocks reached in his 1985 publication.

In essence, Cocks claims that not only did the practice of psychotherapy continue during the Third Reich, but also the institution of psychoanalysis survived during this period as a result of M. H. Göring's leadership. The survival of psychoanalysis and the growth and development of psychotherapy is a theme reiterated throughout his 1985 book and never specifically repudiated in his revised and expanded 1997 edition. Cocks states:

But psychoanalysis as a method did survive among professionals and, under a compulsion, to be sure, shared in the mutual benefit its enforced cooperation bestowed on all the psychotherapeutic schools of thought. . . . "new German psychotherapy" remained essentially a label for the cosmetic assemblage of extant psychotherapeutic orientations. Psychoanalysis was able to adopt a secure, if somewhat defensive and subordinate, position within the institute, where differences, however extreme, by and large remained professional and personal, not political. (Cocks 1985, 15)

He further adds:

The irony was actually a double one: Not only was a Nazi agency facilitating the survival of psychoanalysis, the "Jewish science" they so despised, but the General Medical Society psychotherapists were to benefit from association with their newly stigmatized old rivals, the psychoanalysts . . . this forced association would provide shared benefits far beyond the convenience of shared quarters. (Cocks 1985, 7)

Although Cocks has significantly revised his conclusions between the span of the two editions of his book, the fact that he implicitly indicates that a continuity existed between the way psychoanalysis was practiced on January 29, 1933, and May 8, 1945, leads us to raise an important historical issue. We maintain that because psychoanalysis was considered a "Jewish science" by the Nazi leadership, it was provided what has euphemistically been referred to as "special treatment." (To support our reasoning, at a more appropriate place we will cite the historical record, which reveals how important the fate of psychoanalysis, the "Jewish science," was to the leaders of the Third Reich.) We contend that the psychoanalytic practitioners, their theory, and their method would be so harshly treated that they did not survive. We contend that because psychoanalysis was "Jewish," it received the same treatment that other Jews received. The Nazis followed a similar pattern of treating "Jewish" psychoanalysis the same way they treated the Jewish analysts. They were herded together, monitored, encouraged to emigrate, and one was expelled to Poland only to be recalled to the Göring Institute to serve the state's interests. In 1938, those analysts that were still suspect had their psychoanalytic identities altered; Felix Boehm and Carl Müller-Braunschweig were prevented from performing crucial aspects of their psychoanalytic skill—e.g., training analysis—under the threat of physical harm if they disagreed with the state. One analyst, John Rittmeister, was actually executed for what the Nazis considered a high form of treason—making antiwar posters and propaganda for the Harro

Schulze-Boysen section of the Red Orchestra espionage ring. When the first foreign psychoanalyst visited the German psychoanalysts in Berlin in 1946, his descriptions of what was supposed to have been a psychoanalytic meeting and lecture could only be understood as a regressed caricature of its former identity. John Rickman, a British psychoanalyst, first visited the individual psychoanalysts in their homes. As a result of these individual contacts, he described the behavior of two of the leaders of the re-emerging psychoanalytic movement, Müller-Braunschweig and Boehm, as being regressed and deteriorated. Rickman then observed a lecture given by Müller-Braunschweig to thirty-four students:

> The level of the lecture was low intellectually; was exclusively devoted to sex, praising it as an activity, — and seemed to me far remote from the quality that you expect in a scientific man. [There was practically no reference to the unconscious or to conflict, his handling of the question of sex was crude. . . .]

Rickman expanded on this topic:

> Mueller-Braunschweig's dogmatic and aggressive manner seemed to me to do little, if anything, to pave the way to these seminars which were the pride of the higher German educational institutions. I must say I was profoundly disappointed. (Brecht et al. 1985, 238)

Rickman went on to describe a meeting of the German Psychoanalytical Society that was also run by Müller-Braunschweig. A paper of his former pupil, who had moved to England in January 1939, was going to be discussed. Presentation of this same paper had led her to being admitted to full membership in the British Psychoanalytical Society. Rickman describes how Müller-Braunschweig conducted the meeting:

> In a short time he was denouncing the paper, thumping the table with his fist, saying it was a bad paper, it wasn't psycho-analysis, "and, just think of it, the British Society actually, on the basis of this paper, made her a member!" The theme of the badness of the paper and the stupidity of the British Society recurred during his half-hour's discourse, during which time he was several times corrected, for misquoting the paper or obviously misinterpreting it.
>
> He then asked Dr. Boehm to speak, but realising that something was amiss, apologised for his display of anger but said it was justified by his intolerance of a bad presentation of psycho-analysis. Dr. Boehm repeated the attacks on the paper, got muddled with the theme, and had to be corrected. (Brecht et al. 1985, 238)

These vivid descriptions of two of the leaders of the German psychoanalytic movement argue for a discontinuity or break in the psychoanalytic
movement. Rickman goes on to provide more favorable assessments of
Fräulein Käthe Dräger, Fräulein Marguerite Steinberg, and Dr. Werner
Kemper, suggesting that "not the whole of the whole of the psychoanalytic
movement was in disarray" (Baruch 1999). We have more to say about the
impact of the Third Reich on both Käthe Dräger and Werner Kemper in
chapters 12 and 16 respectively. We give more weight to the cases of
Müller-Braunschweig and Boehm for two reasons. We have more evidence
of their functioning prior to 1933 than we have about other analysts and
this information reveals the significant degree of regression that occurred in
both of them. Secondly, both Boehm and Müller-Braunschweig were
among the leading lights of the German psychoanalytic movement. We
will have more to say about Müller-Braunschweig in chapter 12.

What had happened to the practice and the practitioners of what the
Nazis considered a "Jewish science" led to an important debate within the
discipline of history that has direct implications for the present question of
the survival of psychoanalysis during the Third Reich: the intentionalist-
functionalist or monocratic-polycratic debate. These two perspectives can
be seen as ends of a continuum.

The intentionalist perspective suggests that Nazi policies followed a
specific game plan and that Hitler fully intended to implement the Holocaust from the time he wrote *Mein Kampf*. This perspective suggests that
Nazi ideology was based upon Hitler's obsession with destroying the Jews.
The essential core of this approach was that the policy toward the Jews
started with the April decrees of 1933 and followed a systematic ideologically driven pattern resulting in the "Final Solution" at the death camps
(Dawidowicz 1986; Fleming 1982). According to the intentionalist perspective, the survival of psychoanalysis as well as that of quantum physics
was never in doubt. Psychoanalysis and quantum physics were considered
"Jewish sciences." As "Jewish sciences," both were to be completely eliminated from all aspects of life within the Third Reich and eventually all of
Europe.

The polycratic-functionalist end of the continuum, on the other hand,
considers such "Hitler-centric" interpretations of events as inconsistent with
historical evidence. For these historians, the Nazi state never operated in the
systematic and predetermined way as envisioned by the intentionalists.
These functionalist historians espouse the view that Nazi racial policy
evolved in an ad hoc, improvisational way within a chaotic Third Reich that

was torn apart by competing and powerful forces within the Party and state (Broszat and Mommsen, in Childers and Caplan 1993, 212). The functionalist conclusion is that a great deal of autonomy could be maintained by specific organizations within the Third Reich, as Cocks suggests.

The polycratic or functional-historical perspective espouses the view that Germany did not work in the top-down hierarchically structured way that intentionalists would suggest. Thus, Cocks argues that the Nazi state was dominated by what could best be described as organized chaos or institutional Darwinism. In this way of thinking, the Göring Institute and psychoanalysis were able to survive by finding their niche. Thus, official state policy regarding the elimination of "Jewish psychoanalysis" could go unheeded within the safety of the Göring Institute (Cocks 1985).

We have come to a more intentionalist understanding of the events surrounding the issue of psychoanalysis. Our purpose here is not to disprove the usefulness of the polycratic approach in all areas of historical investigation. Rather, it is our contention that this approach is less consistent with the facts regarding what happened to psychoanalysis in the Third Reich. We are well aware there are no simple answers to these arguments, and only over time can these complex issues be understood more objectively.

Returning to our discussion about Cocks's work, when his first book was published in 1985, it was widely praised for unearthing significant new areas of information about the Third Reich, psychotherapy, and psychoanalysis. However, he was severely criticized by the reviewers for a failure to examine the ethical issues that were intricately involved in the subject he reported (Decker 1998). In 1997, Cocks published a revised and expanded version of *Psychotherapy in the Third Reich: The Göring Institute*. Ironically, the new version has received very little attention, although we believe he has not only corrected his former omissions, but made many additional improvements. It is better written, contains more nuances, and reveals greater insight into the subject. His present findings have a greater breadth and take into account how the history of psychotherapy during the Third Reich relates to modern German history. However, Cocks never actually discusses his former very specific conclusions about psychoanalysis that we have previously cited. Since our major focus is the practice of psychoanalysis and not psychotherapy, we believe his contentions about psychoanalysis made in 1985 still need to be examined, although, as Hannah Decker (1998) has recently stated, we are not as far apart from Cocks's overall position as we were before. However, in viewing the issues involved purely through a psychoanalytic lens, it may seem to the reader that we are further divided than we are and overly critical of Cocks. The problem for us is that almost all that is worthwhile that has been written in English about psychotherapy during the Third Reich has been written by Cocks. In a sense, then, our work must also draw boundaries between psychotherapy and psychoanalysis. Each time we draw that boundary, we will need to reference Cocks.

Part 2
Political Ideology and Psychoanalysis

3

Totalitarianism and Psychoanalysis

FROM THE INCEPTION OF PSYCHOANALYSIS there has been much discussion about its relation to social and political thought, and to various political systems. One question that needs to be posed is whether psychoanalysis, as a theory and a therapeutic technique, requires, or at least favors, any particular political system. Some of the early second-generation analysts such as Otto Fenichel, Edith Jacobsohn, and Annie Reich came to be devoted to a political (specifically Marxist) psychoanalysis (Jacoby 1986). Many of their colleagues were made uncomfortable by this politicization of psychoanalysis. They preferred that psychoanalysis remain "pure" or "politically neutral." For example, Jones in his correspondence averred that psychoanalysis should be politically neutral (Steiner 1989, 52-53). Jones's conception of psychoanalysis as a pure science had developed in accordance with Freud's own belief that the research domain for the field he discovered was a search for psychic truth. Thus, psychoanalysis should not be influenced or contaminated by any political views. The basis for this perspective was rooted in the context of Vienna at the end of the nineteenth century (Steiner 1988, 297). The zeitgeist within which psychoanalysis had been born was the progressive Jewish bourgeoisie climate, which in turn was tied to the Age of Enlightenment. In addition, Jones's stance regarding the political neutrality of psychoanalysis can also be understood as an attempt to steer clear of the two extremist political ideologies that were battling "to the death," so to speak, for control during the 1930s. Most scholars today question whether any system of thought can be completely politically neutral.

A further question is whether psychoanalysts, even if they could maintain a political neutrality, *ought* to do so—and in *all* situations. In his address to the International Psychoanalytic Association Hamburg Congress in 1985, Mayor Klaus von Dohnany censured the psychoanalytic tradition for remaining politically neutral. He bluntly pointed out to the participants of the Congress the harsh consequences of neutrality by all too many intellectuals on the Left in Germany during the 1930s. He criticized psychoanalysis then and now for striving to remain politically disengaged (Wangh 1991, 95). Surely the kind of political ideas that both Otto Fenichel and Edith Jacobsohn believed in did not impair their contributions to either psychoanalytic theory or to patient care. In fact it could be argued that within appropriate boundaries, their opinion about the equality of all human beings is an important strength in the development of empathy for patients. There is, however, no question that when the boundaries within the psychoanalytic frame are broken by political ideas, the end result can be disastrous for the patient.

Riccardo Steiner has published an article in English and French that deals with the subtle distinctions of Ernest Jones's position on political neutrality, and the historical circumstances between 1933 and 1938 in which these differences occurred (Steiner 1988 and 1989). After Hitler was named chancellor of Germany on January 30, 1933, Wilhelm Reich's extreme Marxist beliefs and political action became more than an embarrassment. Many analysts considered it a threat to the institution of psychoanalysis in Europe. Probably with Freud's support, the executive of the WPV met with Reich in April 1933. During that meeting Reich was told that his political action would have to be stopped because of the extreme emotional climate that had been reached in Central Europe. Reich sent a letter to Anna Freud, who was the secretary of the IPA. He indicated that he would comply for one or two years if, in turn, "the IPA makes an official statement of its attitude to my work" to determine if his theory of "Sex-Economy is consistent with my membership" (Steiner 1989, 78). Instead of the official debate that Reich wanted, a more low-key way of coping with this issue was followed by the IPA. In a series of letters to Anna Freud the evolution of Jones's position on Reich's mixing of Marxism and psychoanalysis can be followed. In a letter to Anna Freud dated April 20, 1933, Jones's initial attitude was relatively open-minded and questioning (Steiner 1988, 313). On May 2, 1933, Jones had reached the opinion that "Reich should come to a definite conclusion about which is more important to him, psychoanalysis or politics" (Steiner 1989, 73). In early December Jones met with Reich in London to determine whether his views represented a break in the psychoanalytic tradition, or served as a serious threat to the institutional basis of psychoanalysis in Europe. At this point in Reich's life, he was continually traveling between Denmark and Sweden in order to avoid legal problems. Ten days before their meeting, Reich "had been expelled from the Communist Party because of his association with psycho-analysis" (Steiner 1989, 74). After the interview with Reich, Jones had a four-hour meeting about Reich's situation with several colleagues. The opinion reached was that "on the ground of theory alone, the evidence did not sufficiently warrant his being excluded from the International Association" (Steiner 1989, 74). Regarding the potential danger of Reich's political activities vis-à-vis the institution of psychoanalysis, Jones's letter to Anna Freud states,

> [W]e felt that it would be a serious thing to take up the position that no analyst could be allowed to play an active part in social life and movements, whatever they may be, and we felt that such a question should be decided by the Society of the particular country where any conflict arose between the person's activities and the laws of the country. (Steiner 1989, 74)

The pragmatic conclusion that Jones comes to "is that Reich should be dissuaded from work in any new country (except perhaps Russia)," and "any Group he might found would not receive official recognition" (Steiner 1989, 74).

In a follow-up letter on December 13, 1933, Jones informs Anna Freud that he had met with Reich again and confronted him with the view that he was "imperfectly analyzed," was presenting psychoanalysis in "a misleading way," and no group founded by him would be recognized by the IPA. However, Jones told Reich no steps were being taken to exclude him from membership. At the Lucerne Congress in 1934, according to Jones, Reich resigned, but Reich's story was that he had been expelled. In Reich's case the view that psychoanalysts remain politically neutral won the day.

We end this discussion by reviewing Steiner's position on the implications of totalitarian controls and the practice of psychoanalysis. He astutely points out that

> totalitarian values which rendered it impossible for psychoanalysis to continue to exist, not just on the institutional level but also as a science

since its values had and has as their basis a particular conception of man and human relationships, the respect of the patient as an individual and the fostering of tolerance within clinical practice and in general. These set of circumstances have, *or should have*, the most important repercussions both on the institutional life of psychoanalysis and, to put it succinctly, that which psychoanalysis may be able to contribute to the social sciences. (Steiner 1989, 62)

He goes on to "conclude that the attitude of neutrality which psychoanalysts as clinicians must adopt" cannot be sustained when the political situations threatens the values on which the psychoanalytic tradition is based. "Silence and neutrality in such situations are tantamount to collusion and neutralization" (Steiner 1989, 62-63).

When considering the impact of the major political systems during the twentieth century on psychoanalysis, one must ask, which were workable, which were not? One way to address the relationship between psychoanalysis and political thought is to focus not so much on the politics of the Left versus the Right, but on the degree of freedom and autonomy vis-à-vis control in any given society, whether of the Left or of the Right. What conditions in a society or political system nurture and support the profession and practice of psychoanalysis, and what conditions hinder it? Can we say anything useful about the differences among totalitarian states, authoritarian fascist states, and liberal democracies as to whether they provide a social-political context favorable to psychoanalysis?

We would like to propose as a working hypothesis that, in order for psychoanalysis to be an effective form of treatment, you cannot have a totalitarian system of government. It creates too inhospitable an atmosphere. But before proceeding with this argument, it is necessary to say a word about the ambiguity of the term "totalitarian." The full study of the vicissitudes of the use of the term, since it began to be used in the 1920s and 1930s to describe the nature of the fascist state in Italy, makes for fascinating reading (Gleason 1995) but is beyond the scope of this book. However, for our purposes the following issues need to be highlighted. Throughout the evolution of the use of the term "totalitarianism," one can discern a core of meaning:

[T]he idea of a radically intrusive state run by people who do not merely control their citizens from the outside, preventing them from challenging the elite or doing things that it does not like, but also attempt to reach into the most intimate regions of their lives. These totalitarian elites ceaselessly tried to make their subjects into beings who would be constitutionally incapable of challenging the rule of the state and those who control it. This element—the state's remaking of its citizens and their whole world—had remained central to the term's meaning until this day. (Gleason 1995, 10)

During the 1950s, a professor of government at Harvard University, Carl J. Friedrich, organized a conference on totalitarianism (Friedrich 1954). In his paper he addressed what the Soviet Union and Nazi Germany had in common, despite their many differences. He claimed that, because of the technological advances of the twentieth century, these societies were "historically unique and *sui generis*." He made five points about totalitarian states that are relevant for our investigation:

1) They are ideologically driven, and their ideology makes utopian and messianic claims as to the final perfect society which could be achieved.

2) They have a single mass party consisting of people passionately and unquestioningly dedicated to that ideology.

3) They exert monopolistic control of all means of combat, made possible by modern technological advances.

4) Also, due to these same technological advances, they exert monopolistic control of mass communication (press, radio, motion pictures).

5) The police use terror tactics to maintain discipline and control. Terror tactics are directed against those within the state and outside of it who are designated as enemies or misfits. (Friedrich, in Gleason 1995, 124–25)

Friedrich went on to distinguish totalitarian from authoritarian systems:

Totalitarian societies attempt to shatter all traditional types of authority and to replace them with a new kind of social control. In a very real sense, in a totalitarian society true authority is altogether destroyed. (Friedrich, in Gleason 1995, 125)

According to the military historian John Keegan the roots of the totalitarian states are directly related to World War I. In fact, the totalitarian governments that emerged after World War I were a political means to continue the war. Keegan writes:

It uniformed and militarized its mass electoral following, while depriving voters generally of their electoral rights, exciting their lowest political instincts and marginalising and menacing all internal opposition.

> Less than twenty years after the end of the Great War, the "war to end
> wars" as it had come to be called at the nadir of hopes for its eventual
> conclusion, Europe was once again gripped by the fear of a new war,
> provoked by the actions and ambitions of war lords more aggressive
> than any known to the old world of the long nineteenth-century peace.
> (Keegan 1999, 5)

Keegan's view on totalitarianism adds to the growing view among historians that the two world wars of the twentieth century were in fact one continuous war. In discussing the origins of World War II, Thomas Childers
put it this way: "One hundred years from now" it may be concluded that
"the two world wars of this century in fact constituted one great conflict, a
kind of second Thirty Years War" (Childers 1998, 1). From this perspective, the rise of the totalitarian states was a political means to settle what
had not been resolved by the Treaty of Versailles.

Inherent in totalitarianism is the idea of "totality" as it appears in the
organic thinking of the Romantic philosophers of nineteenth-century
Europe. The whole is greater than the sum of its parts; the individual is
absorbed in the state and individual privacy is of no value. The well-being
of the organic whole is paramount. Thus, the racially based Nazi society
justified getting rid of its Jews and mentally ill much in the same spirit that
a doctor would feel justified in removing a diseased appendix for the well-
being of a patient. The nature of reality is also determined from above and
cannot be questioned. Empirical investigation, trial and error, spontaneity,
and emphasis on reason to arrive at the objective truth (all legacies of the
Enlightenment) were considered unacceptable in this new way of being.

We conclude that despite the ambiguities and potential pitfalls inherent in the use of the term "totalitarianism," it retains its usefulness as a
model, so long as one is willing to specify the criteria by which it is defined,
in this case the core meaning suggested by Gleason and Friedrich's five criteria. Furthermore, its usefulness would be improved if we acknowledge
that totalitarianism may not be an all-or-nothing phenomenon but in the
real world may exist in degrees. One could argue, for example, about the
degree of successful totalitarian control within the Third Reich.

A basic hypothesis in this manuscript is that for Freudian psychoanalysis to be an effective form of treatment, each individual must have a potential for a sense of autonomy and the opportunity to experience one's own
private life in relative freedom. Thus, in authoritarian dictatorships like
Italy and Argentina, in which the government demanded behavioral compliance solely in the public domain, Freudian psychoanalysis could con-

tinue to be meaningfully practiced in the private domain. The specific case documenting the validity of this hypothesis is the Dollfuss-Schuschnigg authoritarian- and fascist-type dictatorship that governed Austria prior to *Anschluß*, during which time psychoanalysis in Vienna flourished. It is a good illustration of the distinction between an extreme form of authoritarian government, in Austria, and a totalitarian government such as Germany during the Third Reich.

The Dollfuss-Schuschnigg regime was not only extremely powerful but it had acted very swiftly to crush socialist-type rebellions during the 1930s. In the early part of 1934, Chancellor Engelbert Dollfuss had put down a Marxist revolt in Vienna by suspending parliament and bombarding the huge socialist housing project in the city until it surrendered (Kestenberg 1994). This is the classical response of fascist authoritarian governments toward threats from the Left (Payne 1980; Griffin 1993). During the 1930s Austria had also manifested its own form of anti-Semitism, albeit a much more old-fashioned and less malignant form than that emerging in Germany. For example, starting in 1934 Jewish physicians were no longer able to obtain positions in the national health care system. This was before the Nazis implemented their racial policies regarding physicians (Proctor 1988, 276). The pivotal difference was that the Austrian government's anti-Semitic actions remained much more circumscribed and never penetrated the private sector of the economy nor the private life of its citizens. Thus, not only did the Vienna Psychoanalytic Institute exist relatively unhindered during this period, but Sigmund Freud felt compelled to support this authoritarian dictatorship from 1934 to 1938 despite its brutal measures against its critics (Roazen 1971, 533-34).

In Germany a new form of regime emerged after 1933 that was quite different from the authoritarian regime in Austria and the fascist government in Italy. On the Night of the Long Knives on June 30, 1934, between 150 to 200 political opponents of Hitler were murdered by the new Nazi elite, the SS. Among the prominent Germans murdered were the leader of the SA, Ernst Roehm; the former second in command of the Nazi Party, Gregor Strasser; and Kurt von Schleicher, General of the Army and a former chancellor of the Weimar government. On July 3, 1934, the true perversion of the regime became obvious when these murders were retroactively classified as legal (Padfield 1993, 158-63; Strasser 1940, 189-203; Toland 1976, 336-52; and Bullock 1962, 290-311).

The next phase of the movement toward a totalitarian government emerged as an outcome of the power struggle between Wilhelm Frick and Hermann Göring during the spring of 1934, and helped create a unique type of government in the Third Reich. In their struggle to gain complete control of police powers in the Nazi state, Heinrich Himmler was the ultimate winner. Himmler was able to unify the police powers of the state to enforce the ideological goals of National Socialism in ways the average German citizen could hardly imagine. Himmler's major prize in acquiring unilateral control of the police was the Gestapo, which Göring had developed and until 1934 controlled. In a series of further moves that culminated on June 17, 1936, Hitler placed all police powers in Germany in Himmler's hands (Fischer 1995, 333-35; Padfield 1993). Thus, Himmler was able to consolidate and centralize all police functions within the SS. The SD (*Sicherheitsdienst*, headed by Reinhard Heydrich) and the Gestapo (headed by Heinrich Müller) were the two most powerful organizations within the Third Reich, and they operated outside the legal boundaries of the regular German court system. The major purpose of the Gestapo and the SD were twofold: the implementation of Nazi ideology and elimination of all opposition to the Third Reich (Snyder 1989, 113-14 and 317-18).

The Gestapo was empowered to use any method on either an individual or group. Thus, with government-sanctioned use of police terror tactics, the regime was able to establish a new form of mass conformity not anticipated previously in Western civilization. The brutal kind of authoritarian state such as the Dollfuss-Schuschnigg government that existed in Austria had been surpassed by the Third Reich with the systematic use of terror and intrusion into private lives. The emergence of a police state organized to terrorize the population served as a means to crush all opposition. The Night of the Long Knives sent a clear message to the German people that could not be easily forgotten. The Third Reich had transformed the nature of government. It had become what is now classified as a totalitarian state.

The very essence of the Nazi totalitarian dictatorship became evident shortly after the Night of the Long Knives was over. The Nazi Party membership in Vienna, armed with its ideological convictions and terror tactics, attempted a putsch against the Austrian government on July 25, 1934. It failed, but Chancellor Dollfuss was assassinated. The Nazi putsch to take over control of another nation was an excellent example of the distinction between a totalitarian state and an authoritarian government. A totalitarian regime believes it has discovered a sacred truth; for the Nazis, that truth was a racial ideology that would entitle them to use any means to implement the end of that truth.

In the final analysis, totalitarian regimes control both public and private life. In authoritarian governments, as in totalitarian regimes, there is the common belief in strong national governments. Both totalitarian and authoritarian governments are firmly committed to pursue nationalistic and aggressive foreign policies. The fascists in Austria had no such ideology whereas the Nazis did.

The next step is to demonstrate the incompatibility of National Socialism's ideology and its totalitarian government with psychoanalysis. With full recognition that not all the consequences of Nazi ideology were stored in *Mein Kampf*, it is our contention that the ideology of National Socialism did have a direct impact upon the fate of psychoanalysis within the Third Reich. The incompatibility between the Third Reich's regime and psychoanalysis will be demonstrated in two ways. First, for psychoanalysis to exist, there needs to be scientific and political freedom; the revision of the social order abrogated such freedom. Second, the Nazis attempted to impose their altered vision of what it was to be a healthy human being on psychotherapeutic practice. They required that people needed to be in harmonious unity with society, their leader, their soul, and the soil—health equals loyalty. We contend that psychoanalysis, as Freud conceived it, assumed the inevitability of conflict among id, ego, and superego, and conflict between the individual and society. Freud conceived of the self in part submitting to culture and yet at the same time being in opposition to it; the self, in a sense, is in a standing quarrel with culture. The eternal struggle between self and culture has been and is a critical dynamic in the evolution of civilization (Freud 1930). Freud's conception of the individual and civilization was totally incompatible with the idea of a harmonious unity of society, soul, and leader.

As has already been indicated, in a totalitarian regime there is no distinction between one's public and private life. In Orwellian terms, people in the Third Reich could be arrested for "thought crimes" (Orwell 1977, 19). An example of a "thought crime" is acceptance of Descartes's philosophy, which is inconsistent with a major principle of National Socialism's ideology, and this in turn makes one guilty. In fact, one of the psychoanalysts at the Göring Institute who eventually was executed was initially suspected for his use of Descartes's phrase *cogito ergo sum* in a formal presentation at the Göring Institute. The psychoanalyst was John Rittmeister, and one of his colleagues present was a very "amiable" man who was affectionately known as Papi, the director of the Institute. Papi's real name was M. H. Göring. He or his wife, Erna, attended every function at the Institute in order to monitor the discussions and thereby ensure their consistency with National Socialism. M. H. Göring was a cousin of the infamous leader of the Third Reich, Hermann Göring.

It was well known that Göring was a member of the Nazi Party, if only because every leadership position would have required Party membership. It was unlikely, however, that the professionals at the Institute knew

Göring also belonged to the Dozentenbund, or Lecturers' Alliance. This was a voluntary section of the Party whose designated function was to monitor the academic and intellectual communities to make sure that individuals in question did not stray from the ideological boundaries of Nazi ideology. In Orwellian terms, Göring was a member of the "Thought Police." It can be hypothesized that such membership in voluntary organizations is evidence of greater commitment to the ideology.

Under such totalitarian systems how can psychoanalysis work? When one has to submit one's mind to the inner logic of an ideological framework such as National Socialism, one must surrender one's inner freedom to such a degree that psychoanalytic exploration must eventually come into conflict with that ideology. In totalitarian states, one's right to perceive differently or to disagree about facts is no longer allowed (Arendt 1973). As the very word "totalitarian" suggests, in Nazi Germany the claim of the regime was on the total person, including that person's private thoughts. In governments in which children are taught by the schools to monitor their parents' ideas and behaviors in their homes, it is hard to imagine how Freudian psychoanalysis could be workable.

Bertolt Brecht's play *The Private Life of the Master Race* is an excellent portrayal of how the world of an ordinary couple is turned upside down once the totalitarian Nazi government used the schools as a means to indoctrinate children to inform on parents whose political views were not in line with National Socialism. In Brecht's play, a casual discussion between a child and his parents slowly unfolds, making clear how Nazi terror has undermined the family's life. At the table, a father's initial annoyance about the government leads him to make sarcastic comments about the Third Reich's failures. The son meanders out of the house as the parents get involved in further deprecating the Nazis. The parents notice that their son has disappeared and start to worry that he has gone to turn them in to the Gestapo. The worry turns to fear and eventually terror as time passes. The parents then blame each other for anti-Nazi remarks, since they are convinced the son has gone to the Gestapo to report them for their anti-Nazi thinking (Brecht 1944). It turns out the son has just gone out for a walk to buy chocolates, but the point about the breakdown in family loyalty and trust is vividly made.

In societies where children are taught to spy on their parents, the privacy of family life no longer exists. Also gone is the reciprocal trust and the customary parent-child roles. In such a nation can a patient really trust his analyst? Can analysts trust their patients or colleagues? In reality, German children did betray their parents to the Gestapo. The situations in which the state had used children to spy on parents often led to their being referred to the children's section of the Göring Institute because of the consequences of severe guilt and ambivalence. It is not surprising that these children had often developed significant problems in loyalties vis-à-vis parents and state (Cocks 1985, 186).

A significant source of incompatibility between psychoanalysis and Nazi ideology is the view concerning the relationship between the individual and society. According to Nazi ideology the concept of *Volksgemeinschaft* (the people's community) assumed that a living biological unity existed between Aryans within that community, and that within that racial unity there were no class distinctions. This concept denied that each individual is endowed with specified rights as a private citizen. The individual exists only as a part of a whole. In other words, "each individual was merely a component atom in the molecular community" (Caplan 1988, 199). Thus, the emphasis on the principle of *Volksgemeinschaft* resulted in a rejection of the Enlightenment's liberal tenets based upon individual rights with limitations on the state's power (Müller 1991, 70).

Despite the importance of the concept of *Volksgemeinschaft* to National Socialist ideology, it has often been treated as a fiction by historians studying the Third Reich. In studying the letters written to the National Socialist German Workers' Party (NSDAP) district leader (*Kreisleitung*) of Eisenach, John Connely (1996) concludes:

> The National Socialist goal of *Volksgemeinschaft* was never achieved in the way the leaders intended, but neither was *Volksgemeinschaft* myth or fiction. Rather, the appeal to *Volksgemeinschaft* became an instrument by which various groups in Germany could pursue interests that were anything but communal. (Connely 1996, 928)

With the local district offices, the concept had a practical and realistic value. For example, in the Düsseldorf region, "Advice Centers" were established at the local level as a means for the party to "build bridges" to the people. The party concluded that these efforts were successful. The district offices tried to resolve disputes in the lives of the German citizens, and were particularly attentive when the citizen appealed to the "racial community." The district leader "could intervene in any issue . . . provided they did not oppose the interests of the higher agencies." (Connely 1996, 899). Connely suggests that the people may not have completely internalized the tenets of National Socialism. Rather they "externalized" or used them in pursuit of their self-interest. The end result, however uncoordinated, tended to leave little room for competing visions of reality. Thus, "what remained was a really existing *Volksgemeinschaft*" (Connely 1996, 929).

The legal breakdown of the autonomy of the individual's guaranteed rights was enhanced by the *Führerprinzip* (the leader principle). Under this principle, Hitler was assumed to be responsible for every aspect of German society, and his authority could not be bound by legal norms of any kind (Proctor 1988, 72; Caplan 1988, 200). Thus, these two basic concepts of the *Führerprinzip* and *Volksgemeinschaft* continued to exert over time an increasing degree of control over the population of the Third Reich. Given the fact that every aspect of life within Germany was influenced by these two concepts, at least to some degree, the very notion that individual autonomy could be respected and the patient could be free to discuss spontaneous thoughts and feelings was inconsistent with the increased Nazification of life.

In the end, Nazi ideology and the totalitarian system (even a less than perfectly successful totalitarian system) would have to destroy the scientific and professional integrity of classical or orthodox psychoanalysis; the freedom of thought that is a necessary part of psychoanalysis could never have survived within the Göring Institute. Without the inherent atmosphere of trust and security, and freedom from the fear of retaliation and punishment, it would be intolerable for the truths one discovers to differ significantly from officially sanctioned ideology. Can meaningful analysis occur in such a setting as the Göring Institute? We suggest that Cocks, who maintains that psychoanalysis did survive, may have uncritically accepted the idea that all the Nazis did was remove the Jews from the practice of psychoanalysis, leaving the science unchanged. For example, he cites the following anecdote:

> The situation was memorably formulated in the words of Franz Wirz, the Nazi Party's Chief Administrator for University Affairs. . . . On this occasion Wirz was responding to traditional yet also newly anxious and "loyal" criticism of Freud from some German psychotherapists at a meeting on 26 April 1936. He noted that he and the party were not so much opposed to the science of psychoanalysis as to its practice by Jews, saying, "We all know that the Wassermann reaction was discovered by a Jew. But no one in Germany would be so foolish as to no longer make use of this reaction." (Cocks 1985, 4-5)

By accepting Wirz's statement as an accurate picture of what happened to psychoanalysis in Germany, the implication is that psychoanalysis did survive. Wirz's analogy accepts the possibility that the method of psychoanalysis, like the Wassermann test, could still be used minus its Jewish practitioners. If we accept this analogy, we fail to understand the need for mutual trust and respect for individual rights that are an essential feature of psychoanalysis. Psychoanalysis is not conducted on a biochemical level of functioning as is the Wassermann test; it is carried out in a social-political context involving certain liberal ideas. A society dominated to a significant extent by an ideology with concepts like *Volksgemeinschaft* and the *Führerprinzip* cannot allow psychoanalysis or even psychoanalytically oriented psychotherapy to function unhindered in its midst. What did survive, as Cocks demonstrated in detail, were various forms of short-term psychotherapy and the neo-analysis of Schultze-Hencke, once it had become properly Aryanized. These "New German Psychotherapies" held that health equaled adjustment to society and productivity within that society.

In summary, we contend that despite opportunities for professional growth, and the continuation of an institutional infrastructure throughout the period, the spirit or *geist* of psychoanalysis at the Göring Institute was altered sufficiently to make applying the term "survival" inappropriate. We realize that this does not preclude, in theory at least, psychoanalysis from being practiced in secret and by people who were on the periphery of the power structure of the Göring Institute. Evidence of this would be very valuable. However, it would not detract from our proposed notion of the essential incompatibility of psychoanalysis and National Socialist ideology and totalitarianism.

We would like to close this section with some observations by others about the pervasive effect of terror and totalitarian governments. Once again, historians enter the debate by stating that the presence of terror is overstated. John Connely stated that open use of terror at the local level was not required for enforcement, although it remained a "latent threat." Terror was "reserved . . . for those outside the *Volksgemeinschaft*" (Connely 1996, 930). Peter Kenez, writing about the Soviet Union, provides a more pointed and realistic appraisal:

> Historians must write about the terror not in order to vent their indignation but because that subject is essential to our understanding. . . . Terror was not a epiphenomenon. It is not a topic like Soviet sports or Soviet opera. Because of the terror, parents talked differently to their children, writers wrote differently, workers and managers talked to one another differently. (Kenez 1986, in Gleason 1995, 142)

The same can be said about the discourse between analyst and analysand during the years of terror of the Third Reich.

4

The Rise and Fall of Marxism within the Psychoanalytic Movement

IN THE PREVIOUS CHAPTER, we began exploring the relationship of psycho-analysis to various political systems, starting with the hypothesized incompatibility between psychoanalysis and National Socialist ideology within a totalitarian system of government. But the National Socialists were not the first nor the only ones to attempt to make psychoanalysis a handmaiden of sorts to a political ideology. There were many attempts to combine psycho-analysis with variations of Marxism since 1909.

At this point it becomes especially important for readers to understand how the events in Europe, particularly in Germany, contributed to the development of two extremist ideologies—Marxism and National Social-ism—after World War I. The four years of carnage on the battlefield had cost Germany the greatest number of soldiers killed in action (1,800,000 compared, for example, to 116,000 Americans) along with the innumerable civilians who starved to death due in part to the Allied naval blockade. Europe and especially Germany were enfeebled by the war while America was virtually untouched. The German hyperinflation of 1923 and the Great Depression of 1929 were factors that contributed to the erosion of faith in nineteenth-century liberalism, international laws, and Judeo-Christian val-ues, while enhancing a depth of anxiety within the German people never experienced in the United States. The feelings of desperation among the

German people helped establish a climate where extreme ideologies such as Marxism and National Socialism were to become prevalent ways of dealing with their distress (Hobsbawm 1994).

In this chapter we will present some of the major attempts to integrate psychoanalysis and Marxism that had become institutionalized within the psychoanalytic movement in Germany. We will start out by describing the example of Ernst Simmel, a man whose Marxist political orientation and his eventual selection of psychoanalysis as a profession were influenced by his work as a physician helping combat troops during the carnage of World War I. His political interests led to his involvement in the Association of Independent Socialist Physicians. We then go on to describe an important subgroup of the BPI, "The Children's Seminar," and their most prominent members, Otto Fenichel, Wilhelm Reich, and Edith Jacobsohn. Next, we portray the inevitable collision course that the psychoanalytic Marxists, the increasingly powerful Nazis, and the psychoanalytic establishment (Freud, Jones, and the IPA) were all following. The IPA, under Jones's direction, tried to avoid the collision by steering the psychoanalytic movement on a course of complete political neutrality. We suggest that the Nazis were successful in eliminating the Marxist influence on all future training of psychoanalysts in Germany. We end our chapter by discussing the one group in Germany that had integrated Marxism and psychoanalysis and did manage to survive the Third Reich, albeit in an institutional form outside the establishment of the psychoanalytic movement. This group consisted of neo-Marxists from the Frankfurt school. We shall describe the original formation of the Frankfurt school, their flight to the United States, their reformation at the New school for Social Research in New York, and their eventual return to Frankfurt am Main, Germany.

The Example of Ernst Simmel

The Deutsche Psychoanalytische Gesellschaft (DPG), or the German Psychoanalytical Society, was founded in Berlin in 1910 by Karl Abraham and was formally recognized by the IPA as a regional society the same year. The members of the DPG in Berlin who most actively opposed the rise of the Nazi Party possessed strong leftist political orientations. The combination of psychoanalysis and Marxism as a means to understand the world was typical of many analysts in Germany and Austria. This might come as a surprise to most Americans, for whom communism is anathema.

As early as 1918 a young Marxist psychoanalyst who had practiced in poor communities from 1908 to 1914 and then served as an army doctor from 1916 to 1918 provided a critical diagnosis of how the "war neurosis" of World War I would lay the groundwork for World War II. Ernst Simmel was typical of many of the analysts who practiced at the DPG. In "War Neuroses and Psychic Trauma," he discusses the disastrous effects of combat on German soldiers who had spent four years on the front lines and the potential for even longer deleterious consequences in the future:

> [I]t is not only the bloody war which leaves such devastating traces in those who took part in it. Rather, it is also the difficult conflict in which the individual finds himself in his fight against a world transformed by war. It is a fight in which the victim of war neurosis succumbs in silent, often unrecognized, torment. (Simmel 1994, 7)

Simmel goes on to point out with great accuracy the prognosis for World War II:

> Whatever in a person's experience is too powerful or horrible for his conscious mind to grasp and work through, filters down to the unconscious levels of his psyche. There it lies like a mine, waiting to explode the entire psychic structure. And only the self-protective mechanism, with its release of waves of affect, and its attachment to an individual organ, to external symptoms, and to symptomatic actions prevents a permanent disturbance of the psychic balance. (Simmel 1994, 8)

Simmel continued to lead the Marxist psychoanalytic philosophical front for many years. In June 1924, the subgroup of psychoanalysts had begun discussing the relationship between politics and psychoanalysis. Simmel chaired another group, called the Association of Socialist Doctors. This subgroup of psychoanalysts was committed to forming a bridge between psychoanalysis and historical materialism (Brecht et al. 1985, 40–41). As early as 1924, Simmel had helped the leftist physician members of the Social Democratic Party break away from that organization and form an independent group, the Association of Independent Socialist Physicians, that was much more radical. Simmel argued that "people do not die from deadly bacteria alone, but rather from the fact that anyone exhausted from brutal exploitation by industry becomes easy prey for whatever germs they happen to encounter" (Proctor 1988, 259 and 260). He listed five demands of the association: the eight-hour work day, occupational health and safety, maternity leave for pregnancy and nursing mothers, laws restructuring child labor, and socialization of health care. The association fought against what it considered a primitive legal code that made abortions criminal, and it demanded greater rights for women to control their own fertility. The members of the Association of Socialist Physicians were clearly a minority of the psychoanalysts and other physician groups in Germany during the Weimar era. However, they were clearly the ideological foes of National Socialism.

Like many groups in Germany, the Association of Independent Socialist Physicians were very slow to take National Socialism seriously. They regarded the Nazi movement as a joke and took the stance that they would not lower themselves to reply to it. One of the major problems that interfered with the liberal and leftist parties from joining forces against the National Socialists was the order from Moscow given to the German Communist Party (KPD). The Communist Marxists were not to cooperate with the Marxists in the Social Democratic Party (SPD) in their protest against National Socialism because the SPD was seen as just as an important enemy as the Nazis; perhaps more, in that the Socialists competed with the Communists for the allegiance of the working class (Kaes and Martin 1994, 309–10).

In 1932, Simmel spoke at a meeting committed to the theme "National Socialism: Enemy of Public Health." In a speech entitled "National Socialism and the Peoples' Health," Simmel criticized National Socialism for regressing to "medieval mysticism" and resorting to the old line of blaming the Jews for natural disasters. Simmel said that today, "we laugh at such explanations, but at one time they cost many Jews their lives" (Proctor 1988, 270-71).

In discussing the Great Depression as it affected the German people, he described their reactions to it as "not understanding what was happening to them" and "mind numbing." The people's reaction to the economic depression after experiencing the hyperinflation of the 1920s was "the same as an expression of an inescapable natural catastrophe." He lamented, "millions that have been living without work, underfed, put together in unbelievable habitats, beaten in body and soul, living in a complete sense of despair." He went on to suggest that, for the young, there would be only one kind of profession, that of not having a job (Simmel 1932, 162-72).

Simmel suggested a remedy to the economic crisis that was having such a destructive impact on Germany. In Marxist terms, he asserted, "the plight of the proletariat should force them to appreciate the genius of Marx and Engels who predicted the current conditions on the basis of selective axioms in the Communist Manifesto in 1848" (Simmel 1932, 162-72). After quoting different aspects of the *Communist Manifesto,* Simmel explained that the social security system in Germany and the medical health programs provided for the workers were not primarily in their interest. Rather, they were only a means to serve the capitalist system by providing back-up workers for industry, with worker patients being only healthy enough to work. In providing services to the workers, physicians allowed for the continuation of worker exploitation as well as their own. Simmel argued that in this system the physicians had lost their autonomy and the idealistic goals of their profession. Physicians now had to work with high quotas of patients as if on an assembly line and were not able to give the time necessary for the individual patient. Like the exploited workers, the physicians serving in this way had to rationalize what they were doing. Simmel called for the complete socialization of all industry and all services as the only reasonable means to remedy the situation.

Only at the very end of his speech did Simmel examine the danger of National Socialism. Despite the fact that the Nazis had received more than 38 percent of the vote in the latest Reichstag election, Simmel's major criticism of National Socialism was left as the last issue to be discussed. Even in exploring the danger of National Socialism, Simmel continued to use classical Marxist interpretations about the rise of fascism throughout Europe. According to Marxist theory, fascism represented the end state of capitalism, and thus capitalism was the core evil to be eliminated. In this dual Marxist-psychoanalytic interpretation of Hitler's Nazi movement offered by Simmel, the inborn drives of aggression and cannibalism do not need to be wholly suppressed or sublimated in capitalism. If fact, these aggressive drives are promoted in capitalism in terms of "killing off the competition." The support of this kind of competition leads to the development of trusts, syndicates, and ultimately the triumph of their aggressive drives. These aggressive drives lead to the end goal of capitalism — great profits. Simmel perceived war as the continuation of the goals of capitalism. War allows for the direct killing of one's rival with the sanction of "being told to do so by a superior." The Jew, Marxist, and any person who thinks differently are the enemy. In this way, the National Socialist movement was seen as a form of emotional regression in its allowing aggressive drives to become manifest. Simmel asserted that Germany needed to awake from this threat, "awake because it is becoming day, the light you see in the sky which comes from the troops of Hitler is nothing else but a fire caused by the collapse of capitalism" (Simmel 1932, 162-72). Thus, even at the eleventh hour, just before the Nazis took power, Simmel still underestimated the horror of National Socialism by associating it with capitalism. By failing to perceive and understand the Nazis for what they really were, the various Marxist groups were denying a reality that Hitler had clearly spelled out in *Mein Kampf.*

The Marxist psychoanalysts remained naïve about the Nazi threat, and most of these analysts were forced to flee when Hitler came to power. An instructive example was Ernst Simmel's own sudden emigration as described by Martin Grotjahn. Simmel was Grotjahn's analyst, and Grotjahn was present in an analytic session when a police friend of Simmel's called to inform him that the Gestapo was going to arrest him. Grotjahn helped Simmel escape out a back window into a backyard and then over a fence. In a later analytic session Simmel admitted they had broken all the regulations for psychoanalytic training and added, "I should be put into an analytic concentration camp" (Grotjahn 1987, 36). The rule Simmel thought he had broken has been called abstinence or neutrality. Anna Freud's well-known dictum that the analyst should remain equidistant from the patient's id, ego, and superego also applies to this "violation." Many contemporary analysts would argue that such an psychic stance is not only impossible but counterproductive.

In looking at the example of Simmel's resistance to National Socialism, we see that it occurred not from the beliefs and principles of a politically "neutral" psychoanalysis but from an amalgamation of psychoanalysis and Marxism. However, like the majority of Marxists who practiced in Germany, Simmel's flight to America ultimately ended a unique era in the history of psychoanalysis.

The Children's Seminar: Marxism's Association with the BPI

Another interesting outcome of the fascinating few years of the Weimar Republic was the attempt at the integration of psychoanalysis and Marxism at the BPI. This attempt combined a broadly based psychological understanding of human nature and a political system based on an economic interpretation of history. It occurred within what became popularly known as the Children's Seminar. The younger members of the BPI met to discuss political ideas and psychoanalysis. Although not all the younger analysts were Marxists, a central core of the Seminar was committed to combining their clinical training with a materialistic conception of history. The materialistic conception of history was predicated on the belief that the modern state was established to maintain the economic basis of society; and that the wealth of the ruling classes had established the state along with its political and legal systems to preserve its own power. It further posited that the end result of doing away with private property and class distinctions would lead the state to wither away until it was nonexistent. Whether or not Marxism and psychoanalysis in their pure forms could ever be integrated in a practical way remains questionable, but Marxism had clearly gained a significant foothold within the BPI and therefore within the psychoanalytic movement.

In 1934, Otto Fenichel published an essay explaining what the members of the Children's Seminar had hoped to accomplish if they had had the time and opportunity. It was entitled "Psychoanalysis as the Nucleus of a Future Dialectical-Materialistic Psychology," and the title reveals the kind of major undertaking that was involved (Fenichel 1967). Given the overwhelming accomplishment of Fenichel's integration of almost all "of the relevant" analytic literature in his classic, *The Psychoanalytic Theory of Neurosis* (1945), and Edith Jacobsohn's well-known expertise in the area of object relations, the promise of their unified efforts to establish a form of integrated psychoanalytic-Marxist theory made that idea appealing, but the question remained as to whether it was practical. They certainly had the intellectual ability to integrate Marxism and psychoanalysis into an encompassing theory of economics, society, and culture, but they were in the wrong place at the wrong time. The Nazis would ensure that a joint effort by them in Germany would fail.

Following the Great Depression of 1929, the psychoanalytic Marxists were using their creative and intellectual abilities to solve problems occurring in the midst of, and in part as a reaction to, the profound social and economic problems that surrounded them. The political events in Berlin were constantly changing, and those living there were very often faced with frightening violence in the streets. The gathering storm of National Socialism was rapidly expanding into more and more aspects of German life. The ominous signs of an apocalypse were on the horizon. The day-to-day turbulence in Europe during the 1920s and 1930s led many intellectuals to the conviction that drastic improvements were needed to fix the constant economic and social changes that kept occurring. If the National Socialist alternative did not fit one's way of looking at the world, another distinct possibility was the reconciliation of Marxism and psychoanalytic theory. The integration of a theory that explained individual behavior with the theory that purportedly understood the reasons for the constant economic crises being experienced seemed a logical solution for many Europeans. Versions of such attempts to integrate Marxism into a wide variety of fields had a long history in Europe and are presently represented in their most refined form by Jürgen Habermas's critical theory (Bernstein 1994, 7).

The intellectual, social, and cultural atmosphere in the United States has never allowed for the legitimacy of Marxist and socialist approaches. America has had the very good fortune of never having been truly confronted with the kind of long and difficult period of economic hard times during which Marxist philosophy could become part of its zeitgeist. The European experience has been entirely different. In Europe, Marxist political philosophy not only amassed enormous popular votes in post–World War II Italy and France, but it also was a major intellectual force before World War I. As most Americans who are acquainted with psychoanalysis will remember, many of Freud's earliest followers were men whose political orientations were far more Left than Right. Those with a Marxist or socialist orientation included Alfred Adler, Erich Fromm, and Wilhelm Reich. Of Freud's early circle, Adler was the only one to join the Social Democratic Party. All three of these psychoanalysts had functioned as orthodox practitioners, but eventually all were labeled as heretics by the orthodox psychoanalysts. While he was still a member of Freud's inner circle, Adler was also the first analyst to attempt an integration between Marxism and psychoanalysis. Adler was probably expounding on the convictions of his wife, a committed socialist, his patient Adolf Ioffe, and his friend Leon Trotsky, when he presented to the Wednesday evening group in 1909 a paper called "On the Psychology of Marxism." In this presentation Adler suggested that Marx had anticipated Freud's concept of instincts and "had taught the proletariat to detect defense mechanisms of the bourgeoisie." Trotsky, of course, would rise to become one of the great leaders of the Bolshevik Revolution, as would Ioffe. In 1908, when Ioffe worked with Trotsky in Vienna on establishing the newspaper *Pravda,* he was also in medical school and was an analytic patient of Adler. Alexander Etkind suggests that the concept of "will to power" that helped lead to the break between Adler and Freud had probably been inspired in part by his Marxist patient (Johnston 1972, 256; Etkind 1997, 230-31). Adler, Reich, and Fromm were eventually all excluded from the Freudian psychoanalytic movement. Once any member had been excommunicated from the fold like these three, no matter how important he had been, he was never allowed to return. From these facts it might be concluded that their Marxist leanings were the reason for their exclusion. However, only in the case of Wilhelm Reich was this in fact true. As we shall make clear, many orthodox psychoanalysts would eventually go to their deaths remaining loyal and committed to both Freud and Marx.

During the early 1920s, the initial results of the Bolshevik Revolution and the early reports of its success impressed many European intellectuals. This optimism about a rational and just political system was seen as the logical outgrowth of the Enlightenment. It led to a meaningful dialogue between psychoanalysis and Marxism. With the glow of optimism from their Russian success, many Marxists perceived that the social and economic liberation promised by Marx was very consistent with the sexual liberation they had read into Freud. Thus, the combination of Marx and Freud had promised to be a good match. One way to look at these theories is that they were extremely complementary. If one accepts the shortcomings of each theory and believes that each theory could be strengthened by the other, an integrationist approach might seem to be a solution for both theories. Thus, what is wrong with Marxism is its complete reliance on rationality and its failure to consider the subjectivity and aggressive nature of human beings. What is wrong with psychoanalysis on the other hand is its lack of a real sense of history and its failure to come to terms with the limitations inherent in the political economy upon which capitalism is built. Thus, an appropriate integration of both theories could offer remedies neither alone would provide (Wolfenstein 1993). From this perspective, the idea of an integration of Marx and Freud made sense.

In the Berlin Psychoanalytic Institute, the issues of Marxism and psychoanalysis were not a purely intellectual question. In the fifteen years that the Weimar government lasted, Berlin was a world of explosive social upheavals and revolutionary politics. It was not a time or place where one could take a peaceful retreat to explore one's inner life without constant reminders that politics was a reality that would not go away.

Yet at the same time, the young analysts and analysts in training were also at the best psychoanalytic training center in the world. Even without the presence of Freud, the Berlin Institute would produce a group of analysts who themselves would cause psychoanalytic revolutions. This would include Karen Horney, Franz Alexander, and Melanie Klein. In this environment of social, cultural, and intellectual unrest, what Jacoby (1986) would call the "political Freudians" were born. In 1922, Otto Fenichel moved from Vienna to Berlin to finish his psychoanalytic training. Fenichel came to an Institute that had been infused by a civic spirit and committed to serving all that came through its doors. Both Max Eitingon and Ernst Simmel had been present at Freud's lecture in 1918 when he asserted that "the large masses of people," as much as the smaller number of rich, all suffer from neurosis. He then dreamed of the day in the future when "the conscience of the community will awake" and provide psychoanalytic care at no cost. Only a few short years later, the Berlin Institute had opened its clinic doors for such a purpose (Jacoby 1986, 65). But it was not only in Berlin that the blue-collar workers, domestics, and laborers were treated (16 percent of the Polyclinic patients were poor), but surprisingly the Vienna outpatient clinic included 24 percent of that same group of poorer patients (Hale 1979, 302; and Kestenberg 1994). In responding to a patient in 1935, Freud confirmed the view that being poor did not prevent one from becoming an analytic patient:

> Now that we have free clinics and the psychoanalytic institutes, the question no longer arises. Anybody can now be analyzed; they may have to wait a little, but everybody has the privilege. Besides, every analyst has a number of free patients. Here in Vienna, for example, every analyst has to treat two free patients. (Wortis 1954, 151)

In Peter Gay's biography of Freud, Gay indicates that in Berlin indigent patients were not inevitably turned over to analysts in training but "at least part of the time to a seasoned practitioner" (Gay 1988, 462–63). When comparable data were obtained in the United States in 1958, it was found that at the outpatient clinic in Chicago 6 percent of those treated were poor patients, and at the New York Institute clinic only 2 percent of those treated were poor (Hale 1979, 306). The generosity of the Europeans in comparison to the American psychoanalysts is consistent with Freud's fears regarding both American medicine and the cultural impact of the United States on psychoanalysis. The dramatic difference between Europe and the United States in providing low-cost psychoanalytic care for the poor was dramatic evidence that Freud's expectations would become real.

In November of 1924, Fenichel, who by this time had become a member of the teaching staff of the Institute, would initiate a course to be given outside the Institute. There are differing opinions of how the Children's Seminar started. Fenichel claimed that Max Eitingon initiated the idea by suggesting that the younger candidates could benefit from meetings run by him outside the formal seminar schedule. Simmel described the origin differently. He claimed that Fenichel, as part of the regular teaching faculty, attempted to introduce the course as part of the regular curriculum, but some of the more senior staff objected to integrating Marxism and psychoanalysis. According to this version, Fenichel's response was, "What of it! If you don't like the way we do it—let us be naughty children." It was without question a left-leaning seminar but was open to conservatives like Harald Schultz-Hencke, and it lasted the life of the Institute (Jacoby 1983, 65–68). However the Seminar came about, there was no question that without Eitingon's support it could never be held inside or outside the formal structure of the BPI. There were a total of 168 meetings, and the number of participants varied from five to twenty-five. The name of Fenichel's last lecture, given in October of 1933 before the group dispersed, was "Psychoanalysis, Socialism and the Tasks for the Future." Apparently there was no rigid political orientation, and the subjects discussed varied from political to technical matters (Jacoby 1986, 62-67).

With the gathering storm of war and most of the Jewish analysts thinking about their personal survival, Fenichel had finally come to the conclusion that the new group of psychoanalysts committed to the Marxist tradition would have to exist in secret. In almost every country close to Germany the fears of being invaded had led to a suppression of civil liberties. The psychoanalytic organization, as well as the countries to which he traveled, were starting to expect the worst as the Third Reich grew more and more aggressive. Before leaving for the United States, Fenichel gave a parting address to a group of analysts in Prague. He stated that at one time he had devoted himself to a psychoanalysis whose authentic task would be "its elaboration into a theory of human culture and society" (Jacoby 1986, 116). He came to the conclusion, however, that such hopes belonged to the distant past (Jacoby 1986, 116). At a time in Europe when fascism was attempting "to make people dumb instead of intelligent," one's purpose in such circumstances was simply the preservation of classical psychoanalysis. He ended with a poem he had written that stated, "Many are oppressed; many are in need; and whoever thinks is threatened." The poem continued: "What once was is past. However, authentic integrity does not know defeat" (Jacoby 1986, 117). The best way to hold on to psychoanalysis was, sadly, for him to flee to America.

Jacoby provides an exceptionally good case about what happened to the political psychoanalysts upon arriving in the United States. He maintains that upon arrival the process of Americanization led to the abandonment of "Freud's bold theorizing and questioning" as exemplified in *Civilization and Its Discontents.* "Against Freud's profound hopes, psychoanalysis became insular, medical, and clinical" (Jacoby 1986, xi). The following evidence supports Jacoby's point of view. The eminent and late lay analyst Reuben Fine published the *History of Psychoanalysis.* On page 449 of the new expanded version of this history, published in 1990, Fine quoted the following traditional Marxist interpretation from Fenichel's collected papers (volume 2, pages 266-67), dated 1944, in which capitalism was considered the cause of fascism:

> The ways of production and distribution, and their contradictions,
> inflict severe frustrations upon individuals of all classes. . . . Today they
> arouse especially feelings of being lost and of "not belonging." [In that
> same vein Fenichel continued by connecting capitalism "not belong-
> ing" to] a longing to have once more an omnipotent person in the
> external world to whom one may submit, losing one's helpless individ-

uality in a magnificent oceanic feeling. This longing forms the psychological condition in the masses which meets the influence of Fascism
halfway. (Fine 1990, 449)

Fine was apparently unable to accept the obvious fact that Fenichel was still
a Marxist in 1944. Thus he would distance Fenichel's statement "back to
his Marxist period, when he was clearly allied with Reich" (Fine 1990,
449). Fine continued to deny that Fenichel held his Marxist views until his
death in 1945. He indicated that the attempt to integrate psychoanalysis
into Marxism collapsed in 1934, contending that when "Wilhelm Reich
was expelled from the International, Fenichel altered his views" (Fine 1990,
108). Fine simply could not accept that Fenichel remained a committed
Marxist after being in the United States for many years, and he distorted
the reality of Fenichel's political beliefs by attributing them to Germany
and Wilhelm Reich. This obvious denial and distortion of reality regarding
Fenichel's political orientation conveys the type of anti-Marxist pressures
that the émigré analysts continually experienced. What might have generated this kind of distortion made by Fine was the obvious failure by Americans in general, and psychoanalysts in particular, to understand any political
position outside the traditional Democratic and Republican Parties frames
of reference. For most Americans then and now, the political position of a
Marxist had only one meaning: a communist who believed in the totalitarian type of government that governed the Soviet Union during the 1950s.
A concurrent idea was that all Marxists believed that the violent overthrow
of the United States government was a necessary prerequisite to reaching
their ends. American political discourse at that time and today has lacked
an appreciation of the subtler distinctions among political systems.

Perhaps as stunning as Fine's characterization of Fenichel's beliefs was
Edith Jacobsohn's silence regarding her own political past (Jacoby 1986,
134). She was a gifted analyst, a significant theoretician who had great
empathy for her patients. At a meeting in Scandinavia after the Nazis took
power in Germany, she showed courage in deciding to go back to Berlin
against Georg Gerö's advice because she did not want to abandon her
patients. Edith Jacobsohn's actions document her sense of duty as well as
great courage. Eventually, many of her patients were arrested, and one was
murdered (Hale 1995, 126). She was imprisoned for two years. While she
was able to cope with Nazi barbarism, after entering the United States she
apparently never discussed her past association with "New Beginnings," the
Marxist group in Berlin to which she had belonged (Lockot 1994c). The
closest Edith Jacobsohn came to discussing her political leanings was in the
obituary she wrote about her friend Annie Reich. Jacobsohn mentions their

participation in the Children's Seminar and a separate study group that dealt with "character" problems and sociopsychological questions. The Children's Seminar was headed by Fenichel and Schultz-Hencke; "the latter often presented deviating views which led to vehement arguments" (Jacobsohn 1971, 335). The inclusion of Schultz-Hencke and Fenichel as coleaders of this group and the intense arguments that occurred lead to all kinds of unanswered questions.

The question must be raised regarding the nature of life in America that led so many avowed Marxists and socialists to become so secretive. How much of their silence was due to their experiences in Europe, the psychoanalytic establishment in the United States, or the kind of "I would rather be dead than Red" philosophy that gripped America from the late 1940s until the 1960s? It is chilling to realize that an individual like Edith Jacobsohn, who was arrested by the Nazis and spent two years in prison without backing down from her political beliefs, upon arrival in America became silent.

Indeed, it remains an irony that the Freudian psychoanalytic tradition that existed in authoritarian nations like Germany and Austria had allowed their Marxist colleagues a place and voice in their institutes, yet upon entering the United States, the legendary symbol of political freedom, the émigré analysts would almost all keep an inordinate silence on their political past.

The Collision Course between the Psychoanalytic Marxists, the Nazis, and the Psychoanalytic Establishment

It appears that the psychoanalytic establishment had decided, in light of the Nazi threat, that for its own protection psychoanalysis needed to separate itself from politics, particularly from the more radical variety. A low political profile was considered essential if psychoanalysts were to have a chance to survive the Nazi storm. As this stance for psychoanalysts was being made clear by leaders of the analytic groups, Wilhelm Reich's behavior became more erratic and disturbed, and he was much more outspoken about his views on Marxist and sexual politics (a promotion of sexual freedom among the working class). He joined the German Communist Party and became a political activist. His Communist Party cellmate, Arthur Koestler, described their door-to-door canvassing and commented wryly, "We sold the World Revolution like vacuum cleaners" (Jacoby 1986, 80). Richard Sterba describes Reich as showing increasing fanaticism in the theoretical as well as the political arena. Reich proposed that a perfect orgasm would prevent or cure any neurosis, apparently drawing from his own experience. He told Sterba that if he did not have an orgasm for two days, he would feel ill and see "black before his eyes." These symptoms disappeared upon having an orgasm. Sterba opines that Reich "defended his thesis so rigorously because his character corresponded . . . to the 'genital narcissist'" (Sterba 1985, 87). The German psychoanalyst Volker Friedrich, however, credits Reich with having made "the only scientific contribution at the Institute which dealt with the growing reality of the National Socialist rule." Reich made this threat clear in June 1932 when he gave a lecture entitled "Mass Psychological Problems within Economic Crisis" (Friedrich 1989, 7). Otto Fenichel was as committed to Marx as was Reich but had an entirely different personal style. The relationship between Reich and Fenichel and their respective interaction with the establishment reveal a great deal about how the psychoanalytic movement responded to the Nazi threat. It is also a revealing study of the relationship between the acceptability of ideas and the style with which they are communicated.

As president of the IPA, Jones had demonstrated a wide variety of opinions about Reich's political beliefs during the Third Reich in his letters to Anna Freud from April to December 1933. In trying to achieve political neutrality for psychoanalysis, Jones encouraged Felix Boehm to talk Reich out of starting an international protest against Edith Jacobsohn's arrest for espionage and her almost one-year imprisonment without a trial. Jones showed a less than empathic attitude toward her, perhaps because his focus was on what this would do to the psychoanalytic movement. Jones was also quite critical of what he described as "ultra Jewish" attitudes on the part of some of the analysts. While he supported Boehm's request to stop the plan to stage an international protest on behalf of Edith Jacobsohn, he also wrote to Anne Buchholtz on June 18, 1936, stating, "It is not true that we have been kept back from concrete action by any advice on the part of [the German protests]" (Brecht et al. 1985, 126). When Fenichel wrote to both Jones and Anna Freud on November 26, 1935, he was attempting to persuade them of the importance of standing firm for principles related to Jacobsohn's arrest and the move to have the Jewish members resign from the DPG (Brecht et al. 1985, 181). Anna Freud apparently was moved, but Jones sent two telegrams to Boehm (November 22 and December 4, 1935) supporting the view that the Jewish members should resign (Brecht et al. 1985, 134 and 136).

Jones's priorities are further revealed by an incident that occurred in 1938, in connection with Richard Sterba's attempts to emigrate with his family from Austria. In his memoirs, Sterba, a gentile psychoanalyst, describes the complexities and the difficulties of his and his wife's decision to leave their homeland. The decision may have been made easier by what he perceived as the understanding and blessing of both Sigmund Freud and Anna Freud. He quotes Anna Freud as saying, "We expected that you would not play the role in Vienna that Felix Boehm plays in Berlin" (Sterba 1982, 159). Sterba proceeded to ask Jones for help in obtaining an immigration visa to England for his family, and Jones turned him down in no uncertain terms. Perhaps, unlike Freud, Jones desired that Sterba serve as the "Boehm of Vienna" and stay in place. Jones indicated he would do "nothing" to help the Sterba family escape. In fact, Richard Sterba learned he would be the last one who would get the IPA's assistance, because according to Jones, "you should have stayed in Vienna together with August Aichhorn as a memory of psychoanalysis for a happier future" (Sterba quoting Jones's letter to him, 1982, 163).

Why did Jones try so hard to keep Sterba in Austria? It makes no sense. The Nazis showed their hand during the *Anschluß* when they took seventy thousand prisoners, including August Aichhorn's son, to places like Dachau. That was why Aichhorn stayed in Austria (Cocks 1985, 187). Sterba concludes that Jones's hope was to move the Jews from the Vienna group to England, while Sterba remained at his post in Vienna. Sterba then traveled to London to meet with Jones and this time was told to go to South Africa rather than expect to be invited to England. Jones's behavior was obviously placing the Sterba family in danger by this point, since South Africa had turned down their application and the Swiss authorities were pressuring them to leave the country (Sterba 1982, 166–67). Jones's behavior must be considered from the perspective that he had originally planned to transfer all the Jewish members of the Vienna Psychoanalytic Institute en masse to England, but most of them chose the United States (Deutsch 1973, 170). This meant there must have been room for Richard and Editha Sterba and their two girls in England. Jones's willingness to place the Sterba family in jeopardy must be considered a failure in integrity. Jones's behavior not only was inconsistent with his previous humane efforts, but it obviously contradicted both Anna and Sigmund Freud's wishes. There appears to be no reasonable explanation or even an obvious irrational motive for Jones's behavior.

The interaction between Reich and Fenichel is both an interesting and illuminating description of how political pressure from the Nazis, Marxists, and the psychoanalytic establishment would lead to dramatically different reactions by these two colleagues and have significantly different outcomes. In 1922, Fenichel arrived in Berlin from Vienna, and the Reichs arrived in 1930. Fenichel supported Reich's early writing in social psychology and endorsed Reich's book, *The Impulsive Character.* Fenichel indicated that Reich showed courage in writing about the relationship between sexual morality and the capitalist system. However, a turning point in their relationship came in 1930. In a review of Reich's *Function of Orgasm*, Fenichel questioned the contention that sexual intercourse is the most important issue in public health. In fact, Fenichel went on to state that experiencing and being able to tolerate some dissatisfaction in sexual desire without disturbance was the "criterion of full health" (Jacoby 1986, 73). Their differences over this issue and many others over the years would lead the two colleagues to their ultimate split. Fenichel had supported Reich, but not totally and unconditionally, and this was something Reich was finding harder and harder to accept (Jacoby 1986, 85-91).

In August 1934, at the thirteenth international psychoanalytical congress in Lucerne, Reich learned that he had been secretly expelled from the DPG a year earlier. Felix Boehm claimed that the initiative for this action came directly from Freud during a meeting in Vienna in the spring of 1933. Freud's request was carried out at an executive meeting of the DPG that summer. Reich was not told because he was out of the country. Reich protested his secret excommunication to the IPA in vain (Nitzschke 1991, 35-36). Despite Reich's belief that Fenichel should have supported him more openly in this matter, they agreed to work together. It was agreed that Fenichel and the other Marxists would work within the analytic organizations to motivate the IPA leadership to actively resist Nazification of the DPG. Reich had agreed to work outside the psychoanalytic organizations but to remain loyal to the inner Marxist circle. Going against his commitment not to join any psychoanalytic organization that would create trouble by causing the IPA to act against him and the organization he joined, Reich proceeded to join the Norwegian Psychoanalytic Association. This action by Reich seemingly discredited both the small Marxist group and the Norwegian Psychoanalytic Association and led to Reich's formal exclusion from the Marxist group (Harris and Brock 1991, 159).

Fenichel would periodically support Reich's work, or criticize it, depending upon the issue involved. Fenichel would have to disagree when Reich stated that with his sexual politics "all humanity can be led directly to heaven or at least into revolutionary action" (Jacoby 1986, 90). Yet, even after their formal split, Fenichel would support Reich in face of attacks by the Viennese psychoanalytic establishment. When Robert Waelder, the Viennese coeditor of an approved psychoanalytic journal, *Imago*, argued that the mixing of politics and science, i.e., psychoanalysis, was unacceptable, Fenichel would respond. Although Fenichel had written an article in

Reich's new journal and was facing expulsion himself, he responded to Waelder with a letter to the editor. In that letter Fenichel declared that many psychoanalysts were committed Marxists and wanted to know how these two sciences were inconsistent.

Fenichel was sent a formal letter by Ernst Kris rejecting his letter for publication; but in an informal letter Waelder sent Fenichel it was alleged that a great embarrassment had been created by Fenichel's letter. Waelder went on to justify what he had previously published. He then requested that Fenichel withdraw his letter of rebuttal. Fenichel not only refused but demanded to know if Waelder's article was the formal public statement that the IPA had promised to publish regarding the status of the Marxists and psychoanalysis. Fenichel agreed that the truthful reason for Reich's being expelled was that he was "too pathological," and his work could not be published (Jacoby 1986, 93). While accepting criticism of Reich's mental status as legitimate, he went on to say that attacking Reich on political grounds was unacceptable. Fenichel suggested that the other Marxists had the impression the IPA did not want them around anymore. With that statement Fenichel threw down the gauntlet for Waelder either to accept or expel the Marxists; but this challenge over principles was never picked up by the establishment. Fenichel obviously was a different case than Reich. He was clearly too healthy, too exceptional a theoretician, and too good a practicing analyst for the psychoanalytic movement to lose. In the world of realpolitik, Fenichel not only knew how to be discrete in face of the Nazi storm, but also knew the power of his own value.

An interesting point in this comparison between these two committed Marxists was that despite Freud's long history of being intolerant of significant dissension, in no way could he have been left out in deciding the fate of Fenichel. Five years after he published *Civilization and Its Discontents,* Freud would accept Fenichel's total commitment to a political system that he, Freud, had denounced as unrealistic and incompatible with human nature. During that same year while Fenichel was in Vienna, the establishment solicited a major essay on psychoanalysis from him. Fenichel and the Vienna group debated back and forth over this article — the Vienna group imploring Fenichel to moderate his tone, and Fenichel asserting the need for the article to be a critique. The work was never published, perhaps suggesting an impasse. However, the effort made reveals the attempt on the part of the Vienna group to keep Fenichel within the fold. During one of his visits Fenichel observed that "they feared me a little bit" (Jacoby 1986, 94). That fear was probably generated by the estimation of Freud's respect for Fenichel. This also suggests Freud's flexibility in areas outside his own theory and clinical judgment. Fenichel was not the same kind of "true believer" as Jones; he was a man who followed the beat of his own drum, and one of those drumbeats happened to be the same as Freud's. Fenichel incorporated in himself the essence and spirit of psychoanalysis as very few ever had before or since, and Freud could value that. Yet Fenichel would dedicate himself to following another drumbeat, one that he would never see to its end. Despite having written a brilliant criticism of Marx, Freud obviously knew that history, economics, and politics were not truly areas of his expertise. The very fact that Fenichel was not thrown out documents for history that Freud could accept opinions entirely different from his own. It gives respectability to the idea that clinical and theoretical psychoanalysis were Freud's only "sacred" areas of intellectual life. Freud's capacity to tolerate Fenichel's Marxism also gives better perspective to the important differences he had with Adler, Stekel, Jung, and Rank. An implication for the psychoanalytic movement was that Freud could give ground to a follower whose own ambitions matched his own. Unfortunately for the world as well as for Fenichel, the right time and place to do his work would last only a few years in Berlin. If it were possible, he needed the lifetime that Freud had to accomplish the task of all tasks, the reconciliation between psychoanalysis and Marxism. And that he never had.

On the other hand, the ultimate conclusion was that the Third Reich eliminated the Marxist impact within the psychoanalytic movement in modern Germany. There are no institutional traces of the Children's Seminar, and thus practicing psychoanalysts in Germany with a Marxist bent practically do not exist. The psychoanalysts who were associated with the Children's Seminar were almost all forced to leave. The few psychoanalysts with Marxist beliefs who continued to practice during the Third Reich were forced to keep their political beliefs to themselves. If they protested in any way, they faced the death penalty. The German psychoanalysts started to reorganize after the end of World War II, when there was no Marxist influence left. Thus, the brief but significant inroads Marxism had made upon psychoanalysis in Germany must be considered a historical discontinuity.

The Frankfurt School

We have described how the Marxist psychoanalysts of the Children's Seminar (i.e., Steff Bernstein, Edith Jacobsohn, Francis Deri, and Otto Fenichel) tended to suppress and/or deny their Marxist leanings when they emigrated to the United States. Fenichel continued the *Rundbrief,* or Circular Letter, but was more discreet in his publications regarding Marxism.

The combination of what happened to the Marxist psychoanalysts in the United States and in Germany meant that by the end of the war, their respective orientations were no longer part of the organizational structure of the psychoanalytic movement. However, there was a continuous amalgamation of psychoanalysis and Marxism outside of the psychoanalytic movement, in the form of the Frankfurt school.

No study of the integration of psychoanalysis with political thought would be complete without a brief look at the Frankfurt school. The Frankfurt Institute of Social Research has provided a left-wing critique of current and past affairs in Germany and in the liberal democracies. From the late 1920s until 1933 there was a reciprocal interaction between parts of the psychoanalytic movement and the Frankfurt Institute of Social Research. The most critical factor related to understanding the Frankfurt Institute is its geographic and historical origin. The Institute was established in the midst of continued crisis and a constant sense of catastrophe within Germany. The continual crisis in Germany had led to a polarization of the Left and Right political forces that dominated German life during the first half of the century. This polarization of the Left and Right consistently reduced the power of the center parties, which therefore could not pass any meaningful legislation. Many who sought a vantage point from which to fight fascism were pushed, so to speak, along the political spectrum toward the Marxist Left. The number of moderates dwindled, and moderation was increasingly viewed as an ineffective position from which to oppose fascism in Italy and later National Socialism in Germany. This polarization in politics eventually led to the collapse of the center during the Weimar Republic, with the consequence that Hitler came to power being able to call attention, somewhat correctly, to the growth of the "Red menace." Intellectuals and academics did not escape this polarization phenomenon.

The Frankfurt school from its inception was a left-wing group of intellectuals trying to understand the nature of fascism and National Socialism. The original Frankfurt Institute was considered neo-Marxist. The failure of the communist revolution to have occurred first in a more advanced Western Europe, as was predicted in classical Marxist theory, led to revisions in that theory. The reevaluation led to the development of a neo-Marxist position. In this revised theory of Marx, there was a rejection of the belief that economic forces were historically the most critical factors leading to revolution. It was more likely that man's alienation from himself and his work, brought about by capitalism, was a condition more significant in creating the need for revolution. The second change in the original Marxist theory was its basic assumption that only the methods of natural science could produce knowledge. It was now accepted that knowledge would be gained by philosophical means, which could never be considered absolute or totally complete. This new form of relativistic Marxism meant it was not only the economic system that had to be modified but the whole culture; each individual's experience of himself must be eventually transformed (Kenny 1994, 360-61). The simple way of differentiating neo-Marxism from classical Marxism was by noting preferences in vocabulary. Neo-Marxists substituted terms such as "alienation" for "capitalism," "reason" for "revolution," and "Eros" for "Proletariat" (Jacoby 1986, 151).

A dialogue between psychoanalysis and Marxism emerged in Germany during the late 1920s and was formalized in 1930. In 1923 the Institute for Social Research was founded as an independent division of the University of Frankfurt. It was originally established as a center for research in philosophy and the social sciences whose philosophical underpinnings were Marxist. The Frankfurt school operated outside the Marxist political parties and was made up of those leftists who were dissatisfied with traditional Marxist theory and philosophy. When Max Horkheimer was appointed director of the Frankfurt Institute of Social Research in 1930, he committed himself to a reevaluation of Marxist theory that would be based upon collective research (Brecht et al. 1985, 56-58). As part of this commitment, Horkheimer invited several prominent psychoanalysts to join the Institute. Those whom he asked to join included Karl Landauer, Heinrich Meng, Frieda Fromm-Reichmann, and S. H. Fuchs. In 1926, the Frankfurt Psychoanalytical Study Group had been established by Landauer, and by 1929 it had grown into the Frankfurt Psychoanalytic Institute under the leadership of Landauer and Meng. It was a multidisciplinary research group that had been established originally for the study of Marxist theory but redirected its focus to examine what had happened to German society during the rise of National Socialism. The founding members of the Frankfurt school, in addition to Max Horkheimer, included Theodor Adorno, Erich Fromm, and Herbert Marcuse. The Frankfurt Psychoanalytical Institute was housed within the Institute for Social Research after they became associated in 1930. Since the Frankfurt Psychoanalytical Institute had become an integrated part of Frankfurt University, it meant that, for the first time in Europe, psychoanalysts could now offer fully accredited university courses. This represented a new window of opportunity for psychoanalysis to become part of mainstream academic life. Given this opportunity, Anna Freud planned to offer a course for students of education in this setting. With this interesting convergence of psychoanalysis and Marxism, new vistas were opened to inquiry. The most obvious issue that required almost immediate study was the rise of fascism, or National Socialism, as it was called in Germany. One of the major problems in the 1920s and 1930s was trying to understand what fascism was and what were its roots (Brecht et al. 1985, 56–69).

As the coalition of interdisciplinary methods was evolving, the National Socialist revolution had become a reality and taken over the Weimar democracy. The Nazis' popularity had clearly reached its peak in July of 1932 with 38 percent of the vote, followed by a loss of more than two million votes four months later. Yet soon thereafter, Hitler snatched victory from the jaws of defeat and became chancellor. While the left wing and liberals ceased to cooperate and instead fought each other, Hitler took power on January 30, 1933. By April of 1933, both the psychoanalytic and social research institutes at Frankfurt were dissolved, and the coalition of professionals brought together to study fascism were fleeing for their lives. The Institute for Social Research dispersed from its Frankfurt location and regrouped within the New School for Social Research in New York City in 1935 and stayed until 1949, when it returned to Frankfurt am Main, Germany.

While still in exile, members of the Frankfurt school were often in Los Angeles. During these periods, the cross-fertilization between academics like Marcuse and Adorno and Berlin clinicians like Fenichel and Simmel was revived for a short time in the unlikely ambience of southern California. Other German exiles also living in Los Angeles during this period included Thomas Mann and Bertolt Brecht. These individuals interacted at meetings of the Los Angeles Psychoanalytic Study Group and Fenichel's literature seminar. In general, Fenichel observed that the Frankfurt school had lost its rigorous Marxist thinking, and he often concluded that the complexity of technology, not the capitalistic economic system, was the core problem. This propensity to blame technology or machinery, rather than the economic system, led Fenichel to observe in 1942 that "Marx today is handled by the 'Marxists' in a very similar way as Freud is handled by the 'Freudians'" (Jacoby 1986, 124). In other words, they had both lost their basic roots. One of the ways that the Frankfurt school survived, however, was by toning down its radical Marxist rhetoric while in America. The Frankfurt school survived and endured in the United States during a very conservative period (the 1950s), and it helped influence the leftist student movement in the 1960s, especially the resistance to the Vietnam War. The more rigorous Marxist psychoanalysts, such as Fenichel, would not provide such a heritage. Their development while in exile in the United States took an interesting turn. They remained loyal to Freud's conceptual psychoanalysis, but subdued or ignored the social-political thought that had been so much a part of psychoanalysis in Europe.

It would be an interesting thought experiment to speculate what would have happened to the members of the Children's Seminar had they not been squelched by the Nazis and forced to emigrate. Is a Marxist society the ideal promulgated by psychoanalytic theory and its particular vison of man? Or is psychoanalysis just as incompatible with Marxism as it is with National Socialism? If one defines Marxism as the original revolutionary and utopian system, we would suggest the latter is true. In *Civilization and Its Discontents* (1930), Freud explicates how the overly optimistic and utopian vision of Marxism does not take into account the universality and ever presence of man's aggressive instinct. Banishing private property, class distinctions, and the exploitative aspects of capitalism would not change human nature. Rather, other opportunities for domination and aggression would have to evolve. Another source of incompatibility was Freud's articulation of the differences between the needs of the individual and the demands of the group or society. This conflict cannot be made to disappear. Man's seamless merging into a classless, harmonious society seems to us as unrealistic as man's mystical union with the *Volksgemeinschaft.*

The question remains whether more moderate neo-Marxists of the Frankfurt school hold more promise for a more realistic amalgamated psychoanalytic Marxism. We will explore this in chapter 14 when we discuss the return of the Frankfurt school to Germany after the war. However, we have presented the view that the most compatible social and cultural context for the practice of psychoanalysis is some form of society characterized by the liberal value of rights inherent in the individual, along with other legacies of the Enlightenment.

5

Jung and Jungian Psychology

The Theoretical Color Bearer for the New German (Nazi) Psychotherapy

IN THE PREVIOUS CHAPTER WE HAVE OUTLINED some of the political-psychological formulations and actions of psychoanalysts on the left of the political spectrum. In this chapter we would like to examine some of the thoughts and deeds of one prominent psychoanalyst, Carl Jung, whose work contributed to the nascent Nazi regime. Our purpose is not to evaluate Jung's theoretical contributions to our basic understanding of human nature. Our assessment of Jung's behavior and attitudes during the Third Reich are not attempts to evaluate his entire theory or pass judgment on his ethical integrity when viewed over the course of his life. His place in the history of ideas, although vigorously debated, is securely established. Our more modest goal is to examine how Jung's words and actions during the rise of National Socialism affected psychoanalysis and the Jewish analysts who practiced it as members of the BPI. We also assess whether or not Jung was prejudiced and whether his freely expressed attitudes contributed to the growing climate of anti-Semitism in Germany.

The first question usually raised about Jung is the highly controversial matter of his racial views. There is much evidence, we believe, that many of Jung's beliefs would today clearly be considered racist. In an essay called "Your Negroid and Indian Behavior" (Jung 1930), he writes that Blacks and American Indians are racially inferior human beings. According to Jung

Racial infection is a most serious mental and moral problem where the primitive outnumbers the white man. America has this problem only in a relative degree, because the whites far outnumber the colored. Apparently he can assimilate the primitive influence with little risk to himself. (Jung 1964, 507-9)

Jung then speculates what would happen with a considerable increase in the proportion of Blacks in the United States:

[T]he inferior man (the Black man) has a tremendous pull because he fascinates the inferior layers of our psyche. . . . He reminds us not so much of our conscious as our unconscious mind—not only of child-hood but of prehistory, which would take us back not more than about twelve hundred years so far as the Germanic races are concerned. (Jung 1964, 507-9)

Jung's theorizing is characterized by the basic assumption that there are racial determinants to the psyche along an inferior-superior continuum. This essay was originally published in 1930, predating Hitler's rise to power and the enforced coordination of all views with National Socialist policy and philosophy, suggesting that those were his genuine views. His views incorporated the concept of exclusivity/inclusivity, which character-ized many social theories of that era.

Jung's social ideas stem from his important concept of the "collective unconscious." According to Jung, the underlying experiences of each indi-vidual contain the collective experience of his or her ancestors. The deposit of the racial past provides what Jung calls a living system of reactions and attitudes determining the individual life in invisible ways. These ancient systems of reactions show themselves in the form of archetypes, or images, that express themselves in the manner of meaningful symbols.

Carl Jung was very involved with the psychotherapeutic and psycho-analytic movements within Germany both before and during the Third Reich. During that time he would often display antidemocratic ideas and his anti-Semitic propensities. In 1933, M. H. Göring, who took over the BPI, promoted Jung to help replace the all-too-Jewish forms of Freudian psychoanalysis with a new German psychotherapy. Jung served the Nazi interests well during the early years. He cooperated with M. H. Göring from 1933 to 1936 and often came to Berlin to give lectures and seminars, and one time he came to give an interview for German radio. In 1934, he coauthored with M. H. Göring a tribute to the psychologist Geheimrat R. Sommer, because "long before the Nazi movement, he recognized the importance of genealogy, eugenics, and race" (Göring and Jung 1943, 313-14), Jung criticized Freud in many ways, and he also reinforced the ideals of National Socialism. He saw his role and purpose as one of helping the German psychotherapists to clarify theory and to improve their practice within the political context. He endorsed Hitler's constant assertions that the individual leader was emerging from the German historical, cultural, and racial soul (Lockot 1985). In his many publications, Jung showed a disdain for democracy because of its denigration of the unique depths of the human soul. Jung made distinctions between Jewish and German science and considered Judaism and Christianity to be different ways of knowing:

> Can one not say there is also a Jewish psychology which bears the marks of Jewish blood and history? Can one not ask what are the particular differences between an essentially Jewish, and an essentially Christian conception? (Proctor 1988, 162-63)

Thus, Jung validated and made respectable the idea that Freud's psychoanalysis was a Jewish psychology that was irrelevant to Aryans (Proctor 1988). He used his own psychological theory to protect German psychotherapists supposedly from Freud's materialism and the ruthlessness of Jewish culture.

When Jung came to Berlin to be interviewed on the radio, it had only been six months since Hitler had been in power. Yet radical changes had already taken place, and the Third Reich was well on the way to becoming a totalitarian regime. The Enabling Act, passed on March 23, 1933, empowered Hitler and shut down the Reichstag. Labor unions had been outlawed, and the only political party allowed in the Third Reich was now the NSDAP. Jung was introduced by Adolf von Weizsäcker in the following way:

> [A]nd now following the talk, you will hear Dr. C. G. Jung, the well-known psychologist from Zürich who juxtaposes his positive teachings to the soul-destroying psychoanalysis of Sigmund Freud. (Lockot 1985, 90)

Adams and Sherry describe Jung's radio speech on the role of special leaders. Jung said:

> As Hitler said recently, the leader must be able to be alone and must have the courage to go his own way. But if he doesn't know himself, how is he to lead others? That is why the true leader is always one who has the courage to be himself, and can look not only others in the eye but above all himself.

Times of mass movement are always times of leadership. Every
movement culminates organically in a leader, who embodies in his
whole being the meaning and purpose of the popular movement. He is
an incarnation of the nation's psyche and its mouthpiece. He is the
spearhead of the phalanx of the whole people in motion. (Adams and
Sherry, in Maidenbaum and Martin 1991, 366)

What we have not seen reported in any English text but documented by
Lockot during that same interview was Jung's warning that

mass suggestion could also overpower the individual and make the
individual unconscious, "therefore it is especially important for mass
movements to incorporate people who do not act from an unconscious
need but from a conscious conviction. This conscious conviction however can only be based on a view of the world." (Lockot 1985, 90)

Jung's presentation was at the very least self-promoting in that it
identified the quality of his own soul leadership. With the exception of
Jung's plea for "self-responsible leadership" (Lockot 1985, 90), the overwhelming gist of the message simply echoes Nazi ideology and propaganda.
In essence, it is a solid endorsement of National Socialism and the *Führerprinzip*. This message supports the principle that one man rules the whole,
but that his subordinates are empowered as little Führers, so to speak (Fischer 1995, 297). Cocks has also thrown more light on the subject of Jung's
anti-Semitic and pro-Nazi attitudes. He has carefully assessed how the
meaning of Jung's statements has been distorted during the process of
translation in a systematic way. He considers this alteration an "editorial
decision . . . designed to cosmetize" and thus alter the historical picture
(Cocks 1997, 147).

In the course of examining Jung's analysis of Hitler and National
Socialism, it is striking how he and Hitler shared one major similarity; they
both believed in mysticism and irrationality as positive human qualities. In
describing Hitler, Jung stated, "The outstanding characteristic of his physi-
ognomy is its dreamy look. I was especially struck by that when I saw pictures taken of him in the Czechoslovakian crisis; there was in his eyes the
look of a seer" (Toland 1976, 497). In another description of Hitler, Jung
indicates, "[He is the] one who is always a bit late to the feast," and "Hitler's power is not political; it is *magic*. Hitler allows himself to be moved by
his own unconscious. He is like a man who listens intently to whispered
suggestions from a mysterious voice and then acts upon them" (Toland
1976, 498).

Roazen has commented, "The closer one is to the Holocaust, the harder
it becomes to take some distance toward the political views that Jung was

associated with" (Roazen, in Maidenbaum and Martin 1991, 216). In this statement Roazen articulates a most important principle in evaluating the ethics of an individual like Jung who supported Nazi ideas before the Holocaust became a historical fact. The other side of the coin, put in his unique personal way, is also just as true: "I am, however, among the lucky ones, born on this continent [North America]; but the accident of geography and history does not spare me the obligation of thinking about the ethical implications that Jung's political commitments entail" (Roazen, in Maidenbaum and Martin 1991, 216). In this regard we also think it is vitally important to identify those individual, social, cultural, and other forces responsible for creating the conditions for the Holocaust. The simple truth is that every human being is responsible for both words and actions; and Jung is not an exception. Because Jung participated with the Göring Institute on a voluntary basis and gave lectures, provided seminars, and the like, his attitudes and verbal statements must be examined to determine his culpability in contributing to an atmosphere in which the Holocaust became possible.

The first question that must be raised is what basis Jung was using to make all his claims regarding the differences between Jewish and Aryan psyches. He considered himself a psychologist, as did Freud. On what psychological data did Jung base his conclusions? He presents no evidence. As best as can be determined, Jung's theories of racial differences between psyches had no basis in any kind of systematic collection of data or any organized observations. While it is true that Freud lacked sufficient empirical data to support his theory about human behavior, there is, without question, clinical data upon which the concepts and theory of psychoanalysis rest. There is no scientific evidence upon which Jung makes his claims.

Prejudice is an ever-present phenomenon. It has been noted by Roazen (1996) that Freud was not free from prejudice. He did not want psychoanalysis to be limited to Jewish thinkers. He allowed this need for a gentile practitioner to determine his choice of Jung as heir apparent, and it was also an important factor in establishing their friendship. While Freud obviously would carry on a struggle with Jung by using psychoanalytic theory, it does not appear that the theory's major concepts were constructed in the service of that prejudice. On the other hand, after Jung split from Freud, he determined that Jewish psychology was not useful in understanding the Germanic mentality. Jung suggested that, as the Christian view of the world loses its authority, the greater menace would be the awakening of the "Blond Beast" that comes from the unconscious of the Aryan European

(Adams and Sherry, in Maidenbaum and Martin 1991, 362–66). It appears that to break from Freud, Jung had directly challenged the very integrity of psychoanalysis by denigrating its value, and limiting its applicability to the Jewish mind.

Another vivid description of the distinctions between the Aryan and the Jew was argued by Jung in one of his books:

> The Jew, who is something of a nomad, has never yet created a cultural form of his own and as far as we can see never will, since all his instincts and talents require a more or less civilized nation to act as host for their development. . . . The "Aryan" unconscious has a higher potential than the Jewish; that is both the advantage and the disadvantage of a youth-fulness not yet fully weaned from barbarism. In my opinion, it has been a grave error in medical psychology up to now to apply Jewish categories—which are not even binding on all Jews—indiscriminately to German and Slavic Christendom. Because of this the most precious secret of the Germanic peoples—their creative and intuitive depth of soul . . . —has been explained as a mass of banal infantilism, while my own warning voice has for decades been suspected of anti-Semitism. This suspicion emanated from Freud. He did not understand the Germanic psyche any more then did his Germanic followers. Has the formidable phenomenon of National Socialism, on which the whole world gazes with astonished eyes, taught them better? (Jung 1964, 165–66; Roazen 1992, 291–92)

In a radio broadcast in Berlin on June 26, 1933, Jung was interviewed by one of his disciples. During that interview Jung indicated the importance of the total human being over the perception of man as the sum of his sexual drives. It is no wonder that when Jung returned to Berlin in 1935 to give a series of lectures on "archetypes," he was received by M. H. Göring with joy and admiration. By this time Jung and M. H. Göring had become closely affiliated leaders of the German Medical Society for Psychotherapy and its official journal, the *Zentralblatt für Psychotherapie.* Jung had taken over leadership of the General Medical Society for Psychotherapy on June 21, 1933. He replaced the previous chairman, Ernst Kretschmer, who was considered "politically suspect" by the Nazis and pressured to resign. After the war, Kretschmer made it clear why he resigned: "I was of the conviction that such a complicated endeavor as the psychotherapy movement could only exist on a free international basis outside of all kinds of political influences" (Lockot 1985, 78–79). The *Zentralblatt,* under Jung's editorial leadership and M. H. Göring's influence, supported the racial goals of National Social-ism and Jung's analytical psychology. The Göring Institute did not need to develop a separate theory of psychotherapy for Germany. Jung's own theory provided an almost perfect match for National Socialism. In a letter to Max Guggenheim, Jung tried to defend his stance regarding his association with the editorial in the *Zentralblatt* that accompanied M. H. Göring's pro-Nazi editorial. In that March 28, 1934, letter, Jung claimed that Jews' "railing at me" for believing in Jewish psychology was shortsighted and "idiotic." He claimed he was not only supporting the Aryan psychotherapists but also the Jewish members of M. H. Göring's society. For this, "the Jews should be thankful to me" (Sklar 1977, 134–37).

Some historical perspective is required to evaluate Jung's claims. By the time this letter to Max Guggenheim had been written, Hitler had acquired full dictatorial power and all Jews had been forced to leave the universities and civil service jobs, and they were not allowed to be leaders of any medical organizations. Jewish professionals and businesses had been officially boycotted; individual acts of violence against Jews by regional and local SA groups were clearly accepted by the police; the Frankfurt Institute for Social Research, which was connected to the Freudian psychoanalytic movement, had been closed, and already between 20 to 24 of the 36 full members of the BPI had been forced to leave Germany (Brecht et al. 1985, 56–75). These events lend an air of bitter irony to Jung's statement that "the Jews should be thankful to me." His claim to have courageously dis-cussed an issue that was on everyone's mind is also meaningless in the con-text of what was happening to Jews on an everyday basis during 1934. It was also far-fetched in light of his correspondence with M. H. Göring regarding the ninth international congress for psychotherapy, which was to be held in Copenhagen on October 2–4, 1937. Since the topic was going to be race and depth psychology, M. H. Göring assumed that "Jung would probably like this topic himself since he had been involved in it for many years" (Lockot 1985, 289). Jung answered this request on March 4, 1937:

> Has the soft-headed doctor who proposed this idea been poked by the devil to suggest we should talk about such a subject, race, and depth psychology in Copenhagen? Such a subject at the moment can be dis-cussed only in Germany. Outside of its boundaries the atmosphere for discussing such a topic is much too heated. (Lockot 1985, 289)

It sounds more like an attempt to justify his own need to air anti-Semitic prejudice in safe havens, and it contradicts everything else he told non-Nazis about his courage. Roazen correctly observes that as a political scientist, the worst of what Jung wrote came in the early days of the rise to power of the Nazis in Germany. Worse still, Jung traveled there to deliver his message; he undertook to make political choices, for which he must historically be held responsible. It was a time when, it will be recalled, Jewish psychotherapists were being forced to flee abroad or were suffering in Germany. (Roazen, in Maidenbaum and Martin 1991, 217–18)

Glover (1956) pointed out long ago that Jung's theory rests upon mystical feelings rather than factual data. On a more personal level perhaps it was a way of saying to Freud, who promoted universal psychic structure, "No we are not the same; you are different." In *Civilization in Transition,* Jung did not renounce his belief in "Jewish" and "Aryan" psychology, despite the abundance of scientific evidence against his position. He returned to the refuge of his Christian roots without an appropriate acknowledgment of his past glorification of paganism. In *Civilization in Transition,* Jung states, "I am grateful to my theological forebearer for having passed on to me the Christian premise, and I also admit my so-called 'father complex.' I do not want to knuckle under to any father and never shall" (Diller 1991, 190–91). This statement was meant to refer to Freud, but is equally applicable to Jung's own father, who was a minister. He claimed his theory to be "but a simple link in the Christian premise." In fact, Jung's exaltation of pagan beliefs was inconsistent with the central tenets of all established Christian religions. His thinking in the 1930s and long afterwards was similar to what is now called New Age. Jung's mythical beliefs in "the primitive and barbarian nature of Aryans," and his call for the worship of the Germanic god Wotan, clearly designate his thinking as anti-Christian as well as anti-Semitic. His later moral outrage at the Germans for being responsible for the Holocaust showed no insight that his own views helped set the stage for that event.

Jung never admitted in a straightforward way that, given the era when he expressed his views on "Jewish" thinking, these views added to the climate of hatred toward the Jews. In 1945, only when National Socialism had been totally defeated and discredited did Jung have the courage to denounce what the Germans had done to the Jews, but he whitewashed his own role by presenting himself as having foreseen this "collective murder" (Jung, in Adams and Sherry, in Maidenbaum and Martin 1991, 390–93).

Let us give the last word to a modern (perhaps postmodern) Jungian analyst. Andrew Samuels (1993) has written an honest, soul searching, and comprehensive review about Jung's anti-Semitism, his racial concepts, and

Nazi leanings. Samuels suggests that the analytical community must come to grips with Jung's "degenerate" propensities and mourn his passing before a meaningful renewal of their psychological movement can occur. Samuels ends the chapter on Jung with the following hopeful message:

> This has been a cautionary tale for depth psychologists who seek to analyze politics and culture. I tried to show that it was Jung's attempt to establish a culturally sensitive psychology of nations that brought him into the same frame as Nazi anti-Semitic ideology. In addition, Jung was absorbed by the question of leadership. Exploring these ideas as thoroughly as possible leads to a kind of reparation, for I think that post-Jungians do have reparation to make. Then it is possible to revalue in more positive terms Jung's overall project. We must couple a less simplistic methodology and a more sensitive set of political values to Jung's intuitions about the centrality of a psychology of cultural difference. If we do so, then analytical psychology has something to offer a depth psychology that is concerned with processes of political and cultural transformation. (Samuels 1993, 336)

This call for reparation is a positive step that all schools of psychotherapy would do well to consider.

Part 3
Hitler in Power

6

The Beginnings of Nazi Rule and the Initial Reaction of the Psychoanalytical Community

HAVING EXPLORED SOME OF THE political ideologies that influenced psychoanalysis before and during the Third Reich, we intend to turn now to what actually happened to the psychoanalytic movement in Germany, and in the BPI in particular, from 1933 to 1945. The events described in this chapter and the following chapters demonstrate, we believe, the degree to which the psychoanalytic movement was demolished in Germany (and Austria) during the Nazi era.

We begin by noting one of the first policies instituted by Hitler's regime when it came to power—the policy of *Gleichschaltung,* or coordination of how individuals and institutions related to each other within National Socialist Germany. *Gleichschaltung* in reality meant bringing the people and institutions into line with Nazi rule. As part of *Gleichschaltung,* on April 7, 1933, the Law of Restoration of the Civil Service was enacted. This was an anti-Semitic governmental action, the first clearly anti-Semitic governmental action in generations. It would initiate an economic boycott of Jews and set quotas for Jewish students in law school and medical school at 1.5 percent. It was ordered that the executive boards of all medical groups had to consist of Aryans. Furthermore, from this date onward all Jews were to be considered foreigners.

Max Eitingon, who was the president of the German Psychoanalytic

Association (DPG), was a Russian-born Jew with Polish nationality. Apparently, Eitingon had anticipated Hitler's coming to power before it occurred, and he traveled to Vienna to discuss its influence on psychoanalysis with Freud on January 27, 1933. Freud continued to correspond with Eitingon about this matter, and while Freud still was not pessimistic about Austria, he did have some doubts: "Vienna is despite all the riots, processions, etc., reported in the newspapers calm, and life is undisturbed. One can be sure that the Hitler movement will extend to Austria—indeed it is already here." Freud encouraged Eitingon to hang on (Jones 1962c, 182). Yet, by April 1933 Eitingon had become convinced that his life was in danger. He had heard the ominous tone and words of the Nazis, none more clear than Joseph Goebbels's nine-minute diatribe against Jews as he introduced Hitler, who then gave his first speech over the radio to the German people. Violence toward Jews was threatened, and Eitingon knew he had good cause for concern (International Films [Producer], and J. Goebbels [Director] 1933).

An examination of what occurred next was gleaned from Jones's correspondence, Michael Molnar's edition of *The Diary of Sigmund Freud, 1929 to 1939*, and Eickhoff's (1995) review of previously unpublished sections of Fenichel's circular letters (*Rundbriefe*). On April 3rd and 8th, 1933, Jones received letters from Dr. J. H. W. van Ophuijsen of the Dutch Psychoanalytic Institute, who sent letters to Jones informing him of the climate in Berlin. Jewish doctors, lawyers, and students were being sent away and prohibited from working. Jews could not get passports to travel abroad. He further advised Jones that it was unwise to send any protest through the mail to the Berlin Institute. It was Ophuijsen's impression that the Nazis scrutinized all international mail very carefully. He thought a letter from Jones might "draw attention to the institute which they have not discovered as yet" (Ophuijsen to Jones, letters dated April 3 and April 8, 1933).

In case the government made demands on the BPI while he was away on a three-week vacation, Eitingon designated both Boehm and Müller-Braunschweig to become the "acting" directors of the Institute under certain conditions. It was feared that the government would demand that Jews be dismissed from leadership positions in all medical organizations, and Boehm and Müller-Braunschweig were gentiles. Eitingon was extremely careful in modifying the power structure and established special conditions for this change of control within the DPG. In the formal agreement that was drawn up, the following stipulations were made: 1) It was in effect from April 11, 1933, to the end of April 1933; 2) a business meeting of all the members in Berlin was to be called immediately if this measure needed to be put in effect (Brecht et al. 1985, 113).

Boehm violated both the spirit and the letter of the agreement by acting unilaterally. On April 8, 1933, Boehm read an order that appeared in the *Medical Journal* stating that all medical organizations had to "Aryanize" their directorships. Instead of informing Eitingon about the notice in the journal, Boehm contacted the government and also set up a meeting with Freud. On April 10, 1933, Boehm went to the Department of the Interior (headed by the Nazi Wilhelm Frick) to learn whether the decree limiting executive committees to Aryans applied to psychoanalysis. Not surprisingly, it did. On April 17, 1933, Boehm visited Freud in Vienna to gain Freud's approval of his plan that Eitingon step down as leader, and for the Jews to withdraw voluntarily from the German Psychoanalytic Association. Freud refused to be drawn into this manipulation but agreed that Boehm could take over leadership if there was a majority vote for this approach. Freud did not think that anything would prevent the Nazis from banning psychoanalysis but thought Boehm's being elected leader would not allow an easy pretext for the Nazis to clamp down. Freud arranged for another psychoanalyst, Paul Federn, to be present in order to witness what was agreed upon. According to Molnar (1992, 146), Freud's "concession" to Boehm "was treading a fine line" and he (Freud) was "grateful for Federn's presence as a witness to guard against distorted reports of the meeting." Freud obviously had come to the conclusion that Boehm's motives lacked integrity. He also did not want to be in a position to be used (Molnar 1992, 146; Eickhoff 1995, 945–56; Sterba 1982, 155–56; and Jones 1962b, 181–83).

By carefully following the specific stipulations of the agreement and comparing it to the actual sequence of events, Boehm's motivation can be reconsidered. Many of Boehm's colleagues considered that his behavior was driven by intense anxiety alone, but in retrospect, one wonders whether he was moved by a growing belief in National Socialism. Otto Fenichel considered Boehm's behavior to be more than a reflection of his anxiety. As Eickhoff states, Fenichel's circular letters reveal "a starkly realistic picture of the events impacting the psychoanalytic community in Berlin during the early years of the Third Reich" (Eickhoff 1995, 948–52). While Boehm was making a skillful appeal to Jones, suggesting that he (Boehm) was preventing the breakup of the association and saving its members from placement in concentration camps, Fenichel had a different interpretation. He reported that behind Boehm's anxiety was the kind of repetition compulsion of the secret diplomacy of the early Nazi regime. In the *Rundbriefe,* it was reported that both Fenichel and Simmel severely criticized Boehm, who

rationalized that "the matter was not of interest to us anymore as we
wanted to leave Germany." Boehm blocked their attempts to have Edith
Jacobsohn attend the board meetings. Fenichel also reported in the circular
letters that by making decisions without listening to the members, Boehm
was already infected with the "Führer principle," —albeit a Führer of psychoanalysis that too often trembled with anxiety. Fenichel considered his
suspicions justified when the Boehm/Müller-Braunschweig board only
approved gentiles for full membership, while Jewish associates with at least
equivalent claims for advancement were passed over. The details of Fenichel's circular letters describe how the Aryan members began refraining
from the slightest contact with their Jewish colleagues. Fenichel's description of the gentiles' professional and personal avoidance of their Jewish colleagues was similar to the fear "of the devil who will grab your whole hand
when you stretch out your little finger" (Fenichel, in Eickhoff 1995, 951).

In the meantime, there occurred an extraordinary meeting of the
DPG at which time Boehm and Müller-Braunschweig's proposal to change
the board had been voted down (Brecht et al. 1985, 112). At this same
meeting, on May 6, 1933, Eitingon resigned his chairmanship from the
Berlin Psychoanalytical Association (Brecht et al. 1985, 84). In writing
about this incident later, Eitingon revealed that it "reminded me of a political event. When two ministers told von Papen they would give way only to
violence, von Papen politely asked what type of violence they would prefer"
(Molnar 1992, 290). Apparently both Freud and Eitingon considered Felix
Boehm not only unfriendly but dangerous to psychoanalysis. A more sym-
pathetic interpretation of Boehm's behavior is offered by Jones at a later
date. In a 1935 letter to Anna Freud, Jones writes of Boehm: "Whenever he
is frightened he tends to go to the authorities and suggest indirectly to
them questions to which, from their side, they can only give one answer"
(Brecht et al. 1985, 131).

In a long letter from Jones to Anna Freud, written in May 1933, Jones
summarized a number of problems that appeared significant for the Berlin
Society at this time. He clearly identified the threat that the Nazis presented to the practice of psychoanalysis. However, he also pointed out how
some of the younger and leftist psychoanalysts were making matters much
worse for themselves by mixing politics and psychoanalysis. In particular,
Jones strongly criticized Reich's idea of psychoanalytic Marxism. In evaluating the prospects of helping German-Jewish analysts emigrate to the United
States Jones doubted that the American institutes would be very helpful,
given their policy of not accepting lay analysts into membership. Jones
clearly pinpointed several significant issues that presented real problems for

the psychoanalytic organizations, institutes, and individual members both in Europe and America (Jones to A. Freud, letter of May 2, 1933).

Unfolding events continued to reveal the increasing dangers that faced psychoanalysis immediately after Hitler was appointed chancellor. One of the most haunting actions that occurred during Hitler's first months in office was the book burnings. There was to be a cultural revolution in which the Jewish-Bolshevik taint was to be purged from Germany. Berlin had the largest burnings, which were organized and executed by Goebbels and which took place across the street from the opera house. They were organized by Humboldt University and were orchestrated in an operatic manner with SA and SS bands playing patriotic music. Over twenty thousand books were burned under nine different categories of German writing by both students and professors:

> The first category was political. Against class struggle and materialism, for community of the people and an idealistic way of life. . . "I commit to the flames the writings of Marx and Kautsky," they chanted. Freud's books were in the fourth category. Joseph Goebbels recited the incantation: "Against soul-disintegrating exaggeration of the instinctual life, for the nobility of the human soul! I commit to the flames the writings of Sigmund Freud." (Molnar 1992, 149)

Freud would later comment in a letter to Arnold Zweig, "What progress we are making. In the Middle Ages they would have burnt me; nowadays they are content with burning my books" (Molnar 1992, 149). For once, Freud underestimated the evil about to take place. Six million Jews, including his four sisters, soon would be murdered.

The law on Restoration of the Professional Civil Service had dramatic consequences for psychoanalysts before the end of the year. The Restoration of the Professional Civil Service would remove Jews from the executive committees of medical societies, from the civil service, university positions, and many legal professions. To classify a person as Jewish the minimum criterion was one Jewish grandparent. In turn, Jews were defined as foreigners without rights. The period between April 7 and December 1933 was to prove critical for the practice of Freudian psychoanalysis if one were Jewish. As indicated, the process of *Gleichschaltung* was a way of totally bringing into line all elements and aspects of society. Each profession had to adhere to the guidelines of National Socialism, and the professional bureaucracies were to be controlled by trusted Nazis (Lifton 1986, 34).

What was the effect of *Gleichschaltung* on professions whose object of study was similar to that of psychoanalysis during this period? In particular, how did *Gleichschaltung* affect the young academic discipline of psychology?

Ulfried Geuter (1992) has provided the definitive work on psychology during the Nazi period. The essential point that Geuter makes about psychoanalysis and psychology is that they went their own professional and scientific ways during the Third Reich (Geuter 1992, 6). Geuter makes a case that initially appears similar to that of Cocks: that psychology not only survived but prospered. Psychology, as Geuter describes it, was able to transform itself from a marginal academic discipline into a state-recognized and sanctioned profession.

As it happened, the psychologists' leadership, as well as its group members, fell into line and cooperated rather comfortably with Nazi ideology. In October 1933, the chairman of the psychology group, Felix Krüger, defined the task of psychology as assisting the mental renewal of the German *Volk*. Apparently, the psychologists who were in the spotlight during the 1933 convention were eager to prove to the new regime how useful they could be. Some psychologists pointed out how their science could be useful in carrying out the upcoming ideological-political tasks. Moreover, the psychologists attempted to distance themselves from the "Jewish contents" and "Jewish theories" connected to the science and to the profession of psychoanalysis.

In psychology, new areas of research were established to demonstrate the validity of the ideology of National Socialism. Geuter indicates that Erich Jaensch's work was one that went out of its way to support the racial ideology of the Nazis, with occasional tirades against "Jewish science." Geuter also describes a research project in comparative psychology by two of Jaensch's pupils—a project that indicates the extent to which psychologists would go in order to support National Socialism. These pupils studied the relationship between "integration type and breeds of chickens." A comparison was made between the northern Nordic chickens and their southern Mediterranean counterparts in terms of their pecking behavior. The results showed that the southern chickens matured sexually earlier, but their pecking behavior was less balanced and more unstable than that of the Nordic chickens. The Nordic chickens pecked with a "firmer 'integration core' more accurately and regularly, and were better at taking their place in the group" (Geuter 1992, 170). This apparently proved that the chicken yard was a useful area to research issues concerning the human racial issues and ability to conform (Geuter 1992, 165-76; Wyatt and Teuber 1944, 223-24, and 238).

Was there no resistance among the psychologists against the views of National Socialism? At least one psychologist stood up and then suffered the fate of others who stood alone. Otto Bobertag was in charge of the test psychology section of the Central Institute for Education and Teaching in Berlin. In 1934, he responded to an article written by Adolf Busemann in 1933 entitled "Psychology in the Midst of the New Movement." Busemann had argued the *Volk* must be developed along the lines and the needs of the soul, and he further maintained that the potential of the German soul be furthered. It was time to expand psychology to include the unique aspects of the German soul, just as National Socialism encouraged the opening up of new living space *(Lebensraum)* for the German people. Bobertag responded that psychology was an invaluable tool to assess many social problems, especially in education. He went on to say that psychology had nothing to do with any "new movement" or ideology; but this obviously anti-Nazi perspective was a lone voice among psychologists. Geuter reports that Bobertag committed suicide on April 25, 1934 (Geuter 1992, 165–70). Furthermore, he suggests that the strategy Busemann proposed was to have a significant impact on the public presentation of psychology during the initial phase of the Third Reich. Felix Krueger, the new chairman of the psychological association, appointed in March of 1933, was eager to demonstrate to the state how useful and important his profession could be in the renewal of the German *Volk.* The führer of the state knew that the *Volk* did not live by bread alone, it required a *Weltanschauung* (Geuter 1992, 55–56, 165–70).

The policy of *Gleichschaltung* was very effective in transforming psychologists to the new ideology. Psychologists would serve Nazi ideological goals at the start of the Third Reich and thereafter as well. Psychologists followed the Wehrmacht's conquest of Poland to help in the most horrendous purposes of the National Socialist Peoples' Welfare Organization (NSV). Geuter reports that the NSV was involved in what was called the "Germanization" of Polish children. In this endeavor, psychologists helped the Gestapo and the SS implement Himmler's decree to steal Aryan-type children from their Polish parents. Psychologists were used to provide an initial identification of Polish children "whose racial appearance indicates Nordic parentage." Those children were taken from their parents and sent to Germany and evaluated for six more weeks to select "valuable blood bearers" for the Third Reich. Those children who failed at the six-week stage of evaluation were murdered. In this way, the psychologists who participated in the "Germanization" program committed a crime against humanity (Geuter 1992, 246–49).

Gleichschaltung was a devastating assault on the political, social, cultural, and professional institutions of the old Germany. Also, the media, such as radio and theater, were brought under jurisdiction of the Reich Chamber of Culture, headed by Joseph Goebbels. While greater German unity did emerge, it did so at a massive cost to the people's rights. There were direct implications for psychoanalysis. By the end of December 1933, the former president of the DPG had resigned and moved to Palestine. Approximately twenty other Berlin Jewish analysts had also emigrated due to serious threats directed toward them. Freud's books had been burned in the infamous Berlin book burnings. The pressure on Jewish psychoanalysts to move away was great. Before other professions were directly faced with dissolution of their groups within Nazi Germany, this possibility was a special burden the Jewish analysts already had to face by December 1935. If the Jewish analysts did not resign, it was possible that the DPG would be dissolved.

One could argue the policy of *Gleichschaltung* was not totally successful (that is, *complete* control was not achieved); we would not argue with this qualification. However, we do argue that the interference and attempts at coordination were sufficiently successful to make a significant change in the scientific conception and practice of psychoanalysis. We contend that psychotherapy and Freudian psychoanalysis were able to maintain their outer form, but as the years passed the very substance of the process was increasingly Nazified.

Hitler was a prime mover in the events surrounding the Restoration law. The law and the boycott of Jewish businesses evoked strong reactions within the Third Reich and abroad. One of those who responded, which Hitler had not anticipated, was President von Hindenburg. The aged field marshall raised himself from his lethargy and protested Hitler's actions against the distinguished Jewish war veterans who were making a living in the civil service. Hitler backed down and compromised in the face of the president's protest. However, the Restoration law would have far-reaching consequences for the German nation, since university professors were to be included under the civil service section. Many Aryan intellectuals realized that the German nation as a whole was going to be the loser. In fact, the intellectual-scientific community was about to lose some of the most brilliant scientists in the world. One eminent German decided to protest. Max Planck told Hitler what a German Jewish chemist, Fritz Haber, had meant to Germany's World War I effort. Haber had synthesized ammonia by the fixation of nitrogen from the air, a feat that saved Germany from immediate defeat at the start of World War I. Nitrates were needed for explosives, and the blockade would have prevented the needed nitrates from reaching Germany. In the dispute that followed, Hitler revealed his ideological rigidity by falling back on his Marxist-Jewish conspiracy theory. When Planck stated that removal of the Jews was tantamount to self-mutilation, Hitler became very angry. He slapped his knee, said no, and called himself a "man of steel." The argument was over (Hilberg 1992, 12-13; Toland 1976, 320-21; and Powers 1993, 35-43).

These two personal interactions with Hitler revealed much about what was to happen on a global scale for Germany. Hitler compromised with the aged ex-military leader Hindenburg, whose role as president was more ceremonial than real. The response Hitler gave to Max Planck was a microcosm of the Third Reich's treatment of Freudian psychoanalysis from 1933 to 1945. By the end of November 1933, the Department of Interior of the Third Reich actually demanded that all the Jewish psycho-analysts would have to resign or the security of the Institute could not be ensured.

What meaning does this have? As old and senile as President von Hindenburg was, there existed the slight possibility he might rally the military to him. This led Hitler to respect the old soldier's opinion. Max Planck was a world-renowned scientist and Nobel laureate. Planck's approach to Hitler stressed the importance of science and reason, and focused on Germany's best interests. He came away empty-handed. Appeals to reason simply led Hitler to respond with ideological slogans about Jews and unrealistic thinking based upon his narcissistic needs.

Hitler's ideological convictions about "Jewish" science had received early support from a surprising source. As early as the 1920s the Nazis had embraced the two Nobel laureate German physicists, Philipp Lenard and Johannes Stark, both eminent figures but ones whose ages or inclinations had prevented them from grasping quantum physics. Lenard's students handed out leaflets in 1922 attacking quantum physics as "Jewish physics." Werner Heisenberg, a young Aryan student, had come to a lecture hoping to hear Albert Einstein discuss his theory of relativity but instead was faced with these "racist" leaflets. He learned that Einstein could not present his lecture because of these protests and that the protests were being made by the graduate students of Lenard. He realized, "[o]ne of my dearest hopes disintegrated. So science, too, could be poisoned by political passions" (Powers 1993, 37). While Heisenberg initially tried to discount such leaflets as a few "crackpot ravings," by 1931 these "crackpots" had made serious inroads into German universities. Ironically, the success of the "crackpots" in debunking the theory of relativity as "Jewish" physics would very early on during the Third Reich ensure that the Nazis would never be able to dominate the world. By forcing Jewish physicists out of German universities, the

Nazis gave the United States and Britain the scientists who could and would help produce the atomic bomb. Lenard and Stark's position that quantum physics was nothing but a phoney "Jewish science" was eventually abandoned by the party and state in favor of a more pragmatic attitude that would help their war aims. However, Heisenberg, who was competent in the area of quantum physics, avoided discussing the reality of an atomic bomb project with those leaders who asked him about it (Powers 1993).

Attacks against "Jewish" physics set the stage for future attacks by Carl Jung and M. H. Göring on Freudian psychoanalysis as being a "Jewish science." From Hitler on down the Third Reich hierarchy, it was clear that all "Jewish" science, art, and literature were "politically incorrect" vis-à-vis Nazi ideology. Toward the end of 1933, it became clear that survival as a Freudian psychoanalyst was going to be a very dangerous experience. As Jones reports: "In November, 1933, two official Nazi psychotherapists met [Felix] Boehm and [Carl] Müller-Braunschweig and told them that the only chance of psychoanalysis being allowed to continue lay in the exclusion of all Jewish members from the Society" (Jones 1962c, 186). These two Nazi officials were both professional members of the SA and turned out to be Kurt Gauger, M.D., and Werner Achelis, Ph.D. These four men would apparently start a dialogue that would contribute in the founding of the Göring Institute (Brecht et al. 1985, 115, 120, 132-40).

7

M. H. Göring

Head of the German Medical Society for Psychotherapy and the Göring Institute

THE GENERAL MEDICAL SOCIETY FOR PSYCHOTHERAPY was established in 1926 with the goal of providing a general forum for debate among the wide variety of psychological schools (e.g., Adlerian, Jungian, Freudian). The organization was committed to offering different modes of psychotherapy that could be provided by physicians. The greatest proportion of its members had a nationalist conservative political orientation, with the exception of those in the DPG who were liberal, largely Jewish, and cosmopolitan. Until April 1, 1933, the world-famous psychiatrist Ernst Kretschmer had been president of the group. With the Nazis in power, Kretschmer realized he would have to resign and return to the psychiatric clinic at the University of Marburg. Kretschmer was very unsympathetic to the Nazis, but he firmly believed that the practice of psychotherapy should be restricted to psychiatrists. The debate over who ought to be allowed to practice psychotherapy found advocates on both sides of the pro- and anti-Nazi divide. When the Nazis came to power in 1933, Kretschmer decided to give up his position as president of the General Medical Society for Psychotherapy.

As Kretschmer resigned his presidency, two new groups took its place. The newly founded German General Medical Society for Psychotherapy was led by Nazi Party member M. H. Göring on September 15, 1933. C. G.

Jung became chairman of the newly formed International General Medical Society for Psychotherapy on June 9, 1933 (Cocks 1985, 47, 107-11). M. H. Göring was "a cousin of the Deputy Führer [Hermann Göring]" (Jones 1962c, 186). He was not Freudian, but he had been analyzed by the Adlerian Leonhard Seif (Cocks 1985,108-11). Göring's new role as leader of the German psychoanalysts, starting on September 15, 1933, initiated a process the Nazis called "salami tactics," the slice-by-slice, slow destruction of psychoanalysis. Among the significant slices cut off were the leadership positions on medical boards. Pressures were exerted on all psychotherapists to read *Mein Kampf.* Kurt Gauger, a physician and member of the SA, demanded that the Psychoanalytic Institute be turned over to the Third Reich. It would be incorporated within the new organization, whose purpose it was to develop an Aryan form of psychotherapy (Brecht et al. 1985, 111-15).

Hitler's rise to power led to M. H. Göring's almost immediate increase in power and professional status. During 1933 he became a well-known and influential psychotherapist almost overnight. In 1933 M. H. Göring started to work cooperatively with Kurt Gauger, who was not only a physician, psychotherapist, and writer, but one of those individuals whose role it was to implement *Gleichschaltung.* Gauger realized that helping M. H. Göring would enhance his own interests, although Gauger's importance eventually diminished after 1936.

M. H. Göring's personality was often described as amiable, but his deeds were those of an ardent Nazi. He had joined the NSDAP on May 1, 1933, and his affiliations within the party were as follows:

a. SA (or Storm Troopers, who were the Brownshirt group prior to Hitler's becoming Chancellor. They were to take on and defeat the communists in street brawls throughout Germany. After Hitler became chancellor, they became part of the police and operated to terrorize citizens.)

b. NS *Dozentenbund* (or the National Socialist Lecturers' Alliance, which was established by the Nazi Party to keep university professors in line with party ideology)

c. NSD—*Ärtzebund*—(National Socialist German Doctors Alliance)

d. NSV (or National Socialist Peoples' Welfare Organization devoted to families, especially mothers and children) (Berlin Document Center)

In a letter to C. G. Jung on August 28, 1933, Walter Cimbal made it clear why M. H. Göring was perhaps the only person to lead the German General Medical Society for Psychotherapy in 1933. He was also the "correct" choice to take over the Berlin Psychoanalytic Institute (BPI) and replace it with the German Institute for Psychological Research and Psychotherapy (the Göring Institute) in 1936. Cimbal described the political atmosphere of the German Society:

> The situation in Germany was thus—that during congress and seminars that leadership had to be taken over by a member of the NSDAP who is going to vouch for the national integrity of the proceedings. Germany in outward ways even today is in a special state in which congresses and meetings are only then legal if they exactly follow the thinking of the government. I personally for example would not want to be responsible for this even though I am an NSDAP, even at that if I had the power to cut off dangerous discussions. Professor Göring could take over this kind of responsibility because of his long political education and because of his close relationship with an important leader of the movement. Because of this he would be much more secure in his discussions, more secure than any of us. (Lockot 1985, 83)

Göring was also a member of the *Stahlhelm* (Steel Helmet), an ex-serviceman's group with extreme conservative roots that had supported Hitler in the April 1932 presidential election. It should also be noted that the *Stahlhelm* was activated along with the SA by Hitler to act as "auxiliary police" after he became chancellor. Göring belonged to both of these groups, which were empowered on February 22, 1933, to combat the political left. All they had to do was put on a white armband with the words "auxiliary police," and these paramilitary groups were transformed into police with the license to bully or kill "undesirables." The historian Klaus P. Fischer suggests this was the equivalent to handing over police matters to the Mafia (Fischer 1995, 271).

As a member of the Lecturers' Alliance, Göring was committed to monitoring his colleagues in terms of their adherence to Nazi ideology (Berlin Document Center). M. H. Göring was described as a very pious Christian who often carried a Bible (Cocks 1985), and as a mild-mannered person whom Ernest Jones described as "amiable." As a psychotherapist his expressed intention was for an integrated Germanic form of therapy to replace Freudian psychoanalysis. In our estimation, M. H. Göring was committed to bringing about a new form of "German psychotherapy."

In a series of letters between 1933 and 1934, M. H. Göring revealed that he was aware that the days of the BPI's autonomy were numbered. In 1935, the BPI was forced to take "Berlin" from its name so it would not be associated with the city. In early 1936, M. H. Göring was given the authority to render an "expert opinion" about the Institute, which was "a prelude to its dissolution" (Cocks 1997, 117). The first three years that the Nazis had been in power was a period of revolutionary changes, but by 1936 they had entered a new phase of stabilization. In that year, the German Institute for Psychological Research and Psychotherapy was established with M. H. Göring as its director (Cocks 1997, 119–20).

As president of the new German Medical Society for Psychotherapy in 1933, and later in 1936, as director of the German Institute for Psychological Research and Psychotherapy (The Göring Institute), M. H. Göring provided a stable and continuous leadership for the twelve years of the Third Reich. One of his first acts was to require all the psychotherapists to read *Mein Kampf.* He also made sure that no Freudian terms were used in teaching about or practicing psychotherapy. This was illustrated in the following excerpt from a 1933 letter from M. H. Göring to Cimbal: "I cannot accept the subjects mentioned in your letter of 21.7 under II; for example, now that Freud's books have been burned, the word 'psychoanalysis' must be removed, so must the words 'individual psychology,' which could perhaps be replaced by 'applied characterology'" (Brecht et al. 1985, 111). In time psychoanalysis became "developmental psychology," and the Oedipus complex became the "family complex."

In concluding his speech to the General Medical Congress for Psychotherapy in 1934, M. H. Göring defended his assignment of *Mein Kampf* as required reading: "I have been attacked because I take it for granted that all members of the Society who are active in writing and speaking have worked through this book [*Mein Kampf*] in all scientific seriousness and recognize it as the basis of their thought." He went on to say:

> I do not care if I am called scientifically incompetent on this account; it is the convictions that matter to me. Today I say "Mein Kampf" must be called a scientific book; it only lacks the scientific jargon which gives so many publications the apparent scientific character which they do not actually possess.

M. H. Göring concludes:

> For that reason I require all of you, before the next Congress . . . to study in detail Adolf Hitler's book and speeches, so that our next meeting may take an auspicious course. (Brecht et al. 1985, 148)

In October of 1936, M. H. Göring gave his inaugural remarks on his new worldview of German psychotherapy, which was to be founded on a non-Freudian, pro-Nazi, and anti-Semitic basis. Thus, the BPI was now led by M. H. Göring, whose ideals were those of National Socialism rather than Freudian psychoanalytic thought (Cocks 1985, 143-45).

After all of these events had transpired, one fact emerged clearly: the Göring Institute was going to be dominated by Nazi ideology. On November 1, 1936, Felix Boehm was once again to travel to Vienna to talk with Freud. He had already told Anna Freud on March 10, 1936, that "the worst thing about life over there (in Germany) is that today one already takes for granted what would have made one's hair stand on end last year" (A. Freud to Ernest Jones, letter of March 10, 1936). Thus, he admitted how compromised his position was continuously becoming. Now Boehm wanted Freud's support for what he had already done. In essence, he wanted permission for having turned over the DPG to M. H. Göring and the Nazi regime after this had already occurred. Richard Sterba's presence with Freud allowed him to note how Freud's genius was still alive during their discussion. Sterba states: "Freud ended the meeting with an admonition to Boehm which I thought was in reality a tactful, indirect condemnation. He said 'You may make all kinds of sacrifices, but are not to make concessions.' But Boehm has obviously made many concessions already" (Molnar 1992, 209). These observations suggest that Freud considered Boehm's integrity as a psychoanalyst too compromised to make an honest discussion of issues possible.

M. H. Göring and his wife, Erna, monitored the seminar groups to ensure that the forbidden terms were not used. Cimbal had indicated such monitoring of the Freudian psychoanalysts was essential, and in a return letter Göring confirmed that the SA member and psychotherapist Gauger had told Müller-Braunschweig that he could no longer let him have a free hand in the training of psychotherapists (Brecht et al. 1985, 111). The extensive Freudian psychoanalytic books were locked up in what can euphemistically be called protective custody. On two separate occasions, M. H. Göring instructed all the psychotherapists that they must violate their Hippocratic Oath and renounce confidentiality when the Third Reich's interests were at stake (Cocks 1985). In fact, in one case a teenage boy of thirteen was turned over by his female therapist to the Gestapo and he was sent to a concentration camp (Lockot 1991a). In the 1997 edition of his book Cocks elaborates on what Lockot revealed to us. A Jungian analyst, Marianne Stark, had been appointed by a German court to provide an expert opinion about a thirteen-year-old learning-disabled delinquent.

During her interview with the youngster she learned he had been stealing rifles from the military for his collection. She took the rifles from him and initially held them in her house. However, since she was hiding a family of Jews, she decided to turn the guns over to M. H. Göring. In the interim, the youngster was arrested on a minor violation, giving M. H. Göring the opportunity to testify. He obeyed Hitler's order to break medical confidentiality and revealed the existence of the youngster's collection of guns to the court. The thirteen-year-old was sentenced to a life prison term. Not surprisingly, with the diagnosis of "psychopath" given by the director of criminal psychology at the Göring Institute, he became a prime candidate for medical experimentation and was infected with tuberculosis. He died in 1947 despite Stark's interventions through intermediaries to save him (Cocks 1997, 238–39).

Given Stark's attempts to intervene on behalf of the youngster, we assume that the gentle, soft-spoken manner of M. H. Göring's "Papi" image had led her to trust in his humaneness. However, this case reveals that M. H. Göring acted according to his previous statements to the members of the Institute when he was faced with the issue of confidentiality in court. It needs to be recognized that by 1942, M. H. Göring was an experienced expert witness. By this time he would have been well aware of how the legal system worked on such matters as well as having a good grasp of the clinical propensities of the director of criminal psychology at the Institute. Given these circumstances, it is more likely that M. H. Göring would have anticipated the probable outcome of the hearings than to assume otherwise.

8

The Freudian Response
to the Nazi Threat
in Germany

Jones and the IPA

As PREVIOUSLY INDICATED, there have been questions about the roles played by Felix Boehm and Carl Müller-Braunschweig, and the correspondence among psychoanalysts in Europe revealed varying attitudes about these two Berlin psychoanalysts. By September 21, 1933, one of the preeminent psychoanalysts of the period, Dr. J. H. W. Van Ophuijsen of the Netherlands, had concluded that both Felix Boehm and Carl Müller-Braunschweig were confirmed Nazis (Ophuijsen to Jones, letter of September 21, 1933). As previously stated, they had tried to talk Freud into having all the Jewish members resign and attempted in a special meeting of the BPI to have the Jewish members of the board removed. Both of these attempts had failed. Van Ophuijsen's opinion was important because his predictions and interpretations of the unfolding events were more accurate than those of any other psychoanalyst, including Freud himself. While Anna Freud and Jones continued to report actions that bothered them about Boehm and Müller-Braunschweig, they tried to give these two gentile psychoanalysts the benefit of the doubt regarding their integrity.

In letters to Ernest Jones in the latter part of 1935, Anna Freud describes Boehm's recklessness in exposing others to danger, and even interprets Müller-Braunschweig's most recent paper as Nazi in nature. In a letter to Jones on December 18, 1935, Eitingon suggests that Müller-Braunschweig was ready

to cooperate with the Nazis. Only Jones believed that Felix Boehm was politically trustworthy. In 1933, he stated in a letter to Anna Freud that "Boehm
has saved psychoanalysis" (Jones to A. Freud, letter of October 10, 1933). Van
Ophuijsen expressed a more skeptical view: "[T]he German Society is not in a
position to fulfill all the written and unwritten conditions imposed by membership of the IPA" (Brecht et al. 1985, 114). In essence, he questioned
whether the DPG should be allowed to continue belonging to the IPA.

During the year 1933, Jones threw himself into the task of saving the
emigrant Freudian psychoanalysts. The Anna Freud–Jones correspondence
reveals how Jones responded to his role as president of the IPA, and took
responsibility for establishing a register for immigrants and played an active
role in their placement throughout the world. While Jones was involved in
the rescue of the emigrants, Boehm and Müller-Braunschweig were confronted on November 18, 1933, by the German Department of the Interior's view that the compromise reached with Jones at the Hague meeting of
October 1, 1933, was not sufficient. The Interior Department once more
insisted that "no foreign Jews" be allowed to work at the BPI (Brecht et al.
1985, 122–24). Steiner reported that there were still more than nine Jewish
Freudian psychoanalysts in Berlin by the fall of 1933 (Steiner 1989, 49).
Since a few more would emigrate before the end of 1933, there remained
only a relatively small minority of Jewish Freudian psychoanalysts eleven
months after Hitler was named chancellor. By December 31, 1933, the
Schloss Tegel Clinic founded by Ernst Simmel in Berlin had been seized by
the Mark Brandenburg SA group, and Max Eitingon, president of the BPI,
had immigrated to Palestine. The two psychoanalysts of significance who
remained at the BPI were Felix Boehm and Carl Müller-Braunschweig.

A major loss of members, candidates, and students had taken place. A
two-year interlude would pass before the next series of significant events
would occur. This relatively peaceful interlude between the Nazi regime
and the DPG ended abruptly in the fall of 1935 with the arrest of Edith
Jacobsohn. On September 15, 1935, the Nuremberg Race Laws were
passed (Cocks 1985, 90). At this period it was also reported by Anna Freud
that two Viennese analysts had already served prison terms in Germany,
and one had broken down under questioning by the Gestapo (A. Freud to
Jones, letter of November 8, 1935). On October 24, 1935, Edith Jacobsohn was surprised in the act of discarding into Gruenewald Lake a suitcase
with documents of the socialist resistance group, "New Beginnings." She
was taken into custody. Both Boehm and Anna Freud saw her behavior as
disloyalty toward the DPG inasmuch as her actions jeopardized the whole
group and their common cause (Brecht et al. 1985, 126).

The arrest of Edith Jacobsohn symbolized more than anything else the loss of the kind of freedom taken for granted in Western democracies. Ignoring her German heritage, the Gestapo arrested her as a foreigner (because she was a Jew) for the crime of "high-treasonable activity of changing the constitution of the Reich by violence" (Brecht et al. 1985, 128). Jacobsohn was arrested for what can only be described as ideological reasons. She had remained a member of a liberal wing of the Social Democratic Party, had discussions of psychoanalysis, fascism, and marxism, and contributed money to political prisoners. Her "high treason" was the possession of anti-Nazi leaflets in her suitcase. On the advice of Edith Jacobsohn's German attorney, Jones started to organize an appeal by both medical and government officials. Learning of Jones's intentions, Boehm sent a frantic message that this action would lead to the dissolution of the DPG. Apparently Boehm had been intimidated again by the Nazis, and his fear led to Jones giving up his course of action. Fenichel was shocked by Jones's behavior, and he was able to convince Anna Freud that Jones was wrong. She, in turn, wrote to Jones on November 24, 1935, informing him that Boehm's personal fears were not based on facts and that regarding Fenichel "from a factual standpoint, I believe he is correct" (A. Freud to Jones, letter of November 5, 1935; Brecht et al. 1985, 181; and Lockot 1994b, 5). Fenichel also wrote an angry letter to Jones pointing out how self-defeating it was for the DPG to fall so quickly into line with Nazi ideology. He gave Jones examples of how the DPG was caving into the Nazis' slightest whims:

> in that it removes the pictures of the Professor [Freud] from the rooms of the institute and replaces them with more "up-to-date" ones [of Hitler]; or by reducing the great number of its Jewish members for racial reasons; or by submitting those written promises whereby the physicians had to make a special choice of the needy patients before helping them. (Fenichel to Jones, November 26, 1935, in Brecht et al. 1985, 181)

For whatever reason, Jones decided to follow Boehm's advice rather than Fenichel's. He would claim to Anna Freud that Fenichel probably just wanted more decisive opposition against the Nazis but did not clearly express himself (Jones to A. Freud, letter of November 28, 1935). If Jones really thought that was Fenichel's meaning, he simply failed to grasp the essential difference between a political versus a principled stance. The end result of Jones's following Boehm's advice on this matter was that Edith Jacobsohn stood trial and was sentenced to two years of penal servitude. At the end of 1937, when it was learned she needed to have an operation, she was placed on "parole" for the operation, which was to take place at the beginning of 1938. She took this opportunity to flee to Prague instead. Due to luck, or guile, or both, Edith Jacobsohn used her medical illness to escape via Prague to New York (Brecht et al. 1985, 127-28).

Brecht et al. (1985) suggest that the Jacobsohn case contributed to the emotional tension of the Aryan members of the DPG, and probably increased their hope that the remaining Jewish members would resign. Just as Jacobsohn's legal case was about to go to trial, another series of events unfolded which would set off an additional crisis for the DPG with different Nazis serving Boehm's self-defeating dependency needs. The group's pain would be played out in another intimidating scenario with Boehm and Müller-Braunschweig serving as intermediaries again. The two gentile psychoanalysts started to meet with Dr. Werner Achelis and Dr. Kurt Gauger, who were both members of the naval branch of the SA as well as professionals. Boehm had initially sought out these two ranking Nazis during a professional meeting in October 1935. He wanted to start a dialogue in order to try to preserve his profession's identity within the context of the Third Reich and the ideology of National Socialism (Brecht et al. 1985, 132-35).

Thus, Boehm started a series of interactions that would facilitate the speed at which new demands would be made upon those psychoanalysts still in Berlin. By the end of November, the Jewish members were once again being asked to resign in order for the gentiles to continue to practice. While requesting another emergency visit from Jones in a letter he had written, Boehm alluded to the question of the Jews. In a brief telegram informing Boehm of a delay in his visit to Berlin, Jones sanctioned the idea that the Jews voluntarily resign. In a strange twist of events before Jones visited Berlin, the Jewish members who initially agreed to voluntary resignations changed their minds once they learned Jones would be present to run the group meeting. In a letter to Anna Freud, Jones blamed this change on Boehm's inadequate leadership (Jones to A. Freud, December 2, 1935, in Brecht et al. 1985, 31). However, the way the group responded suggests another interpretation is possible. Learning of Jones's participation in their next meeting, the Jewish members' hopes were raised. Considering Jones as Freud's chosen heir apparent and president of the IPA, the Jewish members assumed he would be coming to support the idea of their remaining members rather than asking them to resign. Jones of course had previously suggested, "I prefer Psycho-Analysis to be practiced by Gentiles in Germany than not at all" (Jones to A. Freud, letter of November 11, 1935). Given the Zeitgeist that attracted the young Jewish members to join the BPI, it is reasonable to suggest they expected Jones to support the spirit of the

Enlightenment, upon which psychoanalysis had been established, rather than the situationally determined political idea of neutrality. If this was the Jewish members' hope, it never had a chance to happen.

From early in 1933, the transference and countertransference issues within the BPI had to be intense, and it is impossible to conceive how they ever could be resolved. Lockot reports the mixed transference feelings that the German-gentile psychoanalysts would experience toward Abraham, Freud, and Jones and the sense of being abandoned to "Daddy M. H. Göring" who would take over the "fatherhood" (Lockot 1994). At the very least the Jewish members must have experienced various combinations of anger, loss, bitterness, and narcissistic pain. The reexperiencing of the pain of their Jewish history in the country in which they had considered themselves accepted citizens made matters worse. The Jewish members' ultimate pain, however, must have been the fact that their psychoanalytic brothers and sisters—with whom they shared classes, seminars, and analysts—had turned against them so quickly. Long before the Nazis forced them to take action, the gentile members had sought Nazi advice, tried to eject them from the board, and tried to talk them into resigning their membership. Even Jones would be critical of the Jewish members for their "ultra-Jewish attitudes." In a letter to Boehm, written July 24, 1934, Jones states:

> You will know, that I myself regard those emotions and ultra-Jewish attitude very unsympathetically, and it is plain to me that you and your colleagues are being made a dumping-ground for much emotion and resentment which belongs elsewhere and has displaced in your direction. (Steiner 1989, 51)

By December 1935, the Jewish analysts had been forced to resign their memberships, which effectively ended their capacity to practice. Thus, before other Jewish physicians and Jewish attorneys were forced to give up their respective practices, the Jewish Freudian psychoanalysts no longer were able to work in Berlin. It was not until the end of September 1938 that the Nazis revoked the licenses of all Jewish physicians and attorneys within Germany (Proctor 1988, 153; Müller 1991, 58-63). The pace for elimination of Jewish Freudian psychoanalysts was far quicker than for Jewish physicians within other specialties in Germany. Had Jewish Freudian psychoanalysts received special attention from Frick's Interior Department? Why had Jewish Freudian psychoanalysts in Berlin been forbidden to practice so quickly? Did Nazi ideology have any role in this rapid elimination of the Jewish Freudian psychoanalysts?

It is our opinion that the early removal of Jewish Freudian psychoanalysts was not a question of chance but a matter of ideological conviction. It points to the greater vulnerability of psychoanalysis to political manipulation compared with other professions. Both Jews and Freudian psychoanalysis were considered ideological enemies of National Socialism and so it is not surprising that the Jews were pressured into resignation by their gentile colleagues in December 1935. Boehm and the other gentiles were clearly bowing to very specific demands from the Nazi hierarchy. As Cocks (1985) reveals, after the March 1938 *Anschluß*, the very fate of Freud himself was debated by Goebbels, Himmler, and the cousins Göring.

Another factor must be borne in mind. The Nazis were always very aware of the propaganda impact of their actions. While a wholesale elimination of all Jewish professionals was not yet possible by the end of 1935, the Jewish Freudians could be handled without an inordinate international response. In 1935 the Olympics in Berlin was on the horizon, and Hitler wanted this event to be a success. Thus, the wholesale elimination of all Jewish professionals was not yet possible, given the inevitable international reaction to such a move. But the elimination of the most threatening enemy, the Jewish physicists and psychoanalysts, could be carried out without risking a major international response.

Regarding the role of Nazi ideology and the practice of psychoanalysis, a large proportion of the DPG's membership were considered triple threats to the Third Reich. They were analysts, Jews, and marxists. In another strange twist of fate, their initial high level of vulnerability might in the long run have been life enhancing. Their forced removal from the BPI led to their emigration as early as 1935 and, ironically, allowed many of them to escape from continental Europe two years before most other Jewish professionals and thereby avoid the Holocaust.

It is our impression from reviewing Boehm's statements that, if it were not for his constant journeys to the offices of the Department of the Interior on behalf of the BPI, the organization may have been dissolved sometime during 1935 by M. H. Göring. The constant interventions by Boehm and the support given him by Jones seemed to have enabled the BPI to keep its doors open. Jones's comments on Boehm's efforts at one historical moment were that "he must be given the credit for having saved Psychoanalysis in Germany" (Jones to A. Freud, letter of October 2, 1933). But what was it that was saved? The institutional structure remained intact but ominous hints of what was to follow had also emerged. In fact a very strange way of thinking had emerged among those German analysts who stayed on in Berlin. Anna Freud has quoted Boehm as stating "the Berlin Society has gained by the loss of 25 members," and it is obvious why she disagreed with his thinking (A. Freud to Jones, letter of August 7, 1934). Boehm had already grasped the "logical" essence of this Nazi version of Newspeak, and those confronted with it were, at least at first, often too stunned to respond to it quickly and convincingly.

By the end of 1935, the Nazis had delivered one psychological blow after another to the Jewish psychoanalysts in Berlin; they violated their civil rights, took away their professional careers, and stripped them of their citizenship. The racial policies of the Nuremberg Laws were in effect, and the Nazis had shown their utter disdain for the rule of law by murdering well over one hundred political opponents of Hitler on one night and shortly thereafter having the murders declared retroactively legal. As these events had transpired, it was clear that Freud and Jones were still committed to the institutional survival of psychoanalysis in Germany. In the foreword to Cocks's book, *Treating the Mind and Body: Essays in the History of Science and Society under Extreme Circumstances* (1998), Peter J. Löwenberg outlines Freud's obvious lack of humanitarian concerns:

> It is painful and mortifying to read the record of how the leaders of an honored institution, in order to save the organization and promote the careers of the new successors to leadership, humiliated and cast out a large majority of its members to accommodate to a totalitarian state. That a "scientific," or for that matter a "humanistic," society would exclude qualified members for ethnic, racial, religious, or other extrinsic grounds for the sake of the existence of the institution, defies the autonomy of science from political ideology and the morality of valuing individuals that is the humane liberal essence of psychoanalysis itself. (Löwenberg in Cocks 1998, x)

We will return to this tendency to allow humanitarian values to take a back seat to the institutional priorities and theoretical purity when we discuss the postwar reorganization of German psychoanalysis and their readmission into the IPA.

9

The Göring Institute

The Berlin Psychoanalytical Institute Becomes the Göring Institute: The IPA's "Munich Agreement"

Boehm and Müller-Braunschweig started meeting with the Ministry of Culture as early as September 29, 1933, to negotiate the survival of their Institute. In 1934, the two gentile psychoanalysts met with the Jungians and with other psychoanalysts of varying orientations at the home of Kurt Gauger to discuss joining together under a planned new institute headed by M. H. Göring (Brecht et al. 1985, 115).

On February 18, 1936, Felix Boehm was one of the two gentiles who could have assumed a leadership position in the DPG. In that leadership capacity he had to obtain a teaching license for the DPG. Boehm met with the medical division of the German Department of the Interior. (In Nazi Germany, the Department of the Interior was a police regulating agency.) He was told, perhaps by Herbert Linden, that an organization devoted to Freudian psychoanalytic psychotherapy could never be approved. However, if the BPI would merge with other schools of psychotherapy to become part of the new German psychotherapy under the leadership of M. H. Göring, the psychoanalysts could continue to practice. This new psychotherapy institute was to be made up of various schools of psychological thought that would be committed to developing a unique form of treatment called the *Neue Deutsche Seelenheilkunde* (New German Psychotherapy) (Cocks 1997, 157). Thus the institute's administration was committed to create this "New German Psychotherapy" that, by implication, undermined the uniqueness and integrity of the psychoanalytic school of thought.

Boehm met first with Anna Freud; and this was followed by a special conference held on July 19, 1936, in Basel, Switzerland, including Jones, Abraham, Arden Brill, Boehm, Müller-Braunschweig, and M. H. Göring. The psychoanalysts had come to this meeting to obtain a commitment from M. H. Göring ensuring the autonomy of the DPG within this new institute. M. H. Göring made the same kind of lavish promises Hitler had made to Chamberlain concerning the territorial boundaries of Czechoslovakia following Germany's acquisition of the Sudetenland at the Munich Conference. In this case, Göring agreed that the DPG would remain independent within the German Institute for Psychological Research and Psychotherapy, albeit with a submerged identity. It would be allowed to control its own affairs and train its own students. In reality, what happened was that toward the end of 1938, Freudian psychoanalytic training was merged with other schools of psychotherapeutic thought, and the candidates could choose only one emphasis or another by their selection of a tutor (Brecht et al. 1985, 138–40). In the spring of 1936, the DPG had turned the building on Wichmannstrasse 10 over to the German government, and it was renamed the German Institute for Psychological Research and Psychotherapy (*Deutsche Institut für Psychologische Forschung und Psychotherapie*) with the hope that the DPG's integrity would be respected (Cocks 1985, 90). This institute, the Göring Institute, was now in charge of the fate of psychoanalysis in Berlin—and indeed, all of Germany.

Fenichel's description of the two ways Freud's eightieth birthday was celebrated that year (1936) by the Jewish analysts and their former gentile analytic brothers and sisters illuminates the profound changes that had affected the psychoanalytic community. Freud's eightieth birthday was actually celebrated in the newly formed Göring Institute, and formal dress was prescribed; but no Jews were allowed. It was to be an all-gentile affair on the founder's birthday. In another part of Berlin, those Jewish analysts who were former members of the DPG would celebrate Freud's birthday in a less festive way. They would hear a scientific lecture in a private home. Denied citizenship, civil rights, and a professional organization, they considered themselves fortunate to be able to gather at all. Fenichel never learned what happened at the Göring Institute; he was unable to speak to any of his former gentile colleagues. In three years the emotional, intellectual, and social relationships of the finest psychoanalytic institute in the world had been shattered (Eickhoff 1995, 95). The Nazi intent to isolate, dehumanize, and exclude the Jewish analysts from German society had met with complete success. Life for those Jewish analysts had gone from bad to worse, and yet unimaginable and macabre events were still to come.

The Organizational Structure of the Göring Institute

M. H. Göring was named medical director of the German Institute for Psychological Research and Psychotherapy, and Herbert Linden, a psychiatrist, was to become the chief administrative officer. The German Institute was financially supported by the German Labor Front (DAF), by health insurance payments, and by the Nazi Social Welfare Organization. Increased funding came from the German Air Force under the control of M. H. Göring's cousin, Reichsmarshall Hermann Göring. In addition to administration, there were nine other major divisions of the Göring Institute by 1940, five of them concerned with applied psychotherapy:

1. The Educational Counseling Clinic was connected to the youth office of Berlin and treated teenagers fifteen and older individually, with younger children being seen with their parents in combinations of parent counseling, family therapy, and play therapy.

2. The section on expert opinion and catamnesis (clinical histories).

3. The Division of Criminal Psychology.

4. The Division of Diagnostic Testing was oriented toward helping industrial firms.

5. The Outpatient Polyclinic, which was the heart of the Göring organization. (Cocks 1985, 178).

The Göring Institute was to become a major teaching and training center for psychotherapy as well as a research facility. In 1941, the Labor Front alone contributed the equivalent of $135 million to its funding. According to Werner Kemper, a psychoanalyst who directed the Outpatient Polyclinic, 80 percent of the patients were from the middle class. The typical intake of patients included interview, psychological testing, and a physical exam. Kemper estimated that about 50 percent of the cases treated in the outpatient clinic were handled by various modes of short-term therapy. The short-term orientation was congenial with the Nazi emphasis on *Volksgesundheit* (health of the people).

Cocks suggests that one of the reasons the psychoanalyst Gerhard Scheunert was selected to direct the outpatient clinic was his interest in short-term psychotherapy as an efficient, cost-effective means to treat patients and thereby help the Institute in its attempts to have psychotherapy included in the state health insurance system (Cocks 1985, 180–81). Of the approximately fifty psychotherapists who practiced as part of the outpatient clinic, most of them used short-term methods that varied in type and scope depending upon their particular school of thought. Scheunert used a combination of hypnosis, autogenic training, and free association to find what today might be called "core conflicts" of the patient. He claimed that using this approach enabled him to identify and treat an individual within three to four hours. Other practical methods to shorten treatment were the use of alternating sessions with no sessions and Schultz-Hencke's form of neo-analysis, which relied on the rational nature of the ego as the critical element in the cure.

August Vetter was the head of the outpatient psychological testing division from 1939 to 1945, and testing was a customary part of the intake evaluation. Vetter was also a consultant to the I. G. Farben Industry. One of the psychological consultants to the Göring Institute was Erich Jaensch, who was known for his ideological interpretation of test data (Cocks 1985, 146). The typical assessment to provide depth personality data included an impression test developed by Vetter, a drawing test (the Wartegg Test), and a story completion. The impression test was a projective technique that provided the patient with six unstructured forms presented by means of lantern slides. The patient was shown various forms that included patterns of straight lines, patterns of dots, and patterns of shading. Variations of color were included, and the patients' responses were analyzed to determine patterns of both intellectual style and feelings about life's events. The drawing test required the patient to use various kinds of straight lines, patterns of dots, and curved lines that were provided on a "test sheet." Participants were asked to complete the pictures that had been started on the "test sheet." The patient's completed drawing was evaluated by the patient's style of approach and the method used. The story completion test is self-evident. In commenting upon the Germans' use of testing, Col. Paul Fitts, an American psychologist, suggested that, for the most part, the psychologist interpreting the data disregarded exact test scores and relied on clinical judgment. Thus, not using the normative, empirical, and developmental considerations customarily used to make more informed clinical judgments leads to serious questions about credibility and validity. Whether or not these test results were used in evaluating children was not reported, and therefore the initial investigation by the U.S. Army could not determine if clinical judgments about being "untreatable" — or hereditarily disordered — were reached (Fitts 1946). Some cases were handled by depth analysis, including free association and the supine position on the couch. However, even when long-term treatment was considered possible it was usually on a face-to-face basis. The use of hypnosis, autogenic training, massage, gymnastics, breathing exercises, and voice therapy were often integrated into the patient's treatment programs (Cocks 1985).

At its peak in 1941, there were 240 members of the clinical staff including 100 physicians (22 women), 42 academics or psychologists (29 women), and 80 who did not have doctorates (64 women) (Cocks 1985, 177). The essential task of the Göring Institute was to create "the New German Psychotherapy." According to Hans von Hattingberg, the aim of the New German Psychotherapy was to "strengthen belief in the meaning of life and reinforce the link with the higher world of values; it was to convey to the patient the consciousness of being bound and incorporated into the great common destiny of the German people" (Brecht et al. 1985, 152).

The educational counseling service became a formal subdivision under the outpatient program and was directed by Olga von König-Fachsenfeld. Its function was to provide psychotherapeutic assistance to young people who were having difficulty at school. Various types of traditional treatments were provided, including play therapy for children and toddlers, family therapy, as well as group and other forms of individual treatment. "Diagnoses ranged from idiocy and brain damage to various types of neurotic behavior, but the single greatest number . . . suffered from school problems stemming from disrupted family environment" (Cocks 1985, 185). Cocks goes on to say:

> Elisabeth Künkel estimated that about 50 percent of the children who came to the Göring Institute were incapable of integrating themselves in to the community, but only approximately 6 percent were hereditarily disordered and therefore untreatable through psychotherapy. It was the disposition of these latter cases, König-Fachsenfeld has recalled, that brought the shadow of National Socialism into the children's clinic *(Kinderpoliklinik)*. The children could be sent to "safe" homes or asylums; in milder cases the institute would advise bringing the child in for treatment so as to protect him or her from harm from the Nazis. (Cocks 1985, 185–86)

We will return to this awkward description of the nature of treatments provided and the meaning of the "shadow of National Socialism" in the next chapter. The essential ideas for the training of psychotherapists were formulated by the politically altered versions of the three major schools of psychoanalytic thought: the Freudians, the Adlerians, and the Jungians, together with a fourth school made up of psychotherapists who were essentially Nazis and could not be allied with any particular school of thought. In 1938 the three schools of thought were camouflaged as Working Groups A, B, and C, respectively.

After 1938, Working Group A (the Freudian psychoanalysts) was not allowed to hold its meetings in members' homes but only on the Institute's premises. In addition, M. H. Göring or his wife would monitor these meetings to make sure there were no violations, such as using the term "Oedipus Complex." The program of study was to create the medical profession "Specialist in Psychotherapy." The training of psychotherapists was based upon the assumptions that being a physician was not a necessary criterion for being a psychotherapist. The program required at least two years of full-time participation, and it also required a training analysis of at least 150 hours. The training analysis required two to three sessions per week. The medical candidates were required to take courses in the areas of psychology, philosophy, and ethnology. Those candidates with an academic background in psychology who would be trained as psychotherapists at the Göring Institute were to qualify as "Attending Psychologists." They were required to take courses in basic medical areas (i.e., anatomy, physiology, biology, and psychiatry), have adequate supervision, and participate in a training analysis.

In 1938 the Göring Institute was recognized by the Department of the Interior as being one of the most important institutions in Nazi Germany. It was incorporated within the Department of the Interior for its role in providing significant services to the Nazi state. For this honor the Göring Institute sent the following telegram to the Führer:

> In the name of the German General Medical Society for Psychotherapy I offer you, my Führer, a vow of eternal fidelity. At the same time, I announce to you the foundation by the *Reichsärzteführer* of a German Institute for Psychological Research and Psychotherapy, whose supreme task it is to work for the mental and physical health of our people in the spirit of National Socialism. (Brecht et al. 1985, 146)

The Führer replied:

> I thank the German General Medical Society for Psychotherapy for
> their vow of fidelity, and for the announcement of the establishment of
> a German Institute for Psychological Research and Psychotherapy. I
> wish you a great success in your work. (Brecht et al. 1985, 146)

When the Göring Institute was granted financial support from the German
Labor Front in 1939, it became the first publicly financed institute to train
both psychologists and physicians to become professional psychotherapists
in the Third Reich. On January 1, 1944, the Göring Institute was integrated into the *Reichsforschungsrat* (the Research Council of the Reich),
which further consolidated the Institute's importance and power. On July
12, 1944, it became recognized as an essential part of the German war
effort with a priority rating of "second order urgency."

As part of its growing importance within the Third Reich, the Göring
Institute received more funds to support the training of psychotherapists.
The training included a stipulated theoretical course of study, depending
upon one's past educational background. Like all other educational and
professional organizations within the Third Reich, the Göring Institute
had required courses on race, but the hours of instruction between 1936
and 1945 totaled only thirty-one (Cocks 1985, 189–90; Brecht et al. 1985,
146–48).

Those candidates whose prior educational experience had been in academic psychology were identified as "Attending Psychologists," whereas
physicians who completed the training program received what in the
United States would be classified as a "Specialization in Psychotherapy."
Both groups had acquired what could be considered equivalent professional status as "psychotherapists" in terms of their ability to become private practitioners. Both the physician and the psychology graduates were
also eligible to become regular members of the Göring Institute. Other
qualifications for becoming members of the Institute involved being at
least thirty years of age and having five years of professional experience. In
addition to the title of "Attending Psychologist," which took at least two
years of full-time participation in the program, there was a one-year program which enabled a candidate to become a "Consultant Psychologist."
The individuals who acquired the title of "Consultant Psychologist" were
most often already working with children and adolescents as part of their
teaching and social work responsibilities.

Another critical step in the establishment of psychology as an autonomous profession was the result of a commission that had its first meeting at
the Göring Institute in February 1940 with the purpose of creating an

examination for professional psychology. M. H. Göring hosted that meeting and, together with Gustav R. Heyer, advocated the view that full professional status be given those "Attending Psychologists" who were in training to become psychotherapists. The Diploma Examination Regulations (*Diplom-Prüfungsordnung*–DPO) was the culmination of psychology's struggle to become an independent profession. The DPO provided psychology with its own unique identity. Those on the commission considered that psychology could fit the National Socialists' ideological need to provide services to both community and state (Cocks 1985, 27).

However, there remained fierce resistance by many physician groups, as well as by many prominent psychiatrists, regarding the autonomous practice of psychotherapy by psychologists. Max de Crinis, the Director of Psychiatry at the famous Charité Hospital as well as being a leading Nazi spokesperson, was opposed to the establishment of this exam and vowed "to fight it all the way" (Geuter 1992, 229). He stated "that psychologists understand absolutely nothing about medicine, a fact with which we could then immediately confront them if ever they dared to reach out for our domain" (Geuter 1992, 230). Despite a large number of similar protests, on June 16, 1941, the DPO was promulgated, and it was retroactively established as legal from April 1, 1941. The critical prerogative that the medical groups were able to salvage was the requirement that at the Göring Institute the "Attending Psychologists" could practice psychotherapy only with the cooperation or supervision of a physician (Geuter 1992, 246; and Cocks 1985, 194).

The DPO exam required that candidates be evaluated in general, conscious, unconscious, individual, community, characterology, philosophical, ideological, and medical psychology (Cocks 1985, 195). The DPO commission attributed the adoption of the above curriculum to the influence of Jung. The five branches of the Göring Institute allowed for large numbers of psychologists to be trained; their professional identity would be as "psychotherapists." The fact that psychologists were allowed equal access with physicians to be trained in Working Group A to become psychoanalysts represented a unique position within the international psychotherapeutic movement.

Thus, when the *Wehrmacht* reached the zenith of its success during the last month of 1941, it could be argued that, from an institutional framework, psychoanalysis, albeit with its submerged identity, was likewise prospering beyond anyone's wildest imagination in the Third Reich. From a superficial analysis, it was possible to practice "Jewish psychotherapy" without being a Jewish practitioner. From the same institutional and quantitative assessment, the psychology profession also appeared to be a major benefactor of Nazi ideology. During the Third Reich, psychology not only emerged as an autonomous profession, but its practitioners had equal access to training in depth psychotherapy or psychoanalysis as their medical colleagues.

How much can be determined by analyzing the organizational framework of such an institute? On face value in the summer of 1939, the Göring Institute resembled what had existed ten years before. In essence, the Göring Institute was modeled after the BPI, but Freudian terms or ideas on sexuality were never allowed to be mentioned in addition to the numerous other restrictions that have been previously noted. The Freudian element of the organization lost a good deal of responsibility and teaching status. Despite this permanent loss, the Freudians were able to maintain significant influence by clever staffing and by maintaining the directorship of the heart of the Institute, the Outpatient Polyclinic. The fact is that between 1938 and 1945 Working Group A had trained thirty-four psychoanalysts under these conditions (Brecht et al. 1985, 130). By focusing on the power positions they still retained and the number of candidates that had completed their training, the gentile psychoanalysts who remained at the Göring Institute had accepted form rather than function as proof of their survival. In so doing, they had lost sight of the processes necessary for psychoanalysis to survive—namely freedom of thought (or free associations) for both patient and analyst. These were simply withering away from consciousness.

10

The Integration of the Nazi Medical Principles of Healing and Extermination within the Göring Institute

The Roles of M. H. Göring and Herbert Linden

THERE WERE, AMONG PROFESSIONALS, varying degrees of complicity with the Nazis during this troubled period. The practitioners at the Göring Institute were not involved in directly carrying out the most radical goals of the Nazis during the Third Reich, as were the doctors who carried out the grossly inhumane research in the concentration camps or the physicians that made the selection of life or death for the newly arrived inmates as they entered through the camp gates. This chapter deals with professional responsibility, patient care rights, and a pattern of evidence that indicates occurrences of gross abuse at the Göring Institute. The evidence is from Cocks (1985 and 1997), Lifton (1986), Lockot (1985, 1991, 1994), *The Catalog* (Brecht et al. 1985), Friedländer (1995), and Aly et al. (1994).

Previously, we cite a quotation of Olga von König-Fachsenfeld, director of the children's clinic. She stated that "the shadow of National Socialism" was brought into the Institute due to the fate suffered by those children (6 percent of the cases) who were diagnosed as "hereditarily disordered and therefore untreatable through psychotherapy" (Cocks 1985, 185). What Cocks does not make clear is that for the Nazis the term "untreatable" was a code word for extermination. It is now known that many of the "safe" homes or asylums to which the children were sent employed mercy killing or euthanasia on their residents. The conclusion we draw is that as part of its ordinary operating procedures, the Göring Institute participated in the chain of events that inevitably led to criminal murder of German children by the Third Reich. Does this not suggest the tacit acceptance on their part of the Nazified diagnosis "untreatable" as "life unworthy of life"? It would seem that the professionals cannot escape awareness of and responsibility for the uses to which their diagnoses were put.

The leadership roles of M. H. Göring and Herbert Linden in the operation of the Institute requires further clarification. We turn again to the factual information provided by Cocks to understand Herbert Linden, one of the significant leaders of the National Socialists' euthanasia program. Cocks identifies Herbert Linden as a psychiatrist and chief administrative officer of the Institute since its inception, and suggests that when Boehm initially contacted the Medical Division of the Ministry of the Interior on February 18, 1936, to seek continued licensure of the DPG, he had established a relationship with Linden. From that meeting, the idea that the DPG would be incorporated within a general outpatient psychotherapeutic clinic in Berlin emerged. The meeting between Boehm and Linden coincided with M. H. Göring's attempt to solicit the C. G. Jung Society in Berlin to join him in the establishment of a psychotherapeutic institute that would be financed by the Nazi Party. These events apparently led to a compromise between those involved, since the state would never forbid the practice of a useful therapy nor would it allow a psychoanalytic institute dedicated solely to Freudian theory. The compromise reached was that the DPG be integrated within an institute committed to a variety of psychoanalytic theories. When Boehm returned to the Department of the Interior on March 18, 1936, he agreed to the incorporation of the DPG into the "Göring Institute" (Cocks 1985, 143–44).

M. H. Göring

It is our impression that this was another of the compromises made by the DPG that contributed to its own increasing Nazification. This step, however, was a most significant one. On the surface the apparent leader was M. H. Göring. It is our impression, however, that the way the Institute operated was more consistent with Herbert Linden's history of direct authorization for mass murder than it was with the overall behavioral patterns of M. H. Göring.

There is no doubt M. H. Göring was a Nazi. All of his public and private statements consistently were in line with Nazi ideology, and he supported all the government positions. However, there is no evidence that M. H. Göring initiated or sought out punitive actions on his own. He showed flexibility with racial issues at informal discussions within the Institute. He overlooked or did not notice the "racial impurities" of the spouses of those who worked at the Institute. Even though M. H. Göring had personal warmth and a friendly style, he ended up carrying out the most ruthless Nazi policies. The Institute apparently followed Hitler's written authorization to participate in the euthanasia program, and thus violated some of the basic standards of Western civilization. These inhumane activities included the euthanasia program, authorization to murder untreatable homosexuals, and the execution of front-line German troops whose form of "battle fatigue" could create anxiety among the German people. On the basis of M. H. Göring's known verbal and behavioral patterns, it is unlikely that he was the prime mover in ordering these atrocities. We have argued that he was a much more committed Nazi than previously assumed (Cocks 1985, 1997; Spiegel 1975, 1985). We propose that he would cooperate with fanatical orders from those in authority, but giving such orders was not his style.

Let us look more closely at Göring's style of participation. The following evidence provides support for the view that M. H. Göring was a true believer in the fanatical beliefs of National Socialism. Cocks had considered him as the "good" Nazi doctor. In his 1985 publication, Cocks assures the reader that M. H. Göring prohibited staff from the hereditary health court, where presumably the cards were stacked against the patient. It is further suggested that M. H. Göring required specific diagnoses and leaned toward judgments more consistent with psychotherapy as the main recommendation (Cocks 1985, 105). Cocks implies that M. H. Göring played a passively resistant role when it came to the practice of euthanasia. Was the impression Cocks left correct? Findings contradictory to Cocks's contention are found in Lifton's (1986) analysis of the euthanasia program. M. H. Göring is identified as an "ardent" Nazi rather than the prototypical "decent" Nazi that Cocks portrays. Lifton (1986) cites specific evidence contradicting the view that M. H. Göring was not really in favor of euthanasia.

One way to assess M. H. Göring's leadership is to examine the *Witzblatt* (or Joke Newspaper) that portrayed the man on his sixtieth birthday on April 15, 1939. Friedrich cites the following verse (quoted in Friedrich 1989, 12) to demonstrate how clearly and painfully the scientific works, the organization, and the psychotherapy that was provided served the aims of National Socialism:

Proudly unfurled in the whale's hall of fame,
a ring of bronze held tight to the wood announces your name,

And yet there it stood, forgotten, as a barren altar,
Till the era of our disgrace has gone,
Till the Führer's will and holy call
With wondrous violence Greater Germany doth create,
Hooray, hoist high the banner!

So stand we today, a tiny crew
Fighting for a truth that was revealed to us anew,
For a healthy huge Germany our banner does flutter,
You lead us into battle and we follow blind and true,
And oh, how we both love and hate ourselves, too,
And oh, how we desire to clasp the hands of each other,
Hooray, and hoist high the banner!

Göring flatly refused to sign a declaration against the euthanasia program sponsored by a young and courageous psychiatrist, Theo Lang. Lang
had called on M. H. Göring at the Institute on January 20, 1941, and tried
to persuade him to sign a petition to stop the murder of mental patients
(Müller-Hill 1988, 121). When a church leader sought help to protect the
epilepsy patients at his hospital in May 1940, M. H. Göring recommended
"not to undertake anything [in the way of opposition], but only to do this
when we have definite evidence" (Lifton 1986, 91). Göring simply stonewalled the courageous attempts by Pastors Fritz von Bodelschwingh and
Paul Gerhard Braune to stop these so-called mercy killings (Lifton 1986;
Friedländer 1993, 114-15). Thus, the view presented by Cocks that
Göring was a dedicated physician and a pious Christian simply is not consistent with what he said and did when confronted with the challenges in
life that reveal the true nature of a person's character.

M. H. Göring not only followed the most radical mandates of
National Socialism by accepting the practice of murdering those Germans
designated "unworthy of life," he also conformed to Hitler's deceitful style
of foreign policy in dealing with the IPA. The evidence is quite clear that
the arrangements agreed upon with Abraham, Brill, and Jones about the
autonomy of psychoanalysis within the Göring Institute were never going
to be implemented. M. H. Göring, along with Boehm and Müller-Braunschweig, met with the two representatives, Jones and Brill, of the IPA in
Basel during July 1936. In that meeting he promised that the independence of psychoanalysis within the Institute would be respected. However,
in May 1936, M. H. Göring had previously made it quite clear to the
members of the new institute that the ideas and practice of psychoanalysis
would have to be consistent with the idealogy of National Socialism. Dur-

ing his first speech to the members of the Institute, he unequivocally required that the "totalitarian claim" of National Socialist ideology be assured vis-à-vis the practice of psychoanalysis. He further maintained that the "Jewish peculiarities" within psychoanalysis would have to be eliminated (Nitzschke 1991, 41).

M. H. Göring may have been in some ways a kind and benevolent person, but he was not a man tolerant of mistakes, especially if those were ideological in nature. Consider the case of the psychoanalyst John Rittmeister. While M. H. Göring was clinical director of the Institute, the case of John Rittmeister would reveal he was less benign than this role as the fatherly "Papi" would have suggested. As noted earlier, M. H. Göring at first suspected John Rittmeister because of his support of Descartes's philosophy, which called for reasonable doubt of man's perfection (Cocks 1985, 67).

How could Rittmeister's acceptance of Descartes's philosophy lead M. H. Göring to doubt his loyalty to the Third Reich? The answer, we think, reveals the depth of his ideological beliefs. In the first place, Descartes believed that man was a prejudiced being and only by systematic, methodical doubt would he rid himself of prejudice. For those who believed in the ideology of National Socialism there was the essential idea that the Aryans were the "master race," and anyone who could doubt that was suspect. Doubting everything meant one would doubt the master race. The second principle of Descartes that is inconsistent with National Socialism in its simplest form is: *cogito ergo sum* (I think, therefore, I exist). The human capacity for conscious awareness of one's thought is the critical feature distinguishing us from animals. Ultimately, "thinking" would lead Descartes to be an exponent of modern science based upon mathematics and experimentation. National Socialism is based on the romantic philosophical notion that deeply felt intuition, not thought, was the supreme human attribute of the mind (Kenny 1994, 113-19).

If M. H. Göring's suspicion of Rittmeister's loyalty to the Third Reich emerged from these subtle philosophical disagreements with National Socialism, can we doubt he had a firm commitment to its ideology? Was this not his role as a member of the Lecturers' Alliance to ensure that all professors' thinkings conform to Nazi ideology (i.e., to report disagreements of individuals with the Party's ideology)? In general, we believe that M. H. Göring was an enthusiastic Nazi, but he showed variation in his ideological concerns. Issues related to German loyalty elicited his closest collaboration with Nazi ideology while he could be more tolerant about the racial purity of his staff's spouses.

Herbert Linden

Herbert Linden is described as the least known of the major perpetrators of the euthanasia program. He was born in 1899, received his medical license and joined the Nazi party in 1925, and was involved in the inner circle of those who planned the euthanasia program from its inception. Although his major role was bureaucratic, he embraced the extreme virtues of fanatic Nazis. In 1941, his administrative role expanded. He had daily operational control, and he became the driving force of the euthanasia program until the war's end. Linden escaped arrest, interrogation, and trial by committing suicide on April 27, 1945 (Friedländer 1995, 43-44, 190, 200-201).

The Catalog (Brecht et al. 1985) provides specific evidence that Herbert Linden was successful in the Nazification of the Göring Institute. Herbert Linden was the administrator responsible for reorganizing psychiatry and the "New German Psychotherapy" into the twofold process of "healing" and "extermination." Linden was a leader and supporter of the Göring Institute. In that capacity he fostered psychotherapy for the treatable but euthanasia for the untreatable. As previously reported, if psychotherapy failed, the patient was under the threat of euthanasia (Brecht et al. 1985, 162). As leader of the two major front organizations for implementing extermination of the racially impure, Linden had primary responsibility for reintroducing the practice of medicalized murder after the initial protests by German mothers had forced its brief termination.

Other evidence presented in *The Catalog* reveals that Linden was one of the administrators responsible for the euthanasia program for children throughout Germany. He had been appointed head of the State Committee (*Reichsausschuß*) for serious hereditary illnesses in 1939 and State Inspector (*Reichsbeauftragter*) for Mental Asylums in 1941. "Both organizations were a front for the implementation of euthanasia" (Brecht et al. 1985, 162). Linden often took a direct role in deciding whether or not a patient was killed. The Nazi eugenic laws were well known at the Göring Institute and supporting articles were often published in the Institute's publication, *Zentralblatt für Psychotherapie* (Brecht et al. 1985).

According to Aly, "Herbert Linden efficiently and quietly ensured cooperation between state health officials, the authorities in the Führer's Office, and the newly created clandestine special organizations" (Aly et al. 1994, 37). The influence of the supervisory body was widespread and involved almost all facets of the Nazi extermination programs. The supervisory groups had direct ties to the decisions and implementation of the Final Solution (Aly et al. 1994, 23-93; Breitman 1991, 139). In 1940, Linden was also given administrative responsibility to ensure the close cooperation between the

Interior Ministry of the government and the Race Political Office of the Nazi Party (Cocks 1997, 207). In practical terms this meant Linden had the duty to carry out the daily operation of killing those patients designated as racially unfit (Friedländer 1997, 190). Friedländer's findings reveal the full spectrum of Linden's power once he was named Reich plenipotentiary during October 1941 (Friedländer 1995, 157). This title of Reich plenipotentiary conferred on Linden the full power to represent the government (i.e., the Führer) on all matters pertaining to those patients considered to be "life unworthy of life." He was directly responsible for murders in both the adults' and children's euthanasia programs, he ordered the worst aspects of medical research, he had major administrative responsibility over the hospitals and nursing homes in which the killings were carried out, and he also was involved in the decisions resulting in the first murders of handicapped Jews. In this capacity, on December 12, 1940, he issued an order that Jewish handicapped patients be admitted to Bendorf-Sayn Hospital. With this order he became involved in an operation that Friedländer (1995) suggests "foreshadowed, possibly fore-ordained, the final solution" (p. 282).

Michael Burleigh's book, *Death and Deliverance,* further defines the important role that Linden had in the establishment and implementation of the euthanasia program. Burleigh indicates that while there are several versions of how the euthanasia program started, the four major perpetrators were Linden, Professor Karl Rudolph Brandt (one of Hitler's personal physicians), Reichsleiter Philipp Bouhler (director of that part of the Chancellory designated to enhance Hitler's image as Führer), and finally, Victor Brack, an economist in charge of practical matters outside the province of medicine (Burleigh 1994, 93–98, 113, 121, 123–24 and 273–74). These four men were responsible for "a carefully planned and covertly executed operation with precisely defined objectives" (Burleigh 1994, 4). Furthermore, Burleigh states, they "acted conspiratorially, deliberately and methodically to put their ideas into practice. The notions that these policies came about in an ad hoc, contingent or reactive fashion is preposterous. After the war, however, it was the standard line of defense" (Burleigh 1994, 98).

Once the decision was made by Hitler to carry out the euthanasia program and the means of carbon dioxide was chosen, the questions arose of where this would occur, which doctors would be chosen "to turn on the gas valves," and who would select the criteria by which the patients would be executed. The answers to these questions all lead to the conclusion that Linden was responsible for these decisions (Burleigh 1994, 113, 121, and 127–28). When questions or complaints were raised by Germans suspicious that the patients were actually being murdered, Linden was a key figure in maintaining the coverup or negotiating an acceptable settlement (Burleigh 1994, 164-66, 171-75, and 250).

Linden's power increased when he was named Reich plenipotentiary in October 1941. In effect, this meant he was Hitler's personal representative on racial matters. Brecht et al. (1985) revealed that Linden successfully introduced the new Nazi form of treatment at the Institute. The dual role of Nazi medicine was to heal those capable of regaining their health and exterminate those who would remain "unfit" and therefore became a drain on the state's resources. The principle that the purpose of physician and health care organizations was to minister to and heal all the sick was null and void. The Nazi health care organizations and providers had become soldiers of the state. They now had a broader and more significant role: They were the healers of the corpus of the Aryan race, biological warriors fighting the diseased and inferior element that threatened the body of the *Volk*. In the grand scheme of Nazi ideology, the goals of medicine and aesthetics had now become one. The purification of the evolutionary process was to guarantee a beautiful and healthy master race. While the psychoanalysts at the Institute were still far removed from being "willing executioners," under the constant pressure from authority to conform to Nazi ideology, their commitment to the Hippocratic Oath had crumbled. Given this historical portrayal of the chief administrator of the Göring Institute, one must wonder: How fortuitous was the loss of all medical records at Göring Institute toward the end of the war for those members of the Göring Institute who survived?

The evidence on both Linden and M. H. Göring raises questions about other testimony provided to Cocks (1985). For example, the presently available evidence of Nazification within the Institute raises serious questions about Boehm's claim in 1939 to have cured 67 percent of 500 patients of their homosexual behavior, as was reported in Cocks (1985, 209-10). How could one refer to "cure" of homosexuals if one was aware that the alternative to cure was extermination? Such consequences as extermination for "treatment failures" raise the gravest questions about the integrity of any form of psychoanalysis, or any form of psychotherapy for that matter, at the Göring Institute.

The questionable claims for curing homosexuals made by Boehm in 1938 and by Johannes Heinrich Schultz in 1944 are overshadowed by these men's participation in actions that hardly could be considered forms of treatment. In Cocks's 1997 publication, he reveals that Boehm had, in fact, endorsed the death penalty for certain kinds of homosexuals who were members of the armed forces. Boehm was a member of a commission that compared a more liberal Luftwaffe policy on homosexuality published on June 7, 1944, with the more severe policy that included the death penalty, issued by Field Marshall Keitel, chief of the armed forces in May 1943. On December 15, 1944, the commission on which Boehm served supported the "death penalty as a form of treatment" (Cocks 1997, 299).

The Göring Institute had an ongoing working arrangement with the SS to evaluate and treat homosexuals. M. H. Göring, Schultz, and Kalau vom Hofe all took part in working with the SS on this endeavor. What they indicated after the war to Cocks and others was that they tried to keep these homosexual patients from being sent to concentration camps or from being diagnosed as untreatable. As Cocks suggests, Schultz's relationship with the SS was ethically problematic. Schultz had rendered an expert opinion on one case with which Reichsführer Heinrich Himmler was personally concerned. An SS man was sent to the Institute by his family and was under the threat of execution by his superiors. Apparently he was treated by psychotherapy at the Institute, and then Schultz proposed the most bizarre test to demonstrate the man's heterosexuality. He had to demonstrate he could perform sexual intercourse with a prostitute before a panel of experts. (Apparently Schultz admitted this to two secretaries at the Göring Institute.) Cocks correctly indicates that even if this was done to save a man's life, it reveals the Institute was still indirectly supporting the Nazi system of murder. However, when *Der Spiegel* raised the question of whether this method might have been a standard procedure, Cocks states that "if Schultz or anyone else at the Göring Institute was involved in the systematic condemnation of homosexuals to death, then that evidence has yet to be uncovered" (Cocks 1997, 296-97). Yet even Cocks raises the possibility that Schultz told this story to plant a postwar alibi for his work with the SS (303, n. 42). If in fact he was innocent, why would he invent any story? The fact of the matter is that such a method to test heterosexuality has a very sadistic bent. How many potent males could perform effectively in front of such a panel if they knew their life was on the line? Such a method would probably create an inordinate number of false negatives.

Returning to the issue of the euthanasia program within the Göring Institute, by 1990 Cocks admits that his previous claim in 1985, that Göring played a resistant role regarding the euthanasia program, was incorrect. When two colleagues requested his support for their protest, Göring was unwilling to endanger the Institute's position by joining them (Cocks 1990, 312). Schultz was also a firm supporter of the regime's euthanasia policy. He endorsed the Nazi's brutal view of "life unworthy of life" and went on to "express the hope that the insane asylums will soon transform themselves and empty themselves in this way" (Cocks 1997, 235). It is now known that in their professional capacities both Kemper and Boehm were directly involved in supporting the extermination of both homosexuals and soldiers experiencing "battle fatigue." Both men had gradually accepted the Nazi dual role of "healing and extermination."

The fact that Linden's major responsibility was to implement the euthanasia program in 1941, and his propensity was to cover up this program, sheds new light on how he used his role as the chief administrator of the Göring Institute. When Linden's actions are combined with the fact that M. H. Göring stonewalled those individuals who wanted to protest the euthanasia policy, questions arise about the Institute's participation in the extermination program.

It now becomes clear what was meant by "only approximately 6 percent [of these patients] who were [considered] as hereditarily disordered and therefore untreatable through psychotherapy." The most parsimonious explanation of what Olga von König-Fachsenfeld meant when she said that these cases "brought the shadow of National Socialism into the children's clinic" is simply this: these 6 percent of the children were candidates for extermination. The term "untreatable" was a code word like "special treatment" for Jews, and it meant certain death. The terminology "safe homes" was another code word for special facilities where the children were to be given a "merciful death" (Cocks 1985, 185). In retrospect, it is clear what Cocks was describing, and one must wonder whether, as the interviewer, he was all too close to the situation to think of the implications of what Olga von König-Fachsenfeld had said.

We conclude that the overwhelming evidence now reveals that the Göring Institute had incorporated within it the essential, ideological convictions of the NSDAP. The Nazified practice of medicine included roles of both healing and extermination. The administrators of the Institute had accepted the notion that professionals must have values and/or philosophies congruent with the core ideological beliefs of National Socialism. "Special treatment," the euphemism for the death sentence, became feasible for all kinds of mavericks and misfits. The execution of unfit Aryans started within Germany, with their own children, using the military invasion of Poland to cover up the violent nature of eliminating "undesirable" children. It is now estimated that as many as two hundred thousand Aryan men, women, and children were executed during the course of World War II. With Herbert Linden coordinating these extermination programs of "life unworthy of life," the Göring Institute had been brought into projects involving criminal murders.

As members of the Institute, what role did the psychoanalysts play in such criminal activity? While it is clear that the psychoanalysts were not major perpetrators, they were not immune from becoming part of this brutality. By the war's end, Boehm had given up his humane principles and accepted extermination as a way of disposing of "uncured" homosexuals, while Kemper had participated in establishing the death penalty as a special form of treatment for "incurable" forms of battle fatigue. Extermination as a means of treatment had become an acceptable method for two of the most distinguished psychoanalysts at the Göring Institute.

A satirical poem written by one of the students at the Göring Institute probably best portrays both that particular young German's desire to retain psychological truth as well as his or her insight into the essential nature of M. H. Göring's personality. The poem ends with the following powerful lines (Brecht et al. 1985, 153):

> To be freud-less, ah, that were abysmal,
> So full of ourselves, yet so dismal,
> And though dreams are full of "anima" the seeker
> Can utter no glorious "Eureka!"
> The patron of children is Pápi,
> But still in their guilt they're so unhappy,
> None follows the Ego-Ideal,
> For none is the Path of Love real.
> Dear Pápi, your tears must be spilling,
> Your children go on with the killing.
> At last, united, in their graves they've ended,
> And Pápi sobs: "It was so well intended!"

11

"Finis Austriae" (The End of Austria) or "The Stronghold of Jewish Psychotherapy Has Fallen"

IN 1938, THE VIOLENT NATURE OF National Socialism began to reveal itself in its foreign policies. In the beginning of that year, the chancellor of Austria, Kurt von Schuschnigg, was invited to Hitler's Kehlstein, or, as American soldiers renamed it, the "Eagle's Nest." The purpose was to intimidate Schuschnigg into turning control of the Austrian government over to the Nazis. It was obvious to Schuschnigg that he was on the spot at the Eagle's Nest. If he did not placate Hitler sufficiently, the Third Reich was going to use military force to implement the Führer's demands. On the other hand, a complete capitulation to Hitler's demands would at best turn Austria into a puppet state of the Third Reich. The Nazis would have control over the police and military functions. Austria would also be joined at the hip with the Third Reich by having its financial system placed under the control of Hitler. Schuschnigg played a desperate game for time by signing an agreement, but upon returning to Austria called for a plebiscite of the Austrian people to determine whether Hitler's conditions were acceptable. The plebiscite was set for March 13, 1938, but an outraged Hitler ordered German troops to be ready to march into Austria on March 11, 1938. Faced with military invasion, Schuschnigg realized he had lost his gamble. He resigned, German troops entered the country, and on March 13 Hitler proclaimed the *Anschluß* (annexation). Almost immediately, the real violence began: seventy

thousand political arrests in Vienna alone were made, and anti-Semitic programs started with a vengeance. There was bloodshed in the streets of
Vienna, and it was immediately clear that all Jewish psychoanalysts were in
serious danger (Langer and Gifford 1978, 37–41). In his recollections on
the subject of the treatment of the Jews in Vienna, Leopold Bellak (1993)
has recently shared his own experiences, which validate the grim horror
described by Langer and Gifford (1978).

In evaluating the direct impact of *Anschluß* on the Wiener Psychoanalytische Vereinigung (WPV), let us briefly look at Edith Kurzweil's (1996)
description of the New York Psychoanalytic Association's efforts to help
Jewish analysts escape. Kurzweil has relied upon the minutes of the New
York Psychoanalytic Association and those of the Emergency Committee
on Relief and Immigration of the American Psychoanalytic Association as
well as the correspondence of Lawrence Kubie. Kubie was the head of the
Emergency Committee and the prime mover in efforts to save as many as
possible of the Jewish analysts who had been trapped in continental Europe
by the rise of National Socialism. The impression conveyed by Kurzweil
about Kubie has been supported by Judith Kestenberg, M.D., a person
intimately aware of events on both sides of the Atlantic (Kestenberg 1994).
On behalf of the Jewish analysts in Europe, Kubie corresponded with the
membership of the American Psychoanalytical Association, the United
States State Department, and Edward Glover among others. Kubie was acting according to what Kurzweil described as the "friendship and the customary American human instinct to save people suffering from political
repression or natural disasters" in order to "rescue these colleagues" (Kurzweil 1996, 141). Unfortunately, Kubie had chosen the U.S. State Department to work through; he also accepted its advice. Later, evidence would
document that the U.S. State Department throughout World War II had
been significantly influenced by anti-Semitism, which could not have been
helpful to Kubie, the Committee, or the Jewish analysts in Europe. We
learn from Kurzweil's report that in 1938 Kubie sent out two letters about
the horrendous conditions facing the Jewish analysts in Vienna. However,
we never learn if the Jewish analysts in Vienna were ever helped by the
Committee. We only learn that by November 22, 1937, twenty-nine individuals had been saved by the Committee. No other account is given of
those saved, and of course we know that *Anschluß* took place in March
1938. Therefore, the success of the Committee is not clear with regard to
the Jewish analysts in Vienna.

However, a more complete account of what happened emerges from
the eyewitness report of Walter C. Langer, brother of the Harvard historian

William L. Langer. Walter C. Langer was a lay analyst formally trained in Boston and during the *Anschluß* was in analysis with Anna Freud. Langer was an American gentile who quickly grasped the problem his Jewish friends were facing, and he immediately helped rescue five Jews from Austria by driving them to Florence. Upon returning to Vienna, Langer learned that both the number of Jews being rounded up was increasing and the atrocities against them were becoming more vicious.

At this time, Langer was the only American male analyst left in the analytic community, and he was overwhelmed by the enormous number of requests for help. Once he realized the number of people needing help, he came to the conclusion that he would not be able to save many Jews by the kind of heroic driving efforts he had just made across the Alps. It was obvious that in order to escape to the United States, the Jews needed affidavits guaranteeing the financial support of the individual or family until they were able to support themselves. He decided the only practical way to obtain these affidavits from Americans who did not know any of these individuals would be for him to make a personal plea, and he decided to make a quick trip to the United States and make as many arrangements as he could. Just before leaving Vienna, Freud asked him "to personally deliver a letter to Princess Marie Bonaparte in Paris and also a letter to the President of the New York Psychoanalytic Society" (Langer and Gifford 1978, 41). He was more than happy to do this for Freud.

While Langer was optimistic about being able to obtain the affidavits in the United States, his discussion with the Princess in Paris upon delivering Freud's letter revealed that she was much more skeptical about his chances of success. Unfortunately, her assessment was closer to what actually occurred. As Langer describes:

> My reception by the President of the New York Psychoanalytic Society was far from heartwarming. He read the letter from Professor Freud that I had brought and inquired about conditions in Vienna. I asked if he and some of the other member of the Society would sign some of the affidavits . . . , but he declined saying that he would have to take it up with the Board. I pointed out that this was really a matter of life and death. . . . But he declined, saying that he did not know what they would do with these analysts in New York City. (Langer and Gifford 1978, 42)

Langer reported that fortunately he had other friends in New York who were more willing to help, and he obtained a dozen sworn affidavits with the name of the recipient left blank. He then went to Boston, where people "welcomed me with open arms." One of Langer's Boston contacts said "Hell, Walter, . . . I was born in Vienna and I could be one of the thousands of people you describe. What do you want me to sign and how many?" Langer pointed out that he might have to support some of these people after they reached the United States until such time as they were able to support themselves, but this did not deter him. He said, "I'll share my last piece of bread with any of them if we can only get them out." Other people who rallied to the cause were Dr. Felix Frankfurter, then a professor at the Harvard Law School, and Walter Langer's own brother, Professor William Langer. William rallied all the friends he could gather to a library meeting where these issues were discussed. He came away with forty to fifty affidavits. Frankfurter invited him to lunch with four prominent Jews who desperately wanted a report on conditions in Vienna. Langer was put through a "grueling inquiry about the Nazi regime" but came away with fifteen more blank affidavits (Langer and Gifford 1978, 37–54).

Upon returning to Vienna, Langer discovered conditions had become even worse. He gave out the affidavits first to the analytic community, all of whose members escaped. His real soul-searching problem came after the analytic community was rescued. He gave preference to professional people with competence who were married because they needed only one affidavit. He also selected those under forty and in good health. One exception was made. Anna Freud requested an affidavit for her first-grade teacher and her husband, and Langer did not have the heart to deny his analyst's request. Those Jews unable to escape Austria would die in concentration camps. According to the psychoanalyst George Pollock (Keynote Speech 1994), when Freud left Vienna, he had been given only ten exit visas for his family. This meant he had to leave behind many of his relatives, including four sisters, who would not survive.

This episode between Langer and the president of the New York Psychoanalytic Society leaves many unanswered questions. These questions become more important because we know the outcome was the loss of lives that might have been saved. While we know that Kubie was working through the State Department, and we know from Judith Kestenberg that he was esteemed as a man of good will, we do not know whether the president of the New York Society ever informed the Board of Freud's letter or of Langer's request. Why didn't he share with Langer that by that time a system had been worked out by which foreign analysts were being sent to places outside of New York?

For example, Clara M. Happel and Richard and Editha Sterba all went to Detroit, where they were able to establish practices. Martin Grotjahn found work at the Menninger Clinic in Topeka, Kansas, from 1936–38. Why didn't the president send Langer to Kubie, who already was in charge of the rescue mission for Jewish analysts? Why didn't the president, who was also the treasurer of the Emergency Committee on Relief and Immigration of the American Psychoanalytic Association, set up a meeting with Kubie where they both could acquire firsthand information about the actual events that were daily affecting the Viennese analysts? They would have also learned the truth of what was happening on the streets of Vienna instead of relying on one telephone call from Ruth Brunswick and on the United States Department of State's "official" version of the events in Vienna. Edith Kurzweil has given a very positive report of Kubie's and the president's actions on behalf of the Vienna analysts' plight (Kurzweil, in Ash and Söllner 1995, 139-55). However, Kurzweil's review of what the Committee reported to all members of the American Psychoanalytic Association about the events occurring in Vienna can at best be considered a highly cosmeticized version of the truth. To suggest that what was happening in Vienna with the analytic community was being carried out with "official formality and not with mob violence" does not connote at all the violence in the streets nor the terror that the Freud family experienced at the hands of the Gestapo. With Freud's letter in hand for the president to read, it was obvious that Langer was Freud's official psychoanalytic representative on a mission of mercy. Whereas the unsympathetic behavior on the part of our State Department may be attributed in part to its tradition of anti-Semitism, the behavior of the president of the New York Psychoanalytic Society is more perplexing. What led to his response of doing business as usual in a moment of real crisis, uninfluenced by Langer's plea that this was a life-and-death situation? His comment of wondering what they would do with all these analysts in New York suggests the threat of economic competition may have been a motive. This would be consistent with Freud's impression of Americans as being overly concerned with money. In any event, this episode demonstrates that the German gentile analysts were not unique in placing ambition and career over ethical stances. Another possible motive of the president of the New York Society's perplexing behavior is the longstanding schism between the New York group and European group over the issue of lay analysis. When asked by Sanford Gifford about the reason for the American Psychoanalytic Association's longstanding prohibition on lay analysis in America, Langer's response brings us back to the telling events of 1938. He states:

> I do not believe that there is anything that I can add to the problem of
> lay analysis. It never did make much sense to me, particularly since so

many of the outstanding analysts, right from the beginning have been nonmedical and many of our training analysts today were analyzed by them, or by analysts who were analyzed by them. When I think of analysts like Anna Freud, Ernst Kris, Robert Waelder, Erik Erikson, to name a few, I wonder what more they can expect. Confidentially, I sort of had the feeling that the early medical analysts who were instrumental in formulating the politics for our American institutes considered it a most effective way of closing the door to competition, in much the same way that the trade unions have done. This is probably an injustice, but I cannot help but think back on the remark that the President of the New York Psychoanalytic Society made when I approached him for affidavits: "What in the world would we do with all these additional analysts?" (Langer and Gifford 1978, 53)

The entire issue about Langer, the president of the New York Psychoanalytic Society, and the émigré analysts needs further evaluation.

The *Anschluß* made clear how Nazi ideology had a direct impact on the institution and practice of Freudian psychoanalysis. Cocks reveals that one of the first issues to be dealt with by the Nazi leadership was what to do with the Vienna Institute. The more violent faction of the Nazi Party, consisting of Goebbels and Himmler, wanted to throw the whole group into prison. However, the more moderate approach of the German Foreign Office and the opinion of Hermann Göring, who was influenced by his cousin M. H. Göring, would eventually prevail. The Foreign Office and Göring's cousin considered the impact of world opinion on Germany if the renowned Sigmund Freud were to be sent to a concentration camp. Although M. H. Göring's moderate course in dealing with Freud and his followers in Vienna won the day, subsequent actions reveal his less than friendly feelings toward psychoanalysis.

The decision made by the Third Reich was to follow the same course of action originally chosen in dealing with the DPG in Germany. The idea was first to expel the Jews and then incorporate the Vienna Institute, along with its publishing house, within the Göring Institute. M. H. Göring personally charged Müller-Braunschweig with this mission. Müller-Braunschweig was accompanied to Vienna by Anton Sauerwald, an anti-Semitic surgeon who was a member of the Reich Physicians League. Eight days after the arrival of German troops in Vienna, Müller-Braunschweig and Anton Sauerwald met with the directorship of the Vienna Institute and with the ever-present Ernest Jones.

By 1938, Jones had become what we might call the crisis manager

representing Freudian psychoanalytic interests in coping with the continual
Nazi threats to his profession's survival in Europe. Jones had answered the
clarion call once again, this time to make a final effort to persuade Freud to
leave "his home for a foreign land, thus following the road his ancestors
had so wearily trod" so often before (Jones 1962c, 218). Freud's reluctance
to leave Vienna led Jones to make a dash to Vienna; this time he used his
best logic to convince Freud to leave. This gave Jones yet another opportunity both to observe how the Nazis operated and also to interact with the
Nazis for the first time as an unwelcome guest. It also gave him another
chance to help more Jewish analysts and eventually to report to the world
what he had experienced.

During his March 20 visit to Vienna, Jones observed the liquidation
of the Vienna Institute press and clinic. After the exclusion of all Jewish
members and the resignation of non-Jewish members in protest, there
remained only 2 of the 102 members. The Gestapo discovered that Müller-
Braunschweig had betrayed the Third Reich by having sent a letter to Anna
Freud, not only consoling her, but advocating the future autonomy of the
Vienna Institute from both National Socialism and the Göring Institute.
Both Müller-Braunschweig and Anna Freud were interrogated by the
Gestapo.

Since Anna Freud was interrogated for the last time on March 22,
1938, the time frame of this episode was after Müller-Braunschweig had
been in Vienna and already had conducted the meeting with the directors
of the Vienna Institute. Cocks indicates it was M. H. Göring who confronted Müller-Braunschweig and pronounced the letter to Anna Freud as
a "betrayal." M. H. Göring thereafter denied Müller-Braunschweig the
right to teach or publish, and Felix Boehm was prohibited from providing
any training analysis. Finally, the existence and autonomy of the DPG was
eliminated. The DPG dissolved itself on November 19, 1938, and its
members carried on as "Work Group A." M. H. Göring obviously had
come to the conclusion that the Freudian psychoanalysts needed to be
monitored more closely.

The end result in Vienna was that the Austrian Psychoanalytic Society
was officially dissolved on August 25, 1938, leaving behind only a study
group connected to the Göring Institute. M. H. Göring appointed the
neuropsychiatrist Heinrich von Kogerer as its leader and in a letter to him
announced, "the stronghold of Jewish psychotherapy had fallen" (Cocks
1985, 121).

The details of what was considered Müller-Braunschweig's "betrayal"
of the Third Reich during his visit to Vienna to negotiate the takeover of

the Vienna Psychoanalytical Association (WPV) raise issues worth evaluating. The first issue to examine is Müller-Braunschweig's personal motivation for sending such a positive and supportive letter to Anna Freud. What makes this letter confusing is that it was Müller-Braunschweig and his fellow psychoanalysts who had convinced M. H. Göring that incorporating the WPV as a satellite clinic to be a part of their own Institute was a worthwhile venture. Before the letter was even discovered, a meeting had been held in Vienna on March 20, 1938, attended by Jones, Anna Freud, Paul Federn, Müller-Braunschweig, and Anton Sauerwald, a Nazi official who was sent to supervise the Third Reich's takeover of the WPV. During this meeting apparently all the demands made by Müller-Braunschweig, who was representing the DPG and thus acting on behalf of M. H. Göring, had been met. The agreement they reached turned over to the Göring Institute the WPV, its funds, its press (the *Verlag*) and its outpatient clinic. In addition, all of the Jewish members were automatically expelled from the WPV (Brecht et al. 1985, 142; Gay 1988, 621-28; and Cocks 1997, 200-201). All the WPV's facilities were given to Göring's DPG free of cost and the membership aryanized. Why would Müller-Braunschweig risk what he was going to accomplish in Vienna by sending such a positive letter about Sigmund Freud to Anna Freud? In the next chapter we explain how Müller-Braunschweig's contradictory behavior was a function of his intense internal conflicts and ambivalence regarding his dual loyalty to both National Socialism and psychoanalysis.

A second question is even more intriguing. Why would Müller-Braunschweig's letter to Anna Freud be considered a betrayal of the Third Reich by both the Gestapo and M. H. Göring? Apparently, just after Müller-Braunschweig had achieved what appeared to be an enormous success in Vienna with the WPV, he was harshly punished by M. H. Göring. Müller-Braunschweig could no longer enter the Göring Institute, his right to teach and publish was prohibited, and he could not carry out any further training analysis, with one exception being made for M. H. Göring's son. In addition to these personal punishments, there occurred the series of actions concerning the WPV described above. These actions can best be viewed as punitive not only toward the WPV but toward the DPG within the Göring Institute, whose power was being significantly diminished. What about Müller-Braunschweig's letter to Anna Freud was considered such a betrayal that it elicited the significant personal consequences that it did? In the letter he spoke of his "unconditional loyalty" to Sigmund Freud. We propose that what happened can best be understood in terms of the letter as a violation of Nazi ideology, which called for total, undivided loyalty to one's leader, cause, or policy. No nuances or "shades of gray" were allowed. Müller-Braunschweig's "unconditional loyalty" to Sigmund Freud was a direct violation of Nazi views on psychoanalysis as a "Jewish science." If we consider that at the start of the *Anschluß* the more virulent Nazi leaders (Heinrich Himmler and Joseph Goebbels) wanted Freud and his followers thrown in jail despite the expression of international concerns and President Franklin Roosevelt's personal involvement (Gay 1988), then how must they have felt about a "trusted" Aryan's "unconditional loyalty" and commitment to Sigmund Freud and his theory? Taken from this perspective, it is suggested that Müller-Braunschweig's punishment was lighter than what would otherwise be expected. These events in Vienna suggest that Nazi ideology had become a more powerful factor in determining the Third Reich's policy toward Jews and theories considered to be "Jewish science" than it had been before.

Events a few months later would confirm the rising in importance of Nazi ideology and the regime's hostility toward anything Jewish. On November 9–10, 1938, the regime's first officially sanctioned violence and murder of Jews occurred on what is called *Kristallnacht* or the "Night of Broken Glass." Nine days after these barbaric actions against Jews on the streets throughout Germany were taken, the "Jewish science," psychoanalysis, was to be completely aryanized. As Cocks states, by the end of 1938 "psychoanalysis had lost its public life" (Cocks 1997, 201). A "staring contest" between pictures of Freud and Hitler had taken place at the Göring Institute from 1936 to 1938. In 1935, Otto Fenichel had predicted the outcome before the contest took place. "The German Association will not be able to protect itself by removing the pictures of the Professor from the rooms of the institute and replacing them with more 'up-to-date ones'" (Friedrich 1989, 20). By more "up-to-date ones" Fenichel meant Hitler. The short-term staring battle was decisively won by Hitler when Freud's portrait was taken down from its place of honor. The long-term war for the minds and hearts of Hitler's beloved *Volk* would have another outcome, still unfolding today. Psychoanalysis, the "Jewish science," has been available to any German citizen since 1967 if the individual's psychological problems meet the criteria for neurosis (Thöma and Kächhele 1994, 203–4).

Before leaving this discussion on the fall of the "Jewish stronghold of psychotherapy," let us look at Jones's overall actions during the years when the Berlin and Vienna institutes came under Nazi domination. While we point out some of Jones's idiosyncratic weaknesses under certain circumstances, there is not any question about his leadership skill and determination in saving Jewish analysts' lives. During the period from 1933 to 1938, he was president of the IPA, and in 1938 he was president of the British Psycho-Analytical Society (Steiner 1989, 66). In these capacities he had sufficient power to be a significant factor in saving Jewish lives as the tide of the Nazi Wehrmacht came to dominate continental Europe. He did not shrink from the use of that power. In fact, it is hard to conceive of anyone else in the movement who could have used the authority of his position to carry out his responsibilities more effectively and energetically than Jones.

Jones was not only a practical and realistic problem solver, but he also had an enormous capacity to work hard and long (Steiner 1989, 47–50). These abilities would serve the Jewish members of both the DPG and WPV well as the Nazis took power in Germany in 1933 and then in 1938 incorporated Austria into what they call the Greater German Reich. While it would take Jones a relatively long time to realize the Nazis posed a major threat to all human rights regardless of religion, his correspondence with Anna Freud revealed he understood the threat the Jews faced in Berlin. However, his great loyalty to Freud and his role as president of the IPA would lead him to help the Jewish analysts, as well as to follow the best policy to insure the institutional survival of psychoanalysts during the political storm overwhelming Europe. He would do this by emulating Freud and maintaining a stance reflecting scientific objectivity. During the early phases of the Third Reich, Jones clearly stated in a letter to Anna Freud, "My only concern is for the good of psychoanalysis itself," which had as its cost being somewhat insensitive to what he called "Ultra Jewish" attitudes, and perhaps not listening sufficiently to advice from insightful analysts such as Otto Fenichel. On the other hand, Jones's knowledge of the political climates within the psychoanalytic movements as well as the national political and financial atmosphere of both the United States and Great Britain would enable him to begin to make a good match of emigrants with the host nation (Steiner 1989, 41–44).

The end result of Jones's policies was quite clear. Among the Jews who were faced with the onslaught of the Nazi blitzkrieg, the relative percent of psychoanalysts who were exterminated during the Holocaust compared to other professions was quite low (Steiner 1989, 43). Perhaps the most important reason was the exceptional job done by Jones in planning, organizing, and implementing the emigration of Jewish analysts.

It was during the *Anschluß* that perhaps Jones's greatest achievement occurred. Freud's attitude about leaving his home in Austria, in face of the Nazi threat before the Wehrmacht invaded, had always been negative. When the Nazis entered Austria, his attitude seemed to vacillate for several days.

Jones arrived at the WPV's *Verlag* in Vienna just in time to be threatened along with Freud's son Martin, by a gang of SA members. It was during this visit of Jones to Vienna that once again Freud adamantly refused to leave Austria because "it would be like a soldier deserting his post." However, it was Jones's quick reply that, at least on an intellectual level, allowed Freud to accept a decision to leave. Jones quoted second officer Lightoller of the *Titanic,* who was answering a question from a board of inquiry about when he left the ship. Lightoller, having been blown into the water when the boiler exploded, indicated what Jones repeated to Freud, "I never left the ship, Sir, she left me" (Jones 1962c, 220).

Jones had connected with Freud's reasonable nature on March 15, 1938. On March 22, 1938, the Gestapo had taken Anna Freud to headquarters for interrogation. Freud spent a very worried day waiting. Fortunately, she was released. This must have added emotional force to the reasonable decision to emigrate that was being promoted by Jones. Jones had completed his last mission with excellent results. Freud and his immediate family were free to leave Austria. Freud came to see this choice as an opportunity to "die in freedom" (Jones 1962c, 225). As he had done for years, Jones had personally coordinated the efforts of the British Foreign Office with other organizations to achieve his ends.

12

Compromise, Collaboration, and Resistance among the Psychoanalysts during the Third Reich

Carl Müller-Braunschweig, Käthe Dräger, and John Rittmeister

WHAT WE MISS MOST IN COCKS's historical and institutional analysis of what happened at the Göring Institute is a psychological probing into the individuals involved. However, we cannot really fault Cocks for this omission. This is a limitation inherent in historical inquiry, since the field of history has not yet embraced psychohistory as an important part of its mission.

Throughout this book we have mentioned a variety of prototypes or patterns of behavior demonstrated by the psychoanalysts toward the Third Reich. A continuum can be seen to exist among the psychoanalysts from those who joined the Nazi Party and collaborated with the regime (i.e., Gerhard Scheunert) to those who resisted it. The great majority of the psychoanalysts did not join the Nazi Party but showed a propensity to make increasingly greater compromises with their professional standards the longer the regime lasted. In this chapter we intend to illustrate the subtle distinctions in responding that characterized the psychoanalysts. We devote the greatest attention to the case of Carl Müller-Braunschweig, who presents over time a shifting pattern of compromise, collaboration, and resistance. We hope to demonstrate that such a complex prototype of responding is not consistent with the idea of ordinary Germans being "willing executioners," an idea promulgated by Daniel Jonah Goldhagen. We will end this chapter by giving brief portraits of Käthe Dräger and

John Rittmeister, to illustrate two different varieties of resistances to the regime.

A "Fallen" Psychoanalyst

With an awareness that we will never truly know what motivated Carl Müller-Braunschweig's behavior, we have approached the issue of a psychological analysis of his behavior by using the concept of a prototype. That is, we realize that this attempt will at best be an abstraction, not a real analysis. We begin this section with the assumption that Carl Müller-Braunschweig started out as a relatively autonomous and "healthy" individual who was named a member of the Executive Committee of the BPI in 1925. This assumption is supported by the observation of his secretary, Margarete Kohler (Lockot 1985, 119).

In developing the idea of prototypical models as a means of examining the variations in human motivation and responses among the psychoanalysts who had to make some form of adaptation to the terror of the Third Reich, we are clearly not trying to identify any unitary or typical "Nazi personality profile." The existing evidence (Zillmer et al., 1995) and basic good clinical sense dictate that a search for a mythical Nazi profile is on the same level as Jung's conceptualization of distinctive Jewish and Aryan psychological ways of thinking based on race. Our prototypical model's approach rests upon the assumption of diverse and unique personality structures rather than the expectation of any unitary or consistent patterns to emerge among the German analysts.

In this section, then, we provide a prototypical description of the "fall" of a German psychoanalyst whose personality deterioration occurred under the powerful forces of the Nazi totalitarian regime. This section has not been included to present a definitive psychoanalytical study of Carl Müller-Braunschweig. That would be an impossible task, requiring us to have had all the information of his analysis as well as more historical information. Our goal for this section is more modest and limited. Although we do not think that enough information is available to determine the true motivations of his actions during and after the Third Reich, we have, however, found some of the historical facts related to his life during this period to be not only fascinating, but also worth reporting in detail. We think these facts provide us with a starting point in understanding how this German gentile psychoanalyst had been transformed by one of the darkest periods in all human history. We have tried to approach Carl Müller-Braunschweig's life with empathy and respect in order to tell what he did during and after the Third Reich without being moralistic, and yet allow ourselves the right to make judgments. No other period in human history so requires the scholar to seek the psychological truth about individual responsibility with a passion of a neutral scientist, and yet be able at the same time to make judgments about the good and evil aspects of that person. As will be seen, Carl Müller-Braunschweig was a complicated human being whose behavior was hard to understand and hard to judge.

We have made judgments; we consider him to be a "fallen" psychoanalyst because his actions both during and after World War II were unacceptable from the viewpoint of morality in general, and psychoanalytic ethics in particular. At the same time he was capable of courage. We do not believe we could safely say we would have done any better under the same circumstances. We have tried to maintain sufficient psychological neutrality and empathy (a sometimes daunting effort) so that we can report what happened to him in a reasonable way. Carl Müller-Braunschweig's life and career during the Third Reich was marked by painful paradoxes and absurdities. He practiced a "Jewish" science in the capital of a regime whose purpose it became to exterminate everything Jewish; he tried to turn the "Jewish stronghold of psychotherapy" (i.e., the Vienna Institute) into a bastion of the new "German psychotherapy," a task in which he failed in the eyes of M. H. Göring. And yet, he survived all of this and eventually became the founder of an exclusively Freudian psychoanalytic institute in Berlin in 1950 that would be accepted by the IPA.

The introductory descriptive facts about Carl Müller-Braunschweig were acquired from Lockot's (1985) book, *Erinnern und Durcharbeiten* (Remembering and Working Through). Müller-Braunschweig wrote in 1950 in his autobiography that he was born on April 8, 1881, in Braunschweig. His father owned a carpentry shop and was able to afford his son's extensive course of study from the winter of 1901/1902 until the winter semester of 1908. In 1909, when Müller-Braunschweig became familiar with Freud's psychoanalysis, he decided, much to the disappointment of his teachers and friends, to give up his university life and turn to the newly developing science, which in those days was not seen as being part of the university. It is testimony to Müller-Braunschweig's extraordinary depth that, from 1912 until 1914, he studied several semesters of medicine, especially psychiatry, with Karl Bonhoeffer. Müller-Braunschweig originally wanted to obtain an analysis in Vienna, but it was too expensive for him after such a long time in the university. He had his first analysis with Karl

Abraham, which he discontinued, finishing with Hanns Sachs, the specialist in training analysis.

Almost all people who knew Müller-Braunschweig agree that he had a good character and that he was an honest person. Deeply rooted in Müller-Braunschweig's being were loyalty and consistency, but both also had a negative aspect. His strong clinging to things known and based on tradition hindered his self-realization. The courage to try something new was not one of his strengths.

Müller-Braunschweig was married twice. His first wife was Josine Müller. Josine was the first child analyst in Berlin, and she apparently was a severely depressed individual (Lockot 1985, 120). They divorced in 1925 and did not have children. The year Müller-Braunschweig divorced Josine, he married Ada Schott, who had also been trained as a child analyst by Helmine von Hug-Hellmuth in Vienna. They had two children. Ada was a very creative, open, and warm person, and she had a much greater understanding of what National Socialism had in store for Germany.

Other than the times he was teaching, Müller-Braunschweig was rarely at the German Institute for Psychological Research and Psychotherapy. Outsiders saw him as a north German peasant-like type who was blond and a little bit slow. Rubins, the biographer of Karen Horney, describes him as a tall, blond, good-looking man with a calm, deep voice who was especially the friend of Oskar Horney and who carried on lively philosophical religious talks with Karen Horney. Karen Horney was a follower of Freud while in Berlin. After emigrating to the United States, she became a significant proponet of neo-analysis.

Müller-Braunschweig's role during the *Anschluß* exemplified how traumatic psychological stress placed upon an Aryan psychoanalyst who was attempting both to conform to the regime while retaining some degree of integrity proved to be an impossible burden. Carl Müller-Braunschweig was given the task of reorganizing Freud's Vienna Institute into the first Aryan satellite of the Göring Institute in a captive country. During his mission Müller-Braunschweig made several mistakes, including being "politically incorrect" and failing to recruit sufficient numbers of Aryan analysts to establish a satellite institute in Vienna. Müller-Braunschweig's attempts to look good to the international psychoanalytic community and at the same time serve the Nazi cause would both fail. To maintain his good standing with the IPA, Müller-Braunschweig wrote a letter to Anna Freud indicating his personal conviction that the Vienna Institute would retain its independence from the Göring Institute. Müller-Braunschweig's attempt to maintain his reputation with the international psychoanalytic community turned out to be a significant mistake for himself and the other psychoanalysts within the Göring Institute and for the Freuds. Müller-Braunschweig's letter to Anna Freud reveals his way of striking a balance of loyalties between psychoanalysis and National Socialism. The letter to Anna Freud was found easily by the Gestapo when it went to search Freud's home, and Anna Freud was taken to Gestapo headquarters for interrogation. The Gestapo considered the IPA either a subversive or terrorist organization. Having feared such an experience, Anna Freud had obtained from Dr. Schur a sufficient amount of Veronal, a strong barbiturate, to use in case she faced circumstances she considered worse than death.

Thus, while Anna tried to wait patiently in a crowded corridor at the Gestapo's headquarters, the only protection she had was the Veronal. She obviously wanted this waiting to be over, and there are various interpretations about a "mysterious phone call" that finally initiated her being taken to the interrogation room. In her book about these events, Lockot (1985, 121) reveals that under these threatening circumstances, in order to save herself, Anna Freud showed the Gestapo the letter from Müller-Braunschweig. As has been previously reported, the letter to Anna Freud was not only consoling in nature, but also advocated the future autonomy of the Vienna Institute from both the Göring Institute and the influence of National Socialism. This is an exceptionally clear example of Müller-Braunschweig's attempt to balance loyalties to both psychoanalysis and to National Socialism, as represented by M. H. Göring.

Müller-Braunschweig was in total denial of the kind of totalitarian government the Third Reich had become and the total disregard it had for personal rights as well as the methods of terror it so easily used against anyone considered an enemy. In retrospect and from an objective perspective, his punishment for what could have been classified as treason was relatively mild. However, despite these complications, his expressed opinion to Anna Freud that the Vienna Psychoanalytical Association (WPV) would retain its independence, while carrying out M. H. Göring's determination to incorporate the WPV into the German Institute, was typical of the balance he strived to maintain.

Another example of the balance he tried to reach had to do with his publications. In 1935 he published "The National Socialist Idea and Psychoanalysis," in which he supported the global view of integrating psychoanalysis into a new form of "German psychotherapy" (that is, a Nazified form). In that article, he had defended psychoanalysis as being consistent with the goals of National Socialism. He requested that the German government give the DPG the opportunity "to give . . . our Society a specific

German stamp" instead of "the international character . . . with their racial differences" (Brecht et al. 1985, 183). Cocks comments that in the article Müller-Braunschweig had "indirectly but clearly condemned his Jewish colleagues in terms not dissimilar from those employed by the Nazis themselves" (Cocks 1985, 90). An example of Müller-Braunschweig's conflict and ambivalence about psychoanalysis and National Socialism was identified by Volker Friedrich. When Friedrich reviewed Müller-Braunschweig's 1933 article entitled "Psychoanalysis and Weltanschauung," he noted an error in the original publication that revealed internal conflict:

> I noticed with surprise that the title of one of Freud's other works referred to in the article was printed incorrectly. Instead of the correct title, "On the Psychical Mechanism of Hysterical Phenomena," I read "On the Psychical Mechanism of Historical Phenomena." Just as the hysterical symptom represents an unconscious conflict—the symptom, Freud taught us, has a meaning—the printing mistake similarly demonstrates the conflict between honesty on the one side and adjustment and subjection to National Socialism on the other, a conflict which is affectively resisted. (Friedrich 1989, 9)

On the other hand, Müller-Braunschweig was still a competent analyst at this stage of his professional life and published scholarly articles in psychoanalytic journals. Müller-Braunschweig published an article entitled "The girl's first object-cathexis and its importance in penis-envy and femininity" in the *International Journal of Psychoanalysis* (Brecht et al. 1985, 180–83). In 1951, Müller-Braunschweig was able to look back over the years and realize the significant historical markers that documented the deterioration of the practice of psychoanalysis. He reported in 1951 that "I was able to give a presentation during the 15th anniversary of the BPI on February 6, 1935, entitled, 'The girl's first object-cathexis and its importance in penis-envy and femininity,' and less than two years later this presentation was seen as a sign of 'my being full of Jewishness and sexual deviance'" (Lockot 1985, 121). He indicated that from 1933 to 1936 the psychoanalytic nature of his work as researcher, teacher, and practicing psychoanalyst had not been curtailed.

However, other lines of evidence reveal that Müller-Braunschweig showed a pattern of cooperation with National Socialism that apparently was based on his growing identification with the ideology of the NSDAP, or we might say, his identification with the aggressor. We consider the events occurring around the period of the *Anschluß* as leading Müller-

Braunschweig from the position of understandable compromises with National Socialism to what Leo Rangell has referred to as a "compromise of integrity" (Rangell 1980, 208-13).

In a letter to Ernest Jones, Müller-Braunschweig had the audacity to request that the IPA take over the debts of former Jewish members who had previously been coerced to leave the Institute as well as their native country (Brecht et al. 1985, 79). This letter reveals Müller-Braunschweig's insensitivity not only to his former Jewish colleagues' plight after being forced to leave Germany but also to the numerous voluntary efforts Jones had made on behalf of the two gentile psychoanalysts to preserve their autonomy as professionals in Germany and their good standing in the IPA. Jones accepted this request despite a good deal of angry feelings by Jewish members forced to emigrate.

Müller-Braunschweig's acceptance of the Nazi perspective on Jews recently has been further documented. The second letter Müller-Braunschweig sent Jones over this matter suggests the IPA was being inordinately "pressured" to do something for which it was not responsible. These letters also suggest Carl Müller-Braunschweig had, in a very brief period of time, come to accept the National Socialist perspective regarding the way Jewish members of the DPG were to be treated by the regime.

More recent evidence has been provided by the investigations of Regine Lockot. Although Müller-Braunschweig had left no treatment notes or compromising correspondence from the period of the Third Reich, Lockot was provided some information that had not been destroyed and it turned out to be coded. She found someone to decode the information and amongst the material that emerged was a letter to a fascist leader in Italy identifying the Jewish members of the psychoanalytic community in that country (Lockot 1994c). This was further evidence of Müller-Braunschweig's increasing collaboration with the Nazi cause and his willingness to place the lives of Jewish colleagues at risk for no obvious gain. We consider this collaboration a manifestation of his growing identification with the aggressor.

The most blatant indication that Carl Müller-Braunschweig's mission to Vienna during the *Anschluß* created a trauma for him was a letter he wrote to Richard Sterba on May 4, 1938. Sterba was a gentile psychoanalyst who was a member of the WPV but was in Basel, Switzerland, while trying to emigrate from Austria, along with his Jewish colleagues, to freedom in the United States. The letter not only reveals Müller-Braunschweig's complete cooperation with M. H. Göring's demands but it reflects a deterioration in

his capacity to empathize with the obvious motives of others. The letter
(Sterba 1982, 164–65) was sent from Vienna and reads in translation:

Müller-Braunschweig
at present Vienna, 17. Berggasse
(Psycho-Publishing House)   Vienna, IX
                                               Berggasse 7
                                               4/5/38

Esteemed Dr. Sterba,

  I would like to inform you briefly about the local events.
After the resignation [(!) added by Sterba] of the Jewish members, the Vienna Psychoanalytic Society has been absorbed by
the German Psychoanalytic Society. The next task is to construct
out of Berggasse 7 an institute that, like the one in Berlin, per-
mits the different psychotherapeutic schools to work on a basis
of equality. In this way, the possibility of survival and work is
also secured for analysis. For this we urgently need the full cooperation and assistance of the few Aryan members of the Vienna
Psychoanalytic Society. Therefore, I would be very much obliged
to you. . . . As a member of the German Psychoanalytic Society,
you will . . . without further ado, become a member also of the
German Institute. . . .

                  With collegial greetings and HEIL HITLER
                  yours
                  Dr. Carl Müller-Braunschweig

  Given the unlikely fact that Müller-Braunschweig himself would put
in the exclamation point, we have written to Richard Sterba's daughter, Verena Michels, addressing this issue. The letter itself unfortunately has been
lost, but we consider Verena Michels's interpretation of the events related to
her father to be the most accurate: "[M]y guess is the exclamation point is
his and he just didn't bother to footnote it" (Verena Michels 1995). When
Anna Freud had the opportunity to read Müller-Braunschweig's letter she
pointed out that the words "with collegial greetings and HEIL HITLER"
were added after the letter. What was the meaning of this letter? Very simply, Müller-Braunschweig had continued to show the same kind of willing-

ness to cooperate and identify with those in authority, no matter what ideology was expressed. It also revealed how out of touch he was with a man like Richard Sterba, who was obviously in the midst of leaving Austria for the very reasons Müller-Braunschweig was trying to tempt him to return.

> For Müller-Braunschweig, *Anschluß* and his attempt to negotiate the takeover of the WPV for the Göring Institute turned into a watershed experience. It was not until the immediacy of the Vienna experience that he must have realized there was no way to make a reasonable adaptation to National Socialism. He had been confronted by M. H. Göring, a father figure, and interrogated by the Gestapo. He started to live in a world of intense fear. He feared other interrogations, and he feared that his house would be searched by the Gestapo. According to Lockot, "Müller-Braunschweig had lived through a crisis of the soul from which he would never completely recover." (Lockot 1985, 122)

The experiences related to *Anschluß* shattered any sense of self-respect and autonomy Müller-Braunschweig had left and led to significant compromises of integrity. He had failed in his latest attempt to look good to his Freudian colleagues. His letter to Anna Freud had not only been discovered, but this attempt to maintain some loyalty to his psychoanalytic training had been thrown back in his face by M. H. Göring. He was not only confronted by Göring with his lack of loyalty—a quality he valued—but he also would fail to reorganize the Vienna Psychoanalytic Institute (WPV) into an Aryan branch of the Göring Institute. His perceived failures led him to consider M. H. Göring's actions a stab in his back, and he obviously experienced a sense of great humiliation. He felt Göring's prohibition on his teaching, publishing, and his exclusion from the training committee to be losses, which in turn led to depressive episodes (Brecht et al. 1985, 174). Thus, what could hypothetically have been experienced as a means of escaping the limelight and future threats to his life were, in fact, experienced as a narcissistic wound.

   While Müller-Braunschweig had been traumatized by the events after *Anschluß* in Vienna and had made significant compromises in order to survive, he showed one remarkable demonstration of integrity that deserves much credit. When given the opportunity to have all that had been taken away by M. H. Göring at the Institute given back to him if he joined the Nazi Party, Müller-Braunschweig declined (Lockot 1985, 122). This was not a small act of integrity, it was a brave stand.

   During World War II, Carl Müller-Braunschweig's conduct cannot be compared with that of Nazis who carried out the murder of German children, or of those who took an active part in atrocities at the concentration camps or had any role in formulating plans for the Holocaust. His overall behavior was not characterized by the ruthless, primitive, and complete lack of any integrity that all too many Germans presented without any apparent sense of guilt. Müller-Braunschweig's major transgression had occurred while in Vienna during the *Anschluß* when he sent a letter to a fascist leader in Italy identifying Jewish members of the psychoanalytic community. This letter was sent during what must have been the start of the most traumatic period of his life. He was in the presence of the founder of psychoanalysis negotiating the takeover of the Vienna Institute. He was surrounded by acts of enormous violence as over seventy thousand people were arrested on the streets of Vienna by the Nazis' SD and Gestapo. He had obviously written a letter of support to Anna Freud for which he would have to endure much psychological pain.

During the war, Carl Müller-Braunschweig was not allowed to enter the Institute by M. H. Göring's order. While he was deprived of involvement in meetings of the Institute he was asked by Göring to be responsible for lecture organizations. His last version of the curriculum was extremely detailed and documented an extensive teaching experience. M. H. Göring obviously reviewed the curriculum very carefully, and *The Catalog* reports he deleted passages that suggested psychoanalytic thinking but underlined the idea of integrating psychoanalysis into a German psychotherapy. It is our clinical impression from reviewing his status in *The Catalog* that Müller-Braunschweig was suffering from Posttraumatic Stress Disorder (PTSD) with dissociative traits in 1946, and that the experience and symptoms of shock would remain a chronic problem.

Müller-Braunschweig's letter to Gustave Bally of April 6, 1946, probably describes what he and most other Berliners experienced from January 1945 to at least the summer of 1946. After indicating he was thankful that his family all survived the war, he described the way undernourishment lowered his productivity and increased fatigue. An English psychoanalytic representative in Berlin in 1946 had observed that Müller-Braunschweig's eighteen-year-old daughter had fared badly from the Russian soldiery, which at best meant repeated rapes (Brecht et al. 1985, 237). In such a "chronic need, I have lost a good part of my feelings of shame and directly or indirectly let it be known how much one hopes that your foreign friends will send some of the things we do without" (Lockot 1985, 122). This statement by Müller-Braunschweig about the shortage of food in Berlin is well documented (Smith 1990, 245; Fischer 1995, 226, 288, 321, and 346; and Clay 1950, 263-69).

It is our contention that the "fall" of Carl Müller-Braunschweig was to continue throughout World War II and after V-E Day. As stated, Müller-Braunschweig was to have continual problems with depression after *Anschluß*. The humiliations he experienced at the hands of M. H. Göring would bother him long after 1938. The way Müller-Braunschweig was to survive after World War II would continue to reveal significant problems relevant to integrity. The twelve years of living under a totalitarian dictatorship and the traumatic seizure of Berlin by the Soviet troops had a significant effect on him—an effect that continued well after he was free, living in West Berlin. While he would achieve important triumphs during the remainder of his life, the compromises of integrity that started with the rise of National Socialism would continue to plague him. After the end of World War II, he was told by his physician to obtain an analysis, and in 1946 he went to a Jungian (Lockot 1994c). Ironically, despite his own personal choice of a Jungian analyst, Müller-Braunschweig continued to stress the orthodox Freudian psychoanalytic position at the Zürich Congress. He stressed the orthodox position from 1946 to his eventual founding of the *Deutsche Psychoanalytische Vereinigung* (DPV) in 1950 as an exclusively Freudian psychoanalytic training center. By the next year, at the 1951 Congress in Amsterdam, Müller-Braunschweig was able to obtain admission of the DPV as a branch of the IPA.

What do these events mean? We interpret Müller-Braunschweig's ability to obtain treatment from a Jungian after World War II, while simultaneously criticizing the DPG for its acceptance of neo-analysis, less a form of basic hypocrisy than illustrative of the deterioration of his personal integrity and personality structure after twelve traumatic years of the Third Reich. He remained regressed and only a shadow of his former self. Almost all of the psychoanalysts who remained active at the Göring Institute during the war years were considered tainted by the era. It is not hard to imagine that professed allegiance to Freudian orthodoxy after the war could have been thought of as a way of advertising one's dissociation from the Nazi past. As such, it becomes more of a "code word" intended for political ends than a principled commitment to a position (Lockot 1994c). This is clear evidence that the breakdown of Müller-Braunschweig's integrity remained an enduring problem even after the defeat of the Third Reich. His actions suggest to us the hallmarks of the dynamic of "identification with the aggressor." We do believe that Carl Müller-Braunschweig's behavior can only be understood and evaluated in terms of the total context of the rise and fall of the Third Reich. We consider it imperative to accept as true the slow and insidious collapse of psychoanalysis during the Third Reich, for otherwise

Müller-Braunschweig's behavior would appear much worse than it was. His behavior should be seen in the light of his true impotence within a rigid Nazi organization led not just by an ardent Nazi, but by 1945 a fanatic who believed in and followed his Führer's orders to defend Berlin to the death. Müller-Braunschweig's behavior must be understood in the context of the organization to which he belonged, and to which he tried to accommodate: the DPG, which became the Göring Institute, and the totalitarian government that dominated his public and private life.

Milton Mayer's (1955) classic book on Nazi Germany, *They Thought They Were Free: The Germans 1933–45,* describes in a down-to-earth manner how people like Carl Müller-Braunschweig habituated, little by little, to accept being ruled by psychopathic criminals. Müller-Braunschweig's behavior had regressed and his personal integrity had been inordinately compromised.

A brief illustration from Milton Mayer's book can provide some perspective on the overall effects of the Third Reich on individuals like Carl Müller-Braunschweig. We quote from Mayer's section in which a university professor recalls his personal experiences during the Third Reich:

> To live in this process is absolutely not to be able to notice it—please try to believe me. . . . Each step was so small, so inconsequential, so well explained or, on occasion "regretted," . . . one no more saw it developing from day to day than a farmer in his field sees the corn growing. One day it is over his head. (Mayer 1955, 168)

The professor goes on to say:

> [O]ne doesn't see exactly where or how to move. . . . You wait for one great shocking occasion, thinking that others . . . will join with you in resisting somehow. You don't want to "go out of your way to make trouble." Why not? . . . [Y]ou are not in the habit of doing it. And it is not just fear, fear of standing alone, that restrains you; it is also genuine uncertainty. (Mayer 1955, 169)

Mayer's description of the university professor perhaps gives us the best insight into the step-by-step inroads the Third Reich had upon individuals like Carl Müller-Braunschweig. The university professor was able to deny the steady deterioration of human rights until one great, shocking personal experience broke through his denial and he realized the ugly reality that

> everything has changed and changed completely under your nose. The world you live in—your nation, your people—is not the world you

were born in at all. The forms are all there, all untouched, . . . the houses, the shops, the jobs. . . . But the spirit is changed. Now you live in a world of hate and fear and the people who hate and fear do not even know it themselves. (Mayer 1955, 171)

It is this latter description of living in a world of hate and fear, where the people who hate and fear do not even themselves realize it, that comes closest, we believe, to fitting Müller-Braunschweig's professional life and his increasing predicament. Psychoanalytic training had never prepared anyone to cope with the terrors of National Socialism, especially those terrors of the Gestapo and SD. The type of understanding that the university professor portrays and describes helps us begin to understand how individuals like Carl Müller-Braunschweig were constantly being transformed.

However, unlike the university professor, Carl Müller-Braunschweig was to experience the full weight of the totalitarian regime and therefore never had enough freedom to realize what was happening to him nor to understand what was happening to the world in which he lived. His day-to-day professional life was confined within a structured organization (the BPI) that, in the 1920s, Ernest Jones had described as the center of the whole psychoanalytic movement. From 1933 to 1935 Carl Müller-Braunschweig would observe how the best and brightest members were forced to resign and then emigrate. With the Institute reduced to a shell of its former self, Müller-Braunschweig must have been shaken to the very core of his being by the power of the Nazi regime. Shortly after two-thirds of the members had fled, new pressures by the regime would force the BPI to "give" away its entire Institute to M. H. Göring, so that Müller-Braunschweig could, at least, continue with his career.

The power of the Nazis was highlighted by what must have been a shocking deterioration in professional standards when Müller-Braunschweig compared the old BPI with the new Institute that replaced it. With Carl Müller-Braunschweig's former values having already been undermined, the external pressures at the Göring Institute to conform to the ideology of National Socialism and to identify with the aggressor (M. H. Göring) had increased from 1936 to 1938. Given what Carl Müller-Braunschweig must have observed in the streets of Vienna as the Jews and enemies of National Socialism were being rounded up and sent to concentration camps, he had to know from then on his own life would always be at risk.

In conclusion, we have tried to provide a review of Carl Müller-Braunschweig's psychological functioning at the time of the Third Reich. It is impossible to provide a thorough psychological analysis of what specifically did cause the problems he demonstrated over the course of his life. On the other hand, we do think it is worthwhile to try to reconstruct the most obvious influences that led to his deteriorated functioning from 1933 onward. This cannot be a definitive evaluation but it is at least a way to try to understand the impact the Third Reich had on so many of the individuals at the Göring Institute.

Two "Unfallen" Psychoanalysts

While Carl Müller-Braunschweig represents a "fallen" psychoanalyst during the Third Reich, there was, nonetheless, a small number of psychoanalysts who maintained their personal integrity and professional ethics to the bitter end. In this section we shall recall the two whose deeds have since become known, and whose efforts are the only true evidence we have that psychoanalysis, as we know it, was practiced at all in the BPI.

We offer brief portraits of Käthe Dräger and John Rittmeister, two who became part of the resistance to the Nazi regime, each in their own ways. Before presenting their cases, we need to clarify the importance of "heroes" in German history and also discuss how the role of hero can be used to distort reality.

Gerhard Weinberg (1995) reminds us of how difficult it was once World War II started for anyone in Germany to actually resist the Nazi regime. Resistance to totalitarian government is not easy. Most of those Germans who did oppose the Nazis did not live to the end of the war. Yet, those who resisted the Nazis are significant for both Germans and the rest of the world. Weinberg (1995) has pointed out that Germany is becoming the most powerful country in Europe, with the exception of Russia. He states:

> The dramatic success of Germany's physical reconstruction after 1945
> has obscured the far more difficult psychological reconstruction [of the
> German population]. If the German people are to find an integral
> place in Europe and their self-respect, they need a past to which they
> can relate positively. . . . [The Germans need] the signposts, the exam-
> ples, the heroes and the traditions to which a new Germany might hark
> back and relate in the future. (Weinberg 1995, 251)

Weinberg elaborates upon the importance of those who resisted:

> Not perfect men and women making perfect decisions, but fallible
> people facing hard choices and cruel alternatives, the members of the
> resistance provide a basis for a post-Nazi order and point to a future in

which new issues can be measured by a standard of decency. In an age without heroes, in a country where the heroes have too often been those willing to sacrifice the spirit of humanity to the power of the state, a group that tried to assert the opposite—that the state must be subordinated to the elemental rights—stands forth as a standard to which people can adhere and by which they can judge.

However important the role of resisters is for German history, Cocks (1997) warns us of how the role of Rittmeister's resistance has been used in an artful way to avoid guilt. The DPV, DPG, and East Germany all used the name of John Rittmeister to either plead "innocence by association" or to sell a political ideology (Cocks 1997, 388–89). Cocks also points out that "A post hoc fixation on resistance heroes can substitute a wish-fulfilling 'ego ideal' for historical inquiry, obscuring lines of continuity between past and present" (Cocks 1997, 380). With these caveats in mind, the responses of Käthe Dräger and John Rittmeister expand our knowledge of the variety of responses to Nazi Germany's efforts to crush psychoanalysis.

These two Freudian psychoanalysts courageously faced their unique fates and carried out their professional work with grace and dignity. They were heroes. They were not Nordic supermen, but two human beings who maintained their personal integrity and continued to "love and work" when the millions who perished and the millions who watched helplessly must have asked the biblical question, "Why did the heavens not darken and the stars not withhold their radiance; why did not the sun and moon turn dark?" (from the chronicle of Solomon Bar Simpson on the massacre of the Jews on Mainz during the first crusade, 1096 A.D.). These two psychoanalysts, Käthe Dräger and John Rittmeister, not only coped with their own life circumstances in a mature and integrated way but stayed committed to their life's work and the Hippocratic Oath.

Käthe Dräger

Käthe Dräger started her training as a psychoanalyst at the Berlin Psychoanalytic Institute, which in 1936 became the Göring Institute. It is a minor miracle that she survived both the Nazis and then the Soviet occupying forces. She not only survived, she was even able to write an article that described in an objective way what happened to psychoanalysts during the Third Reich. The article she published stated, "But it was not psychoanalysis alone that was destroyed. The spirit was banished from all fields; barbarism prevailed" (Dräger 1972, 202). She also revealed that the Institute "stood on feet of clay." In writing about carrying out psychoanalysis during this period she said, "I think, that in an analysis under the situation of a totalitarian terror regime, transference and countertransference were prejudiced, encumbered and restricted even if patient and analyst shared antagonism to National Socialism. Thus it was inevitable that any unconscious acting out could mean real danger for the patient or for the people related to him, the analyst or for all" (Dräger 1972, 209-10).

In these passages, this survivor of the Nazi regime clearly indicates that the type of psychoanalysis practiced before the Third Reich did not survive it. In Käthe Dräger's article she describes the kind of personal courage and integrity a Freudian psychoanalyst needed during the Third Reich. She made this valid observation about her colleague John Rittmeister:

> A thorough-going opponent of National Socialism was not necessarily a good analyst. However, one who was a good psychoanalyst often did not have sufficient interest in social and political events. If someone combined both, and was engaged in the political resistance, he had to lead a double life. That this might cost one's life was demonstrated by Dr. John Rittmeister. All illegal activities that went beyond passive resistance, such as collecting money, food ration tickets and clothing, helping the persecuted, anything that could be interpreted as organized illegal activity, such as receiving and spreading the news of foreign broadcasting stations or meeting politically suspected persons, was a dangerous risk. Although taken as a whole, such activities were quantitatively of little effect, they had, if successful, a psychological effect on the persons concerned. It provided the feeling that the tyrants were not omnipotent, and it strengthened self-esteem which was, however, impaired by the need for camouflage. (Dräger 1972, 211)

In identifying the double life required by those who combined political opposition with competent psychoanalytic practice, and who survived, she was too modest to say that she was one of the few people to fit those criteria.

The only potential blemish on Käthe Dräger's perception of her surroundings was her gross underestimation of the incidence of Nazi membership among the psychotherapists at the Göring Institute. Dräger reported in her review, "Psychoanalysis in Hitler's Germany: 1933-1945," that at the most, 5 percent of the members of the Göring Institute were also affiliated with the Nazi Party (Dräger 1972, 208). Cocks, however, found that the percentage of Nazis was much higher. In reviewing the records at the Berlin Document Center (BDC), he found that slightly over 36 percent of the early spokesmen and leaders of the Göring Institute were members of the Nazi Party (Cocks 1985, 48).

Was Dräger's underestimation of Nazis at the Institute part of the general cover-up of many professionals of her generation? Was it part of the unconscious and conscious collaboration of many Nazis to hide their past sins? We think the evidence suggests that Dräger never knew the actual percentage of Nazis involved. As a German citizen, Dräger was prohibited by the United States government from having access to the Berlin Document Center, where she would have found the 5 percent figure reported by Werner Kemper to be incorrect. Kemper was a member of the BPI and the DPG in December 1933 and an esteemed teacher, while Dräger was still a candidate (Brecht, Friedrich, Hermanns, Kaminer, and Juelich 1985, 135; Dräger 1972, 205). Kemper, one of the few other psychoanalysts to survive the Third Reich, reported the same 5 percent figure of Nazi membership to both Arthur Feiner and Gerard Chrazanowski in an interview given in 1972 (Feiner 1975, 543; Chrazanowski 1975, 495). Since Kemper had been a senior member of the Institute while Dräger was still a candidate, it was most likely that she learned the 5 percent figure from him. We believe he would have been in a better position to judge the other members' political leanings during the early phase of the Göring Institute. With that exception, we tend to accept as accurate Dräger's overall description of the events at the Institute.

Käthe Dräger was born in 1900, the oldest of three children. She passed her teaching test in 1920 and became interested in marxism as a young adult. As a member of the anti-Stalinist communist group, her life was in danger from both the extreme Left and Right in Germany. Käthe Dräger was caught by the Nazis in 1942, and for her illegal resistance to the Nazis, she was sentenced to teach in Nazi-occupied Poland. In one of Müller-Braunschweig's acts of decency, he requested that she be returned from her position in the east to help the Institute with her skills as a therapist and teacher (Brecht et al. 1985, 175). She was only allowed to return to Berlin on July 1, 1944, where she survived until the end of the war (Lockot 1994, 193–98).

When the British psychoanalyst John Rickman came to Berlin in 1946 to interview and evaluate the psychoanalysts, he said about Käthe Dräger, "She struck me as a person of unusual integrity of character with fine psychological perception." He went on to say that "Fräulein Dräger" would "find herself at home in a liberal culture." In summing up her ability, he said that "in the case of Fräulein Dräger it was high, but that by reason of shyness she would not seem to be suitable for employment in GPRB" (i.e., German Personnel Research Branch of the Control Committee established by the Allies). In a follow-up summary version of his evaluation he indicated that "Fräulein Käthe Dräger was not at all politically minded and was entirely absorbed in psychological thinking" (Brecht et al. 1985, 236). There is specific evidence, however, to contradict the notion that she lacked political mindedness and to suggest that, in fact, such an outward persona was a sophisticated form of camouflage. Käthe Dräger was in fact a committed communist, albeit an anti-Stalinist one. She was also a very "savvy" political person (Lockot 1994c) and the kind of adaptive survivor described by E. J. Anthony as "invulnerable" (Anthony and Cohler 1987). During the Nazi period she gave aid and support to those in danger from the Gestapo, and therefore her life was always at risk. She was not one of the intellectual communists, but "was a leader for the real workers in Berlin, and she helped many families and friends, and lots of them were eventually killed" (Lockot 1994c). After the Soviets conquered Berlin, she stayed on in the city to care for her aging mother, but she was once again in constant danger and under the threat of death, this time because she was not a Stalinist. During the 1940s and early 1950s, individuals like Käthe Dräger were considered enemies of the Soviet "Stalinist" regime. They were often kidnapped in free Berlin and taken to the Soviet zone and then to the equivalent of a concentration camp (i.e., gulag). Thus, she lived all too long under the threat of totalitarian terror. She is the only German analyst of whom we are aware that survived World War II, and who was both a member of the resistance and who remained a committed psychoanalyst. Käthe Dräger, who died on April 12, 1979, never received the recognition that she so well deserved.

John Rittmeister

John Rittmeister was a German-born physician and a trained psychoanalyst who initially moved to Switzerland in 1929 for professional and political reasons. In 1937 he was deported from Switzerland for his communist associations and activities. Against his friends' advice, he returned to Berlin and became the head of the Outpatient Polyclinic at the Göring Institute. He was also a committed communist, and like Käthe Dräger, he was not a Stalinist. His subversive activities, for which he paid the ultimate price of his life, consisted of working with the *Rote Kapelle* (Red Orchestra), a large group of anti-fascist students that operated one of the most powerful spy networks in Germany. These students would meet at Rittmeister's apartment for discussions on political issues. Some time in 1941 Rittmeister became associated with Harro Schulze-Boysen, who was a leader in the Red Orchestra.

John Rittmeister had been recruited into the Red Orchestra as part of

Schulze-Boysen's intellectual, educational, and propaganda brain trust. In this capacity, Rittmeister and his student followers were part of the intellectual resistance to National Socialism. They never were involved in the espionage activities of the group. Yet Rittmeister was one of the intellectuals who helped completely turn the propaganda tables on Joseph Goebbels. The Nazi propaganda expert had opened a major exhibition in Berlin in May 1942 with startling evidence of the desperate poverty existing in Russia. For the purpose of countering communist propaganda of a worker's paradise, the exhibit was given significant radio and press coverage. Having learned about the exhibit in advance, John Rittmeister helped write and paste up huge posters that read: "The Nazi Paradise: War-Hunger-Lies-Gestapo. How much longer?" The SS and Gestapo were infuriated and devoted enormous amounts of manpower to prevent both the espionage and propaganda (Perrault 1969, 270-73).

John Rittmeister was arrested on September 26, 1942, for his part in writing and distributing anti-Nazi educational leaflets. His day in court, January 27, 1943, was the penultimate trial of the Red Orchestra members. Although neither Rittmeister nor any of his younger associates had ever been involved in the very serious crime of passing on secret military information, their resistance being limited to writing, printing, and distributing anti-fascist literature, the prosecutor demanded and obtained from the court the death penalty for all with the exception of any eighteen-year-old males. They were deemed as "furnishing aid and comfort to an enemy" which was tantamount to treason against the country (Tarrant 1995, 99). Rittmeister was condemned to death by the Supreme Military Court on February 8, 1943. In his cell before his death he scribbled on paper bags a philosophical dialogue entitled "The Stages of Morality." In his last letter to his wife, John Rittmeister wrote, "[K]eep your affirmation of life, my loving heart; we do not have to go back into the wilderness nor make the world a wilderness, but mold what we are to become, in the realization of our own true being" (Brecht et al. 1985, 190). John Rittmeister's cell was close to the death chamber. He probably saw and heard the deaths of many of the members of the Red Orchestra who were both tried and sentenced before him. They would have to pass by his cell in small groups going into the small execution chamber. With the exception of the Rittmeister student group, the men were to be hung by "the Austrian method" and the women beheaded. The Austrian method of hanging was very slow strangulation rather than the British method of a quick broken neck (Tarrant 1995, 102-3). The executioners were all attired in tail coats, white gloves, and top hats. The chaplain was not allowed to enter the execution room. The guillotine took an average of eleven seconds of agony before the convicts experienced the mercy of death. On the orders of Adolf Hitler, Rittmeister was executed by guillotine at the infamous Berlin Plötzensee prison on May 13, 1943, along with twelve others (Brecht et al. 1985, 185, 190; Tarrant 1995, 104). These executions were often filmed as if to highlight the themes of cruel sadism and voyeurism that were so prevalent in Nazi ideology and practice. Hitler and the other Nazis apparently enjoyed viewing these brutal executions, but they had nothing to gloat about in terms of the way these victims had faced their fate, with relative calm and serenity.

We have presented these biographical notes on Käthe Dräger and John Rittmeister to pay tribute to their extraordinary courage and to indicate that these two people *did* attempt to keep psychoanalysis alive during the Third Reich. They swam against the current of the Göring Institute, and one of them drowned along the way. Yet, even though they personally did honor to the profession of psychoanalysis, neither would claim that their efforts succeeded in keeping psychoanalysis alive. Quite the contrary, for both of them the Göring Institute signified the end of the psychoanalytic movement in Germany.

Part 4
Psychoanalysis in Germany after the Third Reich: The Long Road Back

13
War's End

Posttraumatic Stress among the Psychoanalysts in Berlin

Those analysts who watched their Jewish colleagues leave Berlin did not have a clue how the next twelve years would treat them. The psychoanalysts who stayed in Berlin would experience increasing stress with each passing year. But the very worst of their experiences would come during the final three months of the Third Reich when Hitler ordered Berlin defended "to the last man" against the Soviets.

In a 1982 article in *Psyche,* Brainin and Kaminer point out the simple irony that, for the non-Jewish German therapists, the experience of bombing and defeat was more significant psychologically than their capacity to empathize with the Jewish victims of the Holocaust (Brainin and Kaminer 1982). This is a significant point for which the evidence is quite convincing. In fact, when most Germans refer to the "Katastrophe" of World War II, they refer to the loss of the war or the bombing of the cities, not to the Holocaust.

It is our contention that for any insight into their Nazified past, members of the former Göring Institute must first come to terms with the effects of posttraumatic stress. The interviews of Müller-Braunschweig and Boehm by John Rickman, a British psychoanalyst sent to evaluate the surviving professionals in 1946, revealed that both of these men were shells of their former selves. The authors suggest that these two Freudian psychoanalysts were exhibiting the dissociative symptoms that were consistent with post-traumatic stress for over a year after Berlin fell to the Soviets. It is our contention that anyone who lived in Berlin from January 1, 1945, to May 8, 1945, must have experienced some form of traumatic stress. It is postulated that John Rickman's conclusion based on the interview data he obtained in 1946 from each individual psychoanalyst needs to be reinterpreted based upon the increased knowledge about the individuals involved and the theoretical advances made in both personality theory and the nature of traumatic stress disorder. The traumatic stress disorder concept pertains to the cumulative effects of each individual's experiences during the twelve years of the Third Reich. The toll of living and working at the Göring Institute during the Third Reich and experiencing the Battle of Berlin was sufficient to have left significant impairments in all but the most "invulnerable" (Anthony et al. 1987) of individuals.

The psychoanalysts of the Göring Institute would experience the most severe stress during the final months of the war along with other Berliners. On February 3, 1945, the American Eighth Army Air Force bombed Berlin in preparation for the Soviet advance against "Fortress Berlin." The B17s came one thousand strong each day at 9:00 A.M. It would take the entire air armada one and a half hours to pass over the city while the bombers dropped their bomb loads. By night the RAF came with its Mosquitos and its special four-thousand-pound "Blockbusters." Sometimes the British hit Berlin at night on two different occasions with the same planes. The RAF came on thirty-six nights between February 13 and April 21 (Read and Fisher 1992, 107, 228–32, 259–60).

In a grandiose and emotional manner, Joseph Goebbels wrote the orders to defend Fortress Berlin. The capital, he said, would be defended to the last man and the last bullet. As usual, Goebbels was very precise in the final commands he placed upon the *Volkssturm* (the peoples' army or home guard). The *Volkssturm* was supposed to consist of men between the ages of sixteen and sixty. But in the defense of Berlin, those chosen were in reality between the ages of twelve and sixteen, and the rest mostly over forty. Just before the last inadequately trained group was marched the few short miles to the German front lines, its members were told that anyone found to be retreating would be executed by hanging from the nearest lamppost. The struggle was to be conducted with 1) fanatical resolution, 2) imagination, 3) every means of deception, artifice, and cunning, 4) strategies of all kinds devised in advance or on a spur of the moment, and 5) above and beneath the ground. The initial brilliance, daring, and almost miraculously quick victories in the beginning of this catastrophic war were only to be surpassed in drama by the horrendous nature of its total and complete defeat during the final hours (Read and Fisher 1992, 250-51). Himmler, a man without any military training, had been given an important military command. He did not even know how to use a gun. It was no wonder that when Himmler set up his battle line in the wrong direction, his command became completely useless (Read and Fisher 1992, 224-25).

Joseph Goebbels's idea of "Total War" became for the Berliners a day-by-day catastrophe. In his diary, Goebbels wrote, "The millions of people in the Reich capital are steadily becoming nervous and hysterical. . . . It is a torture which overstrains the nerves in the long run" (Middlebrook 1988, 327-28). This time Joseph Goebbels understated his case. On April 21, 1945, the last wave of one thousand B17s delivered its payload on Berlin to weaken the city for the Soviet advance. "Fortress Berlin" was now completely in ruins. On April 17, 1945, one of the last symbolic strongholds of Berlin showed its final defiance to the Soviets. The Berlin Philharmonic had played steadily throughout the horror of the bombings from January to April 17. In its last performance on April 12, the Berlin Philharmonic played Beethoven's violin concerto and Wagner's "Twilight of the Gods" (Reuth 1990, 352). On April 19, 1945, Goebbels gave his last speech and once again told the people of Berlin it was their duty to fight to the end (Reuth 1990, 354). By this time the Berlin water works and electrical service had all but stopped working. The last Führer conferences in Hitler's bunker were more like regressed fantasies than reflections of reality. Fake armies and magical weapons were still being discussed. On the streets of Berlin, the SA and the SS were busy hanging deserters from lampposts as a means of brutal punishment, as well as a means to warn others of the consequences of cowardly behavior. The Führer's orders were still being carried out under the penalty of death (Trevor-Roper 1947, 100-109, 119-98, 171). Berlin would now have to endure a constant bombardment of the six thousand tanks blasting their way block by block, and an overwhelming rush of well over two and one half million Soviet troops for another twelve days before the Nazis surrendered Berlin on May 2, 1945. The fighting was not only street by street but house by house and even room by room.

Recent information obtained from the former Soviet Army's archive reveals the final battle for Berlin in 1945 was an unprecedented nightmare in the history of military warfare. Not only did the Germans defend their city to the death, as Hitler ordered, but two Soviet generals used their armies to fight each other for the honor of capturing the capital of the Third Reich. The devastating consequences of this competition between two Soviet armies fighting each other, as well as the Wehrmacht, "to take Berlin At Any Cost" (Documentary, Discovery Channel 1994) meant that 600,000 Soviet troops had perished in this massive waste of human life. The latter report is from a documentary film quoting figures from the Soviet Union's archives. Earlier records that did not include Soviet archival information suggest 304,887 casualties killed, wounded, or missing according to John Erickson (1983, 622), which Gerhard H. Weinberg (1994, 825) considered a conservative figure. German military and civilian casualties were never known, but the new facts of Soviet losses meant that the Berliners must have suffered proportionally. In what must have seemed to the Berliners like an apocalyptic revenge, their capital was being crushed by the Soviets. In comparing the loss of 600,000 Soviet troops in taking Berlin with total U.S. losses of 405,000 for all of World War II, one can perhaps begin to understand what living through the fall of Berlin must have been like (Forster 1973, 256). This was human carnage that almost defies belief, and the one vast gravesite for these Soviet troops remains another great monument to humanity's inhumanity.

The atmosphere of "unreality" that marked the last weeks in the Führerbunker was paralleled to some extent by the Göring Institute until it was taken by Soviet troops. Cocks reports that as early as February 1945, Feliz Scheke, the managing director of the Institute, refused M. H. Göring's order to return to his post in Berlin because the Soviet army was rapidly advancing on the capital. Scheke was called a "defeatist" by M. H. Göring for his realistic appraisal of what would happen to Berlin (Cocks 1997, 346). The same term, "defeatist," was applied to Johannes Heinrich Schultz in the spring of 1945. M. H. Göring tried to convince his deputy director that the leaders of the Institute needed to provide psychological services for the front-line German troops of "Fortress Berlin." Schultz considered such heroics useless in the face of inevitably approaching Soviet triumph. Schultz was also classified as a "defeatist" for his good judgment. Almost to the last moment, M. H. Göring believed in Hitler as he had during the twelve-year Third Reich. He remained a true believer in the ideology of National Socialism and thought Hitler was capable of pulling off a miracle like a Nordic god from Germany's mythological past. As the Soviets were nearing the Institute, he put on his uniform and allowed the SS the "sanctuary" of the Institute. As the Soviets closed in on the Institute, his courage must have failed him for he asked a secretary to bury his uniform in the yard. She refused to take this terrible risk and went to the basement from which she would eventually escape (Lockot 1994c). Göring was captured by the Soviet troops. Shortly thereafter, he died a prisoner of war from typhus.

The final events that marked the existence of the Göring Institute reflect the complexity in understanding the motivation of its leader and the psychoanalysts who worked at the Institute during the Third Reich. In the first place, Kemper claimed that the Institute was destroyed during an air raid (Cocks 1985, 299–300). However, according to Schultz-Hencke the Institute was destroyed by Soviet troops after one of their officers was shot in the back by SS troops from within the Institute (Lockot 1985, 86–87; Brecht et al. 1985, 153; Lockot 1991a and 1994c; and Cocks 1997, 1). The latter explanation is most likely correct. However, the fact that such different impressions have been given about what would seem to be so basic and straightforward an occurrence illuminates the problems involved in trusting the interview data about more complicated and personally revealing matters. The greater part of the truth was destroyed when the records of the Göring Institute were burned with the building, however it happened. Then there is the question about the Red Cross flag. Was it permanent? Or was it used as a trick to deceive the Soviet troops? Joseph Goebbels had ordered a fanatical defense using every deception imaginable to kill as many Soviet soldiers as possible. Was M. H. Göring willingly following the regime's last orders, or was it simply that the SS troops had occupied the building despite M. H. Göring's protest? By this time the Wehrmacht was fragmented and of limited strength. The fact that 600,000 Soviet troops were killed in action in their effort to take Berlin meant that much of the last fanatical defense was in the hands of the *Volkssturm* (Home Guard). The German officers on duty in Berlin and many civilians had taken the last commands of the Third Reich very seriously. Did that resistance include a Luftwaffe officer named M. H. Göring?

When the war was over and Berlin was in shambles, the psychoanalysts who had lived through the war were still faced with the issue of how to continue to survive. Gerhard Scheunert was a psychoanalyst who had become a Nazi during the Third Reich and subsequently helped reestablish the psychoanalytic profession in Germany after the war. He described his feeling after May 8, 1945, as follows:

> We held on to what we had salvaged in ourselves, of psychoanalysis, the old Freudian doctrine. Everything else had to wait until later, there was no other way . . . and so we founded the German Psychoanalytical Association. . . . [W]e set about building an association for the cultivation of Freudian analysis and an analytic training institute, more or less from scratch—an adventure that was ridiculed and fought with a great deal of bitterness and hatred. . . . But this work was also a piece of real reparation for me. (Scheunert 1991 quoted in Friedrich 1995, 265)

Individuals like Scheunert often referred to May 8, 1945, as zero hour.

This belief that they had a new start helped ward off the massive depression that probably would have occurred had they tried to deal with their own guilt by themselves.

What did in fact occur was that the psychoanalysts in Germany knew and even discussed their past among themselves. For example, the fact that Scheunert was a Nazi was no secret. It was known and argued about during the split that took place. Knowing Scheunert was a Nazi, the members of the DPV still elected him their second president, and at the same time this group considered themselves the "true representatives of Freudian psychoanalysis" (Friedrich 1995, 268). What, in fact, followed, whether consciously or unconsciously, was a "conspiracy of silence" among the former members of the Göring Institute that protected them from the German public and the international psychoanalytic community. In a sense this resulted in a self-protective group denial, and the illusion of a brand new beginning—a fictional "zero hour." The belief of being "born again" served to postpone coming to terms with feelings of loss, shame, and the painful memories created during twelve years of Nazi horrors.

John Rickman's 1946 Report to the IPA: The Roles of Transference and Countertransference in Interpreting the Report

The English version of *The Catalog* (Brecht et al. 1985) includes John Rickman's interviews, observations, and ratings from his 1946 visit to Berlin, during which he evaluated the surviving members of the DPG. He interviewed them individually and sat in on one of the DPG's meetings in which the paper discussed was "The Unwanted Child and His Death Instinct" by Hanna Ries. Ries, a former student of Müller-Braunschweig, had fled to England in 1939 and became a member of the British Psycho-Analytical Society during World War II. Müller-Braunschweig read her paper and then criticized it. The degree of Müller-Braunschweig's emotion revealed a great deal and was significant in Rickman's report.

John Rickman was a British psychoanalyst who was asked to work for the German Personnel Research Branch of the Control Commission (GPRB) established by the Allies. It was "set up to supervise the tasks of helping the German people to recover from twelve years of Nazi rule . . . [and] to try to discover and employ people who did not approve of the Nazi regime, and who would be willing to take part in the task of rebuilding post-war Germany" (Brecht et al. 1985, 234). The goal of his mission was to visit the gentile psychoanalysts who were living in Berlin and had survived the war while practicing at the Göring Institute. He had exceptional qualifications for his responsibilities. As a new physician, he had volunteered to work at a

Quaker War Relief Unit in Russia in 1916. His experiences related to psychoanalysis included being analyzed by Sigmund Freud and Melanie Klein, as well as helping Ernest Jones establish the Institute of Psychoanalysis for the British Psycho-Analytical Society. He visited Vienna after the Nazi takeover of Austria to help his colleagues leave (Brecht et al. 1985, 234-35).

It took courage to visit Berlin in October of 1946. The city had been destroyed and the basic utilities had not yet been restored. There were rumors that SS troops were still in hiding waiting for the right moment to attack the Allies. Furthermore, the Americans and British were still (in theory) following entirely different occupation plans for Germany. Americans were committed to the Morganthau Plan, whose goal it was to destroy Germany's industrial base and to reduce the entire nation to a pastoral economy. Britain followed a much more enlightened policy established by its cabinet, whose goal it was to reeducate the German people so they would establish a firm foundation for a liberal democracy. By January 1947, the American policy would change to follow the British model (Pronay and Wilson 1985, 1-3 and 59-69; Braun 1990, 148-50).

During his visit with the German analysts, Rickman conducted himself with grace and showed a humanitarian bent. He went to Berlin to extend the olive branch of peace. It is to his credit that he handled himself with such dignity in the face of the extreme hostility with which he was confronted by Müller-Braunschweig and Felix Boehm. The most important aspect of his trip however was the observations he made that clearly revealed the deep and denied Nazified feelings of Boehm and Müller-Braunschweig. In essence, his report in 1946 shows how much psychoanalysis in Germany had become highly compromised. The technique Rickman used to observe the German analysts' interaction with each other at a membership meeting was designed to assess group process rather than outcome variables. Wilfred Bion gives credit to John Rickman for stimulating the research known as the Northfield Experiment, which is also known for studying leaderless groups (Baruch 1999). The methods used by Rickman were to include "personal interviews on the basis of a friendly colleague conversation" and observation of a scientific meeting to identify group interaction. The goal of the method was to allow for as much spontaneous generation of attitudes as possible (Brecht et al. 1985, 235-36).

One of the significant issues related to the report concerns Rickman's opinion about the degree to which the individual analysts had become Nazified during the twelve years of the Third Reich. Also important was Rickman's opinion regarding the degree of psychopathy the German analysts revealed. After his assessment he concluded:

There are some very fine untroubled spirits in Germany to whom as
colleagues I think we owe every opportunity for affording them development which reasonably we can give. We must also be prepared to
deal with the deteriorated and objectionable personalities. (Rickman
report in Brecht et al. 1985, 239; King and Steiner 1991, 26)

His report thus documented the deteriorated level of functioning that the
two future leaders of rival psychoanalytic groups in Berlin had demonstrated—Carl Müller-Braunschweig and Felix Boehm. The problems and
schisms (see chapter 14) that are still being worked out by the psychoanalytic movement in Germany clearly had some of their roots in these two
founding fathers.

It is interesting to speculate on the possible transference reactions of
Müller-Braunschweig and Boehm toward Rickman. Although Boehm and
Müller-Braunschweig had known Rickman before the war, one can hypoth-
esize that their respective level of object relations had regressed significantly
since that time. Although Rickman extended every level of courtesy to these
two analysts, and despite the probability that his demeanor and approach
reflected his humane Quaker convictions, it is still possible that both
Boehm and Müller-Braunschweig could have seen themselves as the humili-
ated vanquished and seen Rickman as the victor, resulting in shame and
hostility. Rickman states:

The low morale, tactlessness, and indeed spite of Drs. Boehm and
Müller-Braunschweig cannot, I think, be ascribed to underfeeding,
bombing, and the strain of war, nor indeed to twelve years of the Nazi
regime. Those two are most troubled men.

We tend to differ in degree with Rickman giving more credit to the role of
transference and posttraumatic stress disorder in generating their regressed
states. We are aware, however, that one can reasonably disagree about such
interpretations as does Lucy Rickman Baruch (1999). Her point was that
one would then have to explain why Fräuleins Dräger and Steinberg and
Dr. Kemper are not similarly impacted.

In addition to the multiple level of transference-countertransference
issues that must have been elicited during Rickman's individual interviews,
Lockot reports the intense emotional reactions that were displayed at the
scientific group meeting that must have had a complex transferential
nature. According to Lockot, at the meeting Rickman attended

Müller-Braunschweig read the work of Hanna Ries who was his former
student and who had gone in January, 1939, to England. He presented

her lecture entitled, "The unwanted child and his death instinct." She had obtained membership in the British Psychoanalytical Society. We can only assume that such a theme had to trigger very strong subconscious reactions. Didn't it confront the analytical "parent" in Germany with their being guilty of the expulsion of the Jews? That means with their unwanted children but also their siblings and parents. (Lockot 1993, 15)

The German analysts not only had to deal with their guilt for having rejected the Jewish members, but also with the tremendous stress they had endured by staying with Papa Göring. Hanna Ries, the "unwanted child," had been accepted in a warm benevolent way by her adoptive father (Jones) and her new family (the British Society), while the German analysts experienced the pain and hell from British bombers brought on by their father-führer figures (M. H. Göring and Hitler).

However scholars may differ about subtle distinctions, the actual behavioral observations reported by Rickman have become invaluable in understanding the period just after the war—behaviors that the German analysts had not previously shared with any of those who interviewed them. (For those interested readers, the Rickman Report has been included as an appendix.)

14

Postwar Legacies

Theoretical Schisms and the IPA's Denial of Full Membership Status to the DPG: The Historical Relevance of Freud's Letter to Eitingon of March 21, 1933

An examination of what in psychoanalysis survived after Germany's defeat in 1945 brings us to the subject of theoretical schisms. These splits were not a new phenomenon; rather they can be traced back to the beginnings of psychoanalysis and Freud's tendency to view disagreement as heresy. The events of the Third Reich added complexity to the matter, so that the schisms would occur around two distinct fault lines. One fault line divided the traditional Freudians from the neo-Freudians; the second fault line concerned collaboration vs. resistance to the Nazis.

As the National Socialist government began to crack down on the profession in 1933, there is evidence that Freud and Max Eitingon discussed alternative ways of responding. Freud's letter to Eitingon would eventually involve the IPA in this matter of schisms to determine whether or not the DPG could be accepted back into the IPA after World War II. Prior to Freud's letter and the events of World War II, the question of theoretical schisms had been handled within the local institute and with the advice from Freud. However, at the heart of Freud's letter to Eitingon was what could be acceptable as Freudian psychoanalysis after World War II within the guidelines of the IPA. On March 21, 1933, Freud had written a letter of advice to Max Eitingon, the chairman of the Berlin Psychoanalytical Association. That letter deals directly with the issue of the long-term survival of the Berlin Institute and thus the survival of psychoanalysis in Germany. Freud wrote:

1. Let us assume psychoanalysis is prohibited, the Institute closed by the authorities. In that case there is least of all to be said or done about it. You will then have held out until the last moment before the ship is sunk.

2. Let us assume nothing happens to the Institute, but you, as a foreigner etc. are removed from the directorship. But you stay in Berlin and can go on using your influence unofficially. In this case, I think, you cannot close the Institute. True, you founded it and stayed in charge the longest, but then you handed it over to the Berlin group, to which it now belongs. You cannot do it legally, but it is also in the general interest that it remains open, so that it may survive these unfavourable times. Meanwhile, someone like Boehm, who has no particular allegiance [ein Indifferenter], can carry it on. Probably it will not be much attended, either by Germans or by foreigners, as long as the restrictions continue.

3. Again, let us assume nothing happens to the Institute, but you leave Berlin, either voluntarily or under duress. This situation leads to the same considerations as the one I have just mentioned, except that your influence vanishes, and the risk grows that opponents within such as Schultz-Hencke could take over the Institute and use it to further their plans. There is only one thing to be done about that: the Executive of the IPA disqualifies the Institute misused in this way, expelling it, as it were, until it can be absolved. But of course there must be a warning first.

What a miserable discussion! (Brecht et al. 1985, 112)

In his reply to Freud, it was clear that their consultation in Vienna on February 27, 1933, concerning Hitler being named chancellor of the Reich had both men thinking along the same lines. Apparently Eitingon, as president, had anticipated that "Aryans" might be required to be on the governing board and had already appointed Boehm and Müller-Braunschweig to a quasi-legal board to cope with any emergency situations precipitated by the government (Brecht et al. 1985, 112). After having consulted with Freud in Vienna and receiving his letter of March 21, 1933, Eitingon went to these members with the "proposal to leave the decision about the fate of the institute primarily in my hands" (Eitingon to Freud, letter of March 24, 1933). Thus he hoped to use his influence unofficially as Freud suggested. He informed Freud that their response "showed that they are not especially drawn to this proposal" (Eitingon to Freud, letter of March 24, 1933). At an extraordinary general meeting of the DPG on May 6, 1933, the proposition by Müller-Braunschweig and Boehm to change the board was voted down and thus, from a formal point of view, Eitingon was still president. Eitingon, however, knowing that Müller-Braunschweig and Boehm were not going to cooperate with Freud's plan, resigned his chairmanship and decided to emigrate to Palestine (Brecht et al. 1985, 84). At this point, from Eitingon's perspective, not only were the Jews to continue to be persecuted, but the integrity of psychoanalysis in Berlin was in jeopardy.

Freud's hunch about the increased influence that Schultz-Hencke's neo-analytic theory would have upon the DPG turned out to be correct. It would be more than a decade later that Schultz-Hencke's increased influence within the organization would actually be confronted by some psychoanalysts. During the Third Reich, the DPG would go through a variety of changes. To reiterate, initially the DPG was incorporated into the Göring Institute, but eventually, on November 19, 1938, the DPG dissolved itself, to survive as Work Group A at the Institute. Thus in order to "survive," the term "psychoanalytic" had to be dropped, and the DPG no longer formally existed. Thus, "[u]nder Göring's leadership the marginalisation of psychoanalysis and its incorporation into 'German psychotherapy' began" (Brecht et al. 1985, 102). During the period that M. H. Göring led the Institute, the schisms were kept under wraps, and the different groups gave the appearance of working together cooperatively. Schultz-Hencke's power continued to grow and so did the importance of his neo-analytic theory.

The DPG was reconstituted in 1945 with Müller-Braunschweig as president. In a letter to Boehm on October 1945, Müller-Braunschweig describes how Schultz-Hencke had sufficient power and confidence to suggest that his close circle form a group to be called the "Neo-Analytic Group" and become legally approved as a registered association. The DPG that emerged after World War II had a strong subgroup of neo-analysts, as Müller-Braunschweig's carefully worded letter of June 6, 1945, inviting all of the former members back to the society, would reveal (Brecht et al. 1985, 196). Schultz-Hencke had obviously gained power during the years the Nazis were in control, while the Freudians lost some of what they previously had. An uneasy peace existed between the subgroups until Schultz-Hencke, acting as the representative of the DPG at the International Psychoanalytical Congress in Zürich in 1949, presented some of his neo-Freudian concepts to a group meeting, therefore forcing their theoretical differences into the open. As president of the DPG, Müller-Braunschweig tried various ways to convince Schultz-Hencke to resign his membership, and when these attempts failed, he took bold steps as president of the DPG. Müller-Braunschweig established a new orthodox Freudian psychoanalytic organization.

This insistence on theoretical differences is interesting when seen in the context of the psychological trauma of the war and the defeat. The reconstituted DPG that emerged after the war was faced with the challenge of surviving as an integrated group. Its members were faced with the pain of having lived within one of the cruelest regimes in history. How would the psychological trauma affect the individual members, as well as the group's identity? Would the cooperation among the psychoanalysts that occurred during the nine years while M. H. Göring was their only leader and during the twelve years they had lived under National Socialism survive? Or was that cooperation too forced to survive in a freer atmosphere? As already discussed, the conflict emerged between Müller-Braunschweig, who wanted a renewal of traditional psychoanalytic thinking and identity, and Schultz-Hencke, who had developed a neopsychoanalytic approach that prospered during the Third Reich, while "Freudian" psychoanalysis had been suppressed and its members punished by the regime. Schultz-Hencke brought political and financial support from new government agencies by negotiating with them while Müller-Braunschweig was simply committed to regaining an association with the IPA. This conflict polarized the group.

Thus, when in 1949 Schultz-Hencke, as a member of the DPG, presented his own theory in a paper at the International Psychoanalytic Congress in Zürich, in which he used one of his neopsychoanalytic concepts, the paper had wider ramifications. It started a major disagreement between Müller-Braunschweig and Schultz-Hencke that would lead to a split in the DPG. Also at the same 1949 Congress, the DPG reapplied for admission to the IPA. The IPA gave only provisional admission with the condition that its psychoanalytical position be clarified and the issues of collaboration be resolved. The rival groups within the DPG interpreted this provisional acceptance differently. In Müller-Braunschweig's mind, the IPA's conditional acceptance was due to the DPG's permitting of Schultz-Hencke to teach neo-analysis. For Boehm, the criticism of "collaboration" meant what it stated—its links with the Nazi roots of the Göring Institute—but he considered these supposed Nazi roots to be the IPA's simple prejudices against Germans. Schultz-Hencke on the other hand considered the provisional status of the DPG to be unrelated to his theoretical modifications of Freud, but based upon Müller-Braunschweig's personal animosity and the political intrigues with the IPA. In 1949, the members of the DPG rejected the conditions relevant to their full acceptance by the IPA (Brecht et al. 1985, 198; Lockot 1994; Eickhoff 1995).

At this point, Müller-Braunschweig tried once again to get Schultz-Hencke to resign because of his use of the neo-Freudian concepts, but this failed. Since Schultz-Hencke was a popular member of the DPG and the majority of the DPG members accepted his theoretical approach, Müller-Braunschweig's position lacked any prospect of victory. Another orthodox Freudian psychoanalyst failed to convince the board of directors to recast its theoretical approach back to its more Freudian roots; the seven committed Freudians established their own institute without giving up their membership in the DPG. They doggedly had tried to regain control of the old DPG, but they had not succeeded.

Müller-Braunschweig acted decisively in a political move whose spirit and form paralleled Freud's removal of Stekal as editor of the *Zentralblatt* on November 6, 1912 (Roazen 1971, 216; Jones 1962b, 136–37), Jones's method of eliminating the Jungians from the British society in 1919 (Jones 1962b), and the 1933 letter from Freud to Eitingon suggesting ways to prevent the theoretical threat of Schultz-Henke's neo-analysis from denigrating psychoanalysis. Thus, Müller-Braunschweig would follow a traditional political pattern within psychoanalysis that was useful in maintaining its own theoretical identity.

On September 11, 1950, Müller-Braunschweig founded a new association called the German Psychoanalytical Association (*Deutsche Psychoanalytische Vereinigung* or DPV). The major purpose of the DPV was the establishment of an exclusively Freudian psychoanalytical training institute. Müller-Braunschweig's announcement that he established the DPV while he was still president of the DPG stunned and angered many members. The DPG members gave the DPV only a limited chance of success because of the small number of members. Given its small size, the DPV needed the support and recognition of the IPA, and at the 1951 congress in Amsterdam it was admitted as a branch society. At the same congress, Kemper and Boehm requested that the DPG provisional admission status be extended two more years in order to prove its scientific worth to the IPA during that period. The general assembly of the IPA had already voted against extending full recognition. The request for extended provisional status was denied (Brecht et al. 1985, 218). This effectively closed off the DPG from the international psychoanalytic community for many years because of theoretical differences.

The DPV started to grow in Berlin, and eventually it expanded into other cities in the later 1950s, including Heidelberg and Hamburg. Gerhard Scheunert, chairman of the DPV, moved to Hamburg in 1960 and founded the Hamburg Psychoanalytic Institute. In 1995, he gave a deathbed confession that he had been a Nazi Party member. Alexander Mitscherlich founded what was later to be called the Sigmund Freud Institute in Frankfurt am Main. The institute became a recognized center for the DPV in 1960. All of these institutes were helped in their development by training analysts from all over Europe and the United States. The doubts and sense of isolation among the German psychoanalysts were relieved by the support from those foreign analysts who relit the psychoanalytic torch.

By the mid-1970s, the membership in the DPG included practitioners in many other towns and cities in Germany. There were satellite programs in Munich, Stuttgart, and Heidelberg. During the mid-1970s, the DPG was using more Freudian concepts in its psychoanalysis, and eventually the DPG was reintegrated into the mainstream of psychoanalytic thought. At the present time, the Freudian tradition and concepts are represented by the DPG, the DPV, as well as by independent analysts. These Freudian analysts and their Jungian colleagues form an umbrella organization of fifteen hundred members. The formal reintegration of the DPG back into the IPA has become a significant question once again. The executive committees of both the DPG and DPV have recently approved, in principle, that the DPG seek formal affiliation with the IPA. The DPG currently operates outside of the structure of the IPA. It consists of approximately 630 members and 600 candidates in 12 cities in Germany. Otto F. Kernberg, president of the IPA, has indicated that the executive council of the IPA favorably regards this possibility. The IPA will follow its usual procedure in this matter. However, the IPA has recognized that many of the DPG's member organizations already work according to IPA standards, but that is not true of not all of them. Therefore, the IPA Ad Hoc Site Visit Committee would conduct individual assessments in order to insure that these standards are in operation for the various member groups (Kernberg 1999, Tyson 1998). These events point to an attempt at a reversal of the postwar divisive trends.

What were the implications of the post–World War II schisms in the development of psychoanalysis in Germany? The end result of these events may have rectified the theoretical schism as far as the IPA was concerned, but the fact of the matter was that neither the DPG nor the DPV was confronted with its Nazified past.

On face value it was untenable that Jones would not question the admission of the DPV into the IPA in 1951, when he was fully aware of Rickman's opinion of Müller-Braunschweig's incompetence as an analyst and his Nazi leanings (Eickhoff 1995, 953-54). Even more difficult to comprehend is why the entire leadership of the IPA did not raise serious questions about the DPV's admission when the painful reality of the Holocaust was only six years past (Brecht et al. 1985, 234-39; Eickhoff 1995, 953-54). Could the personal and theoretical differences that started with the arrival of the Vienna analysts in London in 1939 (King and Steiner 1992; Roazen 1992, 391-98) continue after the war among the leaders of the IPA and prevent an inquiry into the nature of the Nazi influence in the DPV prior to its admission in 1951?

It would take yet another generation of motivated German psychoanalysts to come to terms with their historical roots (Brecht et al. 1985). Cocks's dissertation and subsequent book, as well as the findings of Lockot (1985, 1988, and 1994a), have helped us to start dealing with the problem that Edith Kurzweil (1985) correctly identified as the "collective amnesia" of the German psychoanalytic community. There have been more recent attempts since the publication of The Catalog (1985) that reveal how German analysts have come to terms with their "collective amnesia." We have elaborated on a recent article by Lockot (1994a), who uses an intriguing metaphor to describe how difficult it was for psychoanalysis to return from its institutionalized psychotherapeutic and Nazified roots within the Göring Institute. In this account, the schism within the DPG resulting in the establishment of the DPV can best be considered a search for a new identity. The end result, however, was to make more complex the task of bringing the disturbing pasts to consciousness. In Lockot's description of the establishment of the DPV in postwar Germany, the behavioral events were similar to that of a transsexual whose identity had been lost in the traumatic events prior to and during World War II. As a result of this traumatic experience, Lockot suggests the "transsexual/DPG" searches for a past identity by a renewed association with the IPA. The unknown factor by both parties in this process is the dissociated experience of the "transsexual/DPG." Seeking a union to make it feel whole, the "transsexual/DPG" slowly manipulates its sought-after and unknowing host into an illicit sexual enactment. The result of this union is the birth or formation of the ethically compromised DPV.

This unconscious process started with Müller-Braunschweig's early attempts after World War II to reach out to the IPA. It continued with his criticisms of Schultz-Hencke's paper on neo-analysis as being "unacceptable" at the IPA's Zurich conference of 1949. Müller-Braunschweig's position that neo-analysis was a major threat to psychoanalysis was supported by Jones during the business meeting of the conference. Jones called Müller-Braunschweig's criticism of Schultz-Hencke's paper an outstanding example of a genuine analyst. Actually, Müller-Braunschweig was scapegoating Schultz-Hencke's neo-analytic theory as if it were a "bad object" that was allowed to exist within the DPG. In this manner he represented the DPV as the true representative of Freud's psychoanalytic theory. In his report about the conference, Jones further distorts the process that has taken place by including selected details of Rickman's 1946 report condemning the German analysts. The final enactment occurred at the 1951 business meeting of the IPA congress in Amsterdam when the DPV's application for membership was unanimously accepted (Eickhoff 1995). During this debate between Müller-Braunschewig and Schultz-Hencke, Jones obviously supported the authenticity of the DPV by his positive comments about Müller-Braunschewig and his selective reporting of what was in Rickman's 1946 report on his visit to Berlin. Jones completely left out Rickman's references to both Boehm and Müller-Braunschweig being politically untrustworthy (i.e., Nazis). By supporting the admission of the DPV into the IPA, the leadership of the world psychoanalytic community had chosen theoretical orthodoxy as a more significant factor in readmission than the Nazification of the members being admitted. In this way the IPA supported the "collective amnesia" of the DPV. By this unconscious process, the Nazification of the German psychoanalysts would remain buried until the young German analysts met the demands made by the IPA in 1977 to come to terms with their Nazi roots.

We return to our original question about the leaders of the IPA closing their eyes to Müller-Braunschweig's regressed functioning and Nazi leanings only six years after the Holocaust. Why would they allow him to form the DPV, be recognized by the IPA, and entrust him with the future of psychoanalysis in Germany considering the fact that the balance of his collaboration to resistance was so precarious? Did they overvalue theoretical purity? Reviewing the events surrounding the acceptance of the DPV into the IPA in 1951, and the rejection of the DPG's appeal for its provisional recognition by the IPA to continue in effect (Brecht et al. 1985, 207–25), suggest to us the following hypothesis. The leaders of the IPA were following one of Freud's last requests. In his letter to Eitingon of March 27, 1933, Freud was clearly concerned that Schultz-Hencke would be able to dilute the purity of psychoanalytic theory. For the leaders of the IPA, the problematic past of Müller-Braunschweig was not nearly as significant as their devotion to

Freud. They were perhaps honoring one of the last requests of Freud, and using a time-honored strategy to ensure that Schultz-Hencke's importance in the DPG would not be allowed to corrupt psychoanalysis.

One German psychoanalyst has raised questions about the DPV "collective amnesia" in a very personal way. Sammy Speier has written a courageous essay in *The Collective Silence* (Heimannsberg and Schmidt 1993, 61–72). He discusses the predicament of being in a training analysis in postwar Germany and the seeming impossibility of dealing with "transference" issues within the DPV. He deals with the problems of raising any significant questions to the training analyst, given the rule of abstinence. In effect, Speier suggests the rule of abstinence not only served to protect the individual training analyst, but German psychoanalysis itself. He points out that the training analyst's usual response to the analysand's questions about the role of psychoanalysis during the Third Reich would be "What is your association, what are you thinking of?" which really means "What on earth are you thinking of, to ask me a personal question?" (Speier, in Heimannsberg and Schmidt 1993, 65). Thus, honest questions and dialogue are avoided, and the working-through process is stonewalled. Speier goes on to make this challenging assertion:

> Gradually I came to realize that behind my fear, and the fear of my colleagues and patients, to question analysts and psychoanalysis was not the fear of opening the door to the parents' bedroom and witnessing its "primal scene," but rather the fear of opening the door to the gas chamber. (Speier, in Heimannsberg and Schmidt 1993, 65)

We have quoted many German analysts who have raised significant issues about their profession, but not one has taken the kind of direct personal approach Sammy Speier has taken. Speier's essay continues its no-holds-barred confrontation with not only the DPV, but in fact with the whole postwar German psychoanalytic tradition. He points out:

> The teachers who trained today's psychoanalysts belong to that generation whose life history bears the stamp of the Nazi dictatorship and the mass extermination it brought about. The psychoanalysts in postwar Germany were not, as one would like to imagine, men of the "founding hour" only, but rather men of the final hour as well, and that has important implications for the new generation of psychoanalysts. The fact that we have an unadmitted and unresolved history of genocide behind us is a state of affairs which we would prefer to suppress and deny. (Speier, in Heimannsberg and Schmidt 1993, 61–62)

Speier goes on with his unrelenting criticism of the DPV. He indicates that when many of the DPV members were questioned on how they conducted themselves in the years 1933–45, their reaction was "monstrous." The questions that had not been answered since World War II led to rage reactions and accusations of disloyalty toward those who asked the questions.

In this extremely disquieting essay, Speier really raises questions about the IPA's role in this process of "collective amnesia." Despite the fact that he does not accuse, he points out:

> Many psychoanalysts in the DPV live with the fantasy that they
> received the Jewish blessing of the International Psychoanalytic Associ
> ation in 1950. That date was to have marked the painless birth of a
> German psychoanalytic society after Auschwitz. But so far as I know,
> painless births occur only under anaesthesia; and all too many DPV
> members today still give the impression of being anaesthetized. (Speier,
> in Heimannsberg and Schmidt 1993, 70)

What Speier does not question in his often brilliant, sometimes abstract, sometimes concrete evaluation of some of the serious problems of postwar German psychoanalysis is the part played by the IPA. After all, how could there be a perception of Jewish blessing of the DPV without the IPA's supporting that collective denial he so correctly finds as an unacceptable state of affairs?

The Catalog (or "Here Life Goes On in a Most Peculiar Way: Psychoanalysis before and after 1933")

One of the most important documents that has shed light on the psychoanalytic movement in Germany both during and after the Third Reich was published in 1985. It is referred to as *The Catalog,* but is actually entitled *Here Life Goes On in a Most Peculiar Way: Psychoanalysis before and after 1933* (ed. Karen Brecht, Volker Friedrich, Ludger M. Hermanns, Isidor J. Kaminer, and Dierk H. Juelich).

One of the reasons this document was published was to meet the demand of the International Psychoanalytical Association (IPA) in 1977 that the German psychoanalysts come to terms with their Nazified past. While the IPA Programme Commission had initiated this request for the collection of documents in 1977, it was apparently unaware that this same idea had already risen in the minds of a few younger German analysts whose work was generally supported by the DPV. In any case, the IPA request elicited a much needed airing of differences among a wide range of German psychoanalysts in the journal *Psyche.*

It is interesting to note the significance of the formal title of *The Catalog.* The title, *Here Life Goes On in a Most Peculiar Way,* comes from a sentence in a letter written by John Rittmeister, the analyst executed by the Nazis, to friends in Switzerland. The letter, written on October 15, 1939, some six weeks after Germany started World War II, opens by stating, "[T]here is a world of difference between us now, but we have not forgotten you." And the letter goes on to say, "Here life goes on in a very peculiar way, sometimes as though there were nothing the matter."

The Catalog is a collection of significant historical documents that relate to the practice of psychoanalysis in Germany. The documents cover the growth of the psychoanalytic movement in Germany from its inception to the rise of the Third Reich and the fifteen years after its fall, and include photographs, a variety of professional and personal letters, newspaper and journal articles, speeches, memos, and personal recollections. These documents are systematically arranged to provide an overview of the persecution of Jewish analysts and the defamation of psychoanalysis itself during the Third Reich. There is ample evidence of the forced emigration of the Jewish analysts from Germany and the impact the Nazis had upon both the practice of psychoanalysis and the analysts who remained in Germany. In particular, *The Catalog* examines the influence of the German Institute for Psychological Research and Psychotherapy (the Göring Institute) on the practice of psychoanalysis. The events after World War II, including the reconstruction of the DPG and the founding of the DPV, are also recorded.

The Catalog's editorial comments reveal a brave, genuine attempt at coming to terms with National Socialism's impact upon psychoanalysis. *The Catalog* was originally published in German in 1985 by Kellner Verlag of Hamburg. The authors of this manuscript acquired an English version of *The Catalog* in December 1993, published once again by Kellner Verlag, but this version has no new publication date.

The Catalog is the kind of professional self-evaluation that Christian Pross recommends for German physicians in order to come to terms with their roots in National Socialism. In the introduction to *Cleansing the Fatherland: Nazi Medicine and Racial Hygiene* (Aly et al. 1994), Pross concludes that speculation based on interview data alone is insufficient to understand the truth of what happened to medicine during the Third Reich. Only a careful analysis of historical documents, diaries, letters, and describing what the Nazis actually did—rather than what they said they did—will reveal historical reality and individual responsibility. Pross documents the new wave of German physicians and psychoanalysts who built upon the courage of psychoanalyst Alexander Mitscherlich (see next section), whose testimony at the Nuremberg doctors' trials in 1947-48 (Aly et al. 1994) told the truth about the monstrous decisions he observed made by physicians, decisions that turned them into licensed killers. Until the end of the 1970s, former Nazis who participated in unacceptable medical practices involving their Hippocratic Oath were able to retain their important academic positions.

The introduction and the preface to the English edition of *The Catalog* follows the spirit and form of what Pross proposed. *The Catalog* presents significant historical information describing how it came to be published. It originated as an accompaniment to an exhibition that was held in conjunction with the International Psychoanalytical Congress in Hamburg in 1985. The history of the 1985 congress held in Hamburg, the exhibition, and *The Catalog* are all relevant to understanding the issues currently being investigated.

In 1977, at the IPA congress in Jerusalem, a controversial compromise had to be reached about the organization's next meeting place. The German Psychoanalytical Association had felt secure enough in 1977 in Jerusalem to propose that the next IPA congress be held in Berlin. For the Jewish analysts, Berlin was an emotional reminder as the Nazi capital of the Third Reich. For the Jewish participants at the 1977 Jerusalem congress, the idea of the next meeting being held in Berlin elicited overwhelming psychic pain. The IPA respected the meaning that Berlin had for its Jewish members, and the city was rejected as the site for the 1985 congress. The IPA's refusal of Berlin in turn created much anguish for the German analysts. Finally, a compromise position was worked out, whereby the 1985 congress would be held in Hamburg. In order to better understand the choice of Hamburg over Berlin, we asked one of the children of an émigré Jewish analyst about this issue. Peter Happel, the son of Clara Happel, despite his young age at the time, has a remarkable memory about those who emigrated to the United States. He remembers that among those German Jewish analysts who emigrated, there were great hopes that some form of revolt would take place in Hamburg (Happel 1994). Hamburg's reputation as a liberal city was based upon the communist uprising that occurred there in 1923. The émigrés' hopes about Hamburg would never materialize, but for many Jews who had been able to escape Germany by ship, the last place they left was now the first place to which they returned after more than forty years. From the perspective of the Jewish émigrés, the historical role of Hamburg as being a free member of the Hanseatic League meant it was more a commercial center than a symbol of German nationalism as was Berlin. This made Hamburg more acceptable. As it happened, not only was the 1985 IPA Congress held in Hamburg, but also that same year the first three major books about the impact of the Third Reich upon the practice of psychoanalysis in Germany were published (Cocks 1985; Lockot 1985; Brecht et al. 1985). It is now clear that 1985 was a watershed experience for not only German psychoanalysis but perhaps for the entire IPA as well.

According to Volker Friedrich, the group of German psychoanalysts that was formed to assess the Nazi impact on their profession faced some difficult moments. In the first place, their job was made more difficult because of the break in the written records and documents that occurred from the end of 1938, when the DPG was disbanded, until the end of the war. However, this was not the only cause of difficulty. Each document reviewed by the group elicited the same kind of heated controversies that typically accompany any historical discussion of the effects of National Socialism on any aspect of German life today. Volker Friedrich described how the interpersonal atmosphere among the German analysts became personally threatening because "we suspected each other—in a continuous process of alternating roles and positions—of being Nazi perpetrators." Friedrich correctly points out how often in discussions like these, the "Nazi introject" is passed back and forth like a "hot potato" from person to person in attempts to come to terms with the "paranoid world of the Nazis" (Friedrich 1990, 628). The Hamburg congress was the first international psychoanalytic congress in Germany since 1932. It raised many painful issues for Jewish members and in particular émigré psychoanalysts. There were symbolic as well as personal issues involved in attending the congress. There were very painful memories that had to be encountered and worked through. Many wondered whether the official return of the IPA to Germany could be interpreted as condoning the extermination of six million Jews. A majority of the Jewish psychoanalysts were concerned that the congress would be a betrayal of the memory of their parents, grandparents, and other relatives who had been killed in concentration camps. These personal issues were not easy to resolve. The congress also raised questions for the German analysts. The German analysts had to deal with their family's and their profession's wounds related to the Holocaust. During the proceedings, groups of analysts and psychiatrists raised questions about NATO's aggressive war-like policy toward the Soviet Union. Attacks upon the liberal democracy's stance toward the Soviet Union detracted from the purpose of this special congress, but they served to underline how political issues would simply not disappear as a problem and that psychoanalysis could not avoid them (Kurzweil 1989, 304–5).

Margrit Wreschner Rustow has written an article that described the IPA's 1985 congress in Hamburg. She describes the intense emotional feelings that she experienced returning to the Germany that she was forced to leave as a child. She states that "it took much soul searching and an overcoming of strong, conflicting feelings to attend the congress . . . even after the decision to accept the invitation of the German Psychoanalytical Association had finally been reached" (Rustow 1987, 203). According to Rustow, both the gentile German analysts and the foreign Jewish analysts experienced different sources of psychic pain, and the tension level was high. Rustow quotes the opening remarks of the president of the German Psychoanalytical Association (DPG), Dieter Olmeyer:

> We stand before you, deeply distressed and deeply anguished, but also fully conscious of that course of events that was set into motion by Germans. It is only possible to work through things which are accessible to the conscious, which can again and again and ever more clearly become conscious, which can and must be remembered. The mere passing of time has not healed any wounds, has not cleared the way for any new developments. In . . . recent years, German psychoanalysts have increasingly attempted to become conscious of, and come to terms with, the guilt, the shame, and the mourning which they as Germans have to bear.

He elaborated upon what happened during the Third Reich:

> Psychoanalysis shared the fate of all scientific disciplines for which freedom of thought and absolute truthfulness are of supreme importance and which endeavor to guide mankind on a path which will enable people to understand each other and treat each other in a humane way: it was suppressed, outlawed, and destroyed in National Socialist Germany. (Rustow 1987, 204)

Martin Wangh was a Jewish psychoanalyst born in Germany, forced to flee, and he too had returned. Wangh participated in some of the planning conferences before the congress. Wangh had expected the Hamburg congress to allow the German psychoanalysts to continue the process of coming to terms with their Nazified past. Many of the younger German analysts had started to confront the stonewalling and resistance of their training analysts who wanted no questions raised about what had happened during the Third Reich. Younger analysts, acting in what they believed to be a time-honored way of "remembering and working through," found criticism and even dismissal from training centers when they tried to honestly assess the past. During the planning stage for the congress, Wangh's proposal to support the German psychoanalysts' self-examination during this congress was opposed by the president and some of the Jewish executive officers of the IPA. One Jewish executive officer challenged Wangh's idea by stating, "How could we go to Hamburg and be so offensive to our hosts? It would be tactless. How would it be if he came to Israel and spoke there about the war in Lebanon?" Wangh was shocked by this equation. This incident among the leaders of the international psychoanalytic community reveals how difficult and daunting the task of "remembering and working through" the meaning of the Holocaust remains for Jews and non-Jews alike. Denial and resistance regarding the catastrophic events during the Third Reich are ever present, and they are powerful forces acting to evade or distort the truth.

A compromise was required to decide how much time would be allocated by the congress to the issue of the Nazi influence on psychoanalysis during the Third Reich. Although only one day had been given to the topic of the "Nazi Phenomenon," the restrictions wilted due to the German psychoanalysts' determined effort to confront their past. The German psychoanalysts had organized an extraordinary collection of photographs, documents, and professional articles that were exhibited in such an effective way that the focus of the congress remained on the Nazis' effect on psychoanalysis after the war was over.

The findings of this extraordinary congress were published thereafter in what is referred to as *The Catalog*. The whole purpose "has been to search out the traumatic sequences in order to allow what has been lost to find a voice." The confrontation "had its effects in many ways and many directions. Where this whole process will lead is still open" (Brecht et al. 1985, 77). The result so far has revealed that the German psychoanalysts have started to rise to the standards of the founders.

The Frankfurt School after the War: Mitscherlich and Habermas

In the postwar period in Germany, two intellectuals continued the dialogue between psychoanalysis and political thought: psychoanalyst Alexander Mitscherlich and a professor of philosophy, Jürgen Habermas, who was a product of the teachers of the first-generation Frankfurt school.

Alexander Mitscherlich was a free thinking left-wing student when Hitler came to power. He left Germany to study medicine in Zürich, and when he returned for an illegal visit, he was imprisoned. When the Third

Reich had fallen, Mitscherlich helped the Allies in their investigation of what Nazi doctors had done to prisoners in concentration camps. He was outraged by the barbaric crimes committed in the name of medicine, and he gave public lectures stressing Germany's need to return to its humanistic roots. He cast himself as the conscience of Germany's past crimes, and he saw the only way for Germany to become redeemed was through psychoanalysis.

While psychoanalysis in Berlin would have a different rebirth, Alexander Mitscherlich would pave the way for psychoanalysis to have a new start in Heidelberg. In 1949, Mitscherlich was funded by the Rockefeller Foundation to open a psychosomatic clinic in Heidelberg. He had come to believe that a psychoanalytic understanding of psychosomatic theory was the ultimate cure for the souls and bodies of the German nation. The clinic became the basis for the founding of the Sigmund Freud Institute in Frankfurt am Main. Mitscherlich's public domain was his constant questioning of the underlying psychological factors in Germany that led to the Holocaust. It was his hope to eradicate the boundless aggression and prejudice that led to genocide. He was tireless in his efforts to expose and understand the dynamics of anti-Semitism. Two of his major publications were *Society without the Fathers* and *The Inability to Mourn,* both attempts to examine the psychological effects of the Nazi era on every German and to search for factors related to a national psyche. While Mitscherlich's public posture did much to enhance the image of psychoanalysis in Germany, his main contribution to the professional field was to reiterate the study of psychosomatic medicine originally addressed by Ernst Simmel and Otto Fenichel.

Mitscherlich's contribution to the psychotherapeutic revival in Germany also included his founding of the journal *Psyche* in 1947. The journal has encouraged the continued debate about the Nazification of psychoanalysis during the Third Reich. Discovery after discovery about how the Third Reich altered psychological and psychoanalytic practice has been published, making it more difficult to forget about what happened during the war.

Mitscherlich's tremendous influence was a focus on a multidisciplinary approach, so when Max Horkheimer and Theodor Adorno returned from New York, they became allies with Mitscherlich, and for a period, the Frankfurt school had returned to its roots. Also, for a time, Mitscherlich found common cause with the Frankfurt school's new star student, Jürgen Habermas. In 1958, at a philosophical symposium, a young group of intellectuals attempted to deal with the criticisms aimed at psychoanalysis by countering it with their own arguments. This group of young intellectuals argued that causal validations do not need to be tested by a scientific standard, as the followers of Karl Popper's logical positivism had argued. According to these intellectuals, psychoanalysis had its own scientific method at arriving at truth—interpretative insights. Interpretative insights or hermeneutics, as it would be called, was a means of legitimizing psychoanalysis in a new way. Among its supporters were George Klein, Roy Schaefer, and Jürgen Habermas. For the young Habermas, psychoanalysis had already been incorporated into his understanding of the world.

Jürgen Habermas today is considered one of the most important social scientists in the world. His work synthesizes many trends and themes in Western thought, and he attempts to offer an expanded conception of rationality, allowing us to criticize in a reasonable way our society and the direction it has been taking us. He is attempting to provide a critical analysis of contemporary advanced capitalism within the liberal democratic framework. His intellectual heritage can be traced to his major teachers, Herbert Marcuse, Max Horkheimer, and his mentor Theodor W. Adorno, all part of the Frankfurt school tradition. In his work, Habermas tries to reconnect science and ethics. Unlike other major critics of modernity and rationality, such as Heidegger on the Right and Marcuse on the Left, Habermas is attempting to salvage the Enlightenment's value of reason by modifying and expanding the concept.

Habermas's first exposure to psychoanalysis occurred at a most significant moment for the young intellectual and aspiring academician. The occasion in 1956 was a centennial commemorating Freud's birthday, which also marked the date of Marcuse's first academic return to Germany after the war. Habermas wrote,

> I should mention that the international conference of *Freud in der Gegenwart,* where Marcuse lectured side-by-side with famous analysts such as Alexander, Balint, Erikson, and Spitz, was the first opportunity for young German academics to learn about the simple fact that Sigmund Freud was the founding father of a living scientific and intellectual tradition. (Habermas, in Bernstein 1994, 68)

Habermas went on to say that Marcuse's first lecture sounded "strange and radical" at a time when Freud and Marx were "dead dogs" and practically unknown at German universities. Habermas continued, "For us, the research assistants at the Institute of Horkheimer and Adorno, this was the moment when we faced an embodiment and vivid expression of the political spirit of the old Frankfurt School" (Habermas, in Bernstein 1994, 68). It was in that first encounter between Habermas and Marcuse that the meaning of Freud and Marx and the ultimate meaning of the Frankfurt school's exile in New York became clear to him and why the centennial conference had been organized by Mitscherlich.

In formulating his project, which began in the 1960s and continues today, Habermas was to incorporate aspects of Freud's thinking. Habermas's ultimate goal has been to reformulate and to elaborate upon the theory whose essential task is nothing less than the complete emancipation of that part of humanity living within those states/countries who are governed by a legitimate form of liberal democracy. In this approach Habermas is truly carrying out the original purpose of the Frankfurt school, which was a multidisciplined integration of knowledge to advance what was called critical theory, which would lead to a society that supported human freedom and personal autonomy, and limiting as far as possible the unnecessary constraints of social order. In sum, Habermas has established core principles of historical materialism and class struggle within psychoanalytic theory. This formulation renews the Frankfurt school's ties to its own past.

While an examination of Habermas's critical theory is beyond the scope of this volume, it is perhaps worthwhile to note some additional details in this unique intellectual's life. Habermas was a teenager in Germany at the end of World War II, and what he learned about his country has had a lasting impact on him and has remained a cardinal focus and emotional driving force for his work. In an essay entitled "The German Idealism of Jewish Philosophers," he documents this experience:

> At the age of 15 or 16, I sat before the radio and experienced what was being discussed before the Nuremberg Tribunal; when others, instead of being struck silent by the ghastliness, began to dispute the justice of the trial, procedural questions, and questions of jurisdiction, there was that first rupture, which still gapes. Certainly it is only because I was still sensitive and easily offended that I did not close myself to the fact of a collectively realized inhumanity in the same measure as the majority of my elders. (Bernstein 1994, 2)

For those Germans who were so moved to learn the truth and were willing to listen to the daily pain about the Third Reich, the Holocaust, and the German people, this had to be a devastating and disorienting experience. Habermas's willingness to listen and tolerate the pain would serve him, Germany, and the world well. At this early stage of Habermas's life, despite the specter of the carnage that dominated Germany during his adolescence, he obviously had achieved a level of psychological identity and must have been a profoundly curious young man.

At approximately fifty-five years of age, Habermas discerned a challenge, a slow erosion of the truth about the Third Reich; this must have been reminiscent of what he had heard over the radio forty years before. The historical truth about the Holocaust was starting to slip away, and it was historians, this time, who were starting to distort the motivational factors related to the Holocaust. Habermas must have read one too many articles that diminished or even whitewashed the reality of the Holocaust. In 1986, he decided to assume his historical obligation as a significant intellectual in West Germany and confront these distortions of the truth. The ethical imperative for him simply to tell the truth contributed to the start of the historical controversy in Germany known as the *Historikerstreit* (Historians' Debate).

The *Historikerstreit* is a debate among German intellectuals, for the most part historians, regarding the singularity or uniqueness of the Holocaust. Why is it important for our understanding in this psychoanalytic investigation to discuss the *Historikerstreit?* The first reason is because the *Historikerstreit* parallels the younger German psychoanalysts' attempt to come to terms with their own Nazified past vis-à-vis those conservative forces within the psychoanalytic movement who would prefer to let sleeping dogs lie. Thus, it is of the utmost importance for the rest of the world to appreciate the forces within Germany calling for a continual process of reexamination of the issues and questions related to the Holocaust, opposing those forces that, as Richard Wolin has aptly stated, "want the very posing of the question itself null and void" (Wolin 1995, ix). Another reason, of course, is to document Habermas's contribution and thus demonstrate the kind of impact psychoanalysis has had on one of the most important political philosophers of the twentieth century.

This debate, which erupted in the spring of 1986, was building for a number of years. It is helpful to note some significant events that were going on at that time in Germany and the West. Some saw this debate as an apparent reaction to the aftermath of President Reagan's statement during his 1985 trip to the Bitburg Cemetery, where German soldiers were buried, some of whom were members of the SS. Reagan suggested that they too were victims along with the victims of the Holocaust. The occasion marked the fortieth anniversary of Germany's defeat in World War II. Many Germans, who began reflecting on their national identity and the role they had played internationally since their defeat, appreciated Reagan's position. In addition, 1986 marked the beginning of the 1986–87 Bundestag electoral campaign. At around the same time there appeared publications by several German historians—Ernst Nolte, Michael Stürmer, and Andreas Hillgruber—who voiced a desire to reevaluate and revise, where appropriate, the Germans' understanding of themselves as actors on the world stage.

The controversy was about a nation's memory and its image of itself.

The controversy spread, and eventually focused on a plan for a museum in Berlin that would define Germany's role in the Holocaust during World War II, and its overall national history. The touchstone for this national debate was an article by Ernst Nolte, "The Past That Will Not Pass: A Speech That Could Be Written but Not Delivered," published in a Frankfurt newspaper after a speech Nolte was supposed to give to a group of German intellectuals was canceled for unknown reasons. The implication was that certain intellectuals had prior knowledge that Nolte was going to redefine the nature of the Holocaust and therefore the group moved to deny him an open forum because of the content of the speech. In fact, when it was published, the article did equate the atrocities carried out in the extermination concentration camps with similar crimes committed by the Soviet Union, Turkey, and the Khmer Rouge.

Yet, Nolte had already gone further than just equating the Third Reich with the then Soviet Union. He had already suggested in 1980 that Hitler's policy for the Final Solution could be better understood as a preemptive strike against the Jews who, Hitler had reason to believe, would be enemies of the Reich. Nolte based this on Chaim Weizmann's statement made in the first days of September 1939, to the effect that Jews all over the world would fight on the side of England during this war. Nolte considered the horrible firebombing of Hamburg in 1943 by the Allies, before they knew of the Holocaust, as evidence of "a desire to destroy the civilian population" (Knowlton and Cates 1993, 8).

In his 1980 lecture he already had elaborated on this hypothesis of irrational fear of annihilation as a motive for the Holocaust:

> Those who do not wish to see Hitler's annihilation of the Jews in this connection are perhaps led by very noble motives, but they are falsifying history. In the legitimate search for direct causes, they overlook the chief preconditions, without which all other causes would have been ineffective. Auschwitz is not primarily a result of traditional anti-Semitism and was not just one more case of genocide. It was the fear-borne reaction to the acts of annihilation that took place during the Russian Revolution. (Knowlton and Cates 1993, 13–14)

In response to Nolte and similar articles by Hillgruber and Stürmer, Habermas argued that they were trying to throw off moral constraints and establish a revisionistic narrative in order to equip Germans with a conventional nationalistic identity replete with a national history. Habermas concluded his 1986 article, "A Kind of Settlement of Damages: The Apologetic Tendencies in German History Writing" with the following:

The unconditional opening of the Federal Republic to the political culture of the West is the greatest intellectual achievement of our postwar period; my generation should be especially proud of this. This event cannot and should not be stabilized by a kind of NATO philosophy colored with German nationalism. The opening of the Federal Republic has been achieved precisely by overcoming the ideology of Central Europe that our revisionists are trying to warm up for us with their geopolitical drumbeat about "the old geographically central position of the Germans in Europe" (Stürmer) and "the reconstruction of the destroyed European Center" (Hillgruber). The only patriotism that will not estrange us from the West is a constitutional patriotism. Unfortunately, it took Auschwitz to make possible to the old cultural nation of the Germans binding universalist constitutional principles anchored in conviction. Those who want to drive the shame about this fact out of us with phrases such as "obsession with guilt" (Stürmer and Oppenheimer), those who desire to call the Germans back to conventional forms of their national identity, are destroying the only reliable foundation for our ties to the West. (cited in Knowlton and Cates 1993, 43–44)

Habermas responded to Nolte's public redefinition of the previous historical understanding of the Holocaust in an uncharacteristic manner. He usually writes in a highly abstract style, and in a very measured and impersonal way. The table thumping and moralistic approach of some of the first-generation members of the Frankfurt school was never his style, but he changed his approach regarding the *Historikerstreit*. One can only guess why he responded as he did. Perhaps he heard in Nolte's words a new version of an old theme: the beat of Hitler's famous National Socialist drum and with it the start of another torchlight parade down Unter den Linden. Or perhaps he remembered that the academicians' response in the 1930s to the growth of National Socialism was denial, slight embarrassment at its excessive rhetoric, and perhaps some polite criticisms in their scholarly journals. In any case, it was a strong attack that left no doubts what he thought Nolte was conveying. Habermas had learned the lesson of World War II well; here was one German who was going to stand and fight. In Habermas's pointed attack on Nolte, one sees the intellectual heir of Marcuse and Adorno, the founders of the Frankfurt school who were forced to flee their fatherland. The tradition of Landauer, Fromm, and Frieda Fromm-Reichmann still has a worthy representative in Germany.

Part 5
Some Conclusions

15

The Continuity vs. Discontinuity of Psychoanalysis during the Third Reich

IN THIS FINAL SECTION, WE WOULD LIKE to return to our starting point in the book—namely, to the question of whether or to what extent psychoanalysis survived in Germany during the Third Reich. As we indicated earlier, the books by Geoffrey Cocks (1985, 1997) have taken the position that a historical continuity within the psychoanalytic movement did, in fact, exist during the Third Reich. Our purpose has been to examine this claim. In so doing, we have concluded that Cocks presents a limited view when one considers the crucial defining qualities of the psychoanalytic endeavor.

In Cocks's updated and revised edition of *Psychotherapy in the Third Reich: The Göring Institute* (1997) there are some important departures from the original book (1985) that inspired our investigation into this area. He no longer uses the word "survival" regarding psychoanalysis. Instead, he provides a very rich and meaningful discussion of the continuities and discontinuities within the history of psychotherapy across the period before, during, and after the Third Reich. This puts the history of psychotherapy in a larger context of the history of professionalization in modern Germany and in the West. He states:

> Nazi Germany did not represent a clean break with either the past or
> the future. The Nazi system itself was much more riven with disconti-
> nuities than earlier studies of the aims and actions of its leaders had led

us to believe. These discontinuities in the structure of National Socialism in power, however, allowed for social and economic continuities
with developments before 1933 and after 1945, thus lodging the Nazi
years more firmly into the course of modern German history. (Cocks
1997, 401)

There is much in the above with which we would agree, were we looking at
psychoanalysis as an individual example of the general case of professions
jockeying for power and support from the state. In fact, we find Cocks's last
chapter in the 1997 edition about psychotherapy and the course of German history to be illuminating. However, our lens in evaluating this historical information is slightly different from Cocks's. The focus of our study is
the practice of psychoanalysis. But psychoanalysis represented more than a
profession. It was a revolutionary vision of man in modern society. As such,
it was an idea or set of ideas that informed the method of psychoanalytic
treatment. Our interest was and is in the fate of this idea, and the defining
qualities of this set of ideas, we maintain, must be considered when evaluating the "survival" or continuity versus discontinuity issue. It was Freud's
vision that Hitler hated the most. The ideology of National Socialism rests
on the complete trust of one's Aryan intuition. In Freud's vision we see a
belief in powerful unconscious motivation and in insight and reason to
mediate the demands of our instincts, the demands of reality, and the
demands of conscience. We also see people being given the responsibility of
balancing their commitment to themselves versus society. There is yet
another problem with the emphasis on structure and process within the
larger framework. The issue of professional integrity becomes lost or irrelevant. We have come to realize, however, that looking at individual dynamics and the integrity of individual decisions without understanding the
structural conditions of the particular historical time is just as incomplete
as the reverse approach.

Hannah S. Decker has pointed out a major improvement in Cocks's
latest publication:

When Cocks first published in 1985 he was praised for his research but
chastised by many reviewers for his lack of a moral stand. In the second
edition, published last year, Cocks has revised many of his earlier views.
He now clearly states that Matthias Heinrich Göring was an enthusiastic Nazi who kept Freud's books locked up, that the members of the
Göring Institute were opportunists in their efforts to promote themselves individually and professionally and that by their services they
helped racist society and a murderous regime function. He clearly

states that it is not the thesis of his book that Nazi Germany provided a positive environment to practice psychotherapy for the advancement of science, knowledge and human services in general. But Cocks does say that psychotherapy as an institutional and professional entity faired better under National Socialism than might have been expected and has been assumed. (Decker 1998)

In this regard, we consider Decker's opinion to be correct. However, at another juncture in his latest book, Cocks takes a stance with which we have some concern. In the 1997 edition of Cocks's book, he presents his own position about the professional integrity of the psychotherapists at the Göring Institute when he describes his own reactions to interviewing them in the early 1970s:

> At the time I had not found evidence that any of the members of the Göring Institute had been involved in atrocities, but I was bothered by an understandable desire on the part of the people I was interviewing to justify and defend their activities in Nazi Germany, including their acquiescence, or worse, in the purging of Jewish colleagues. But I decided that I should take advantage of the fact that I was a foreigner who had no other purpose than to describe accurately and dispassion-ately the history of this group of aspiring professionals. The wrestling with the moral consequences could be and has been more successfully carried out by professional descendants in Germany. This did not mean that I would not evaluate the moral consequences of the profes-sionalization of psychotherapy in Germany between 1933 and 1945. (Cocks 1997, 388)

We admire Cocks's commitment to an objective and rational analysis of the facts he found. We also appreciate the need for standards of behavior and sensitivities that one should be aware of when a guest in another's nation. We are, after all, human beings before we are scholars. Notwithstanding such sensitivity, the proposition that the moral issues of psychoanalysis dur-ing the Third Reich best be left to the present-day German psychoanalysts suggests these issues are uniquely German, with no relevance for us in this country at this time. Responsibility to deal with moral and ethical issues of what we study has become increasingly important, as we have witnessed the uses and abuses of science and other areas of study in this century. It is in this context that restraints on any scholar's mandate to deal with ethical issues of one's area of study, be that history, physics, psychology, or genetics, become highly problematic.

The functionalist concept of "organized chaos" is a critical issue in making the argument that psychoanalysis survived the Third Reich, contrary to what two significant psychoanalysts previously concluded (Jones 1962c; Thomä 1969). Does the preponderance of evidence support the view that there were enough gaps or spaces within the organization, out of reach of the totalitarian control, so that the continuity of psychoanalysis was effected? Let us review what occurred. The DPG had been incorporated within the Göring Institute in 1936, and subsequently in 1938 it was disguised by calling it "Working Group A." In this camouflaged way it survived, submerged within the Institute with other schools of psychotherapy. The Göring Institute was established to develop a new integrated form of depth psychotherapy consistent with the essential principles of National Socialism. According to Cocks (1985 and 1997), the psychoanalytic group had survived in the disorganized Nazi regime with its multitude of competing and conflicting agencies. A corollary of this functionalist position is that the vast majority of organizations in the Third Reich were not essentially motivated by ideological goals, but by the more practical goal of treating patients with psychological conflicts or neuroses.

Let us now look at how this was done, and how it presented opportunities for professional growth for psychoanalysts. Cocks helps us here by explaining that apart from the treatment dealt out to those individuals described as presenting "genetic disorders" or as "asocials" like the Jews, homosexuals, Slavs, etc., who were to be eliminated through extermination and sterilization, there was nonetheless an opportunity for psychotherapy in Germany. He concludes that psychotherapy could cash in on the Nazi idea of "'care and control' for the racially pure 'Aryans' who comprised the majority of the people living in Germany" (Cocks 1985, 12). The biological and racial standards of "life unworthy of life" would not fit the typical Aryan who exhibited the more common neurotic conflict that was manifested by most Germans. This view resulted from an ideological as well as psychological definition of mental disorders within the master race. We must note that the very admission that "care" was tied to "control" within the ideological framework of a health care system leads us to the conclusion that psychoanalysis was incompatible with the kind of therapeutic procedures that survived in the Third Reich. The Nazi ideology and German *Zeitgeist* from the mid-1930s until the end of World War II were antithetical to the freedom of thought and respect for differences that is a necessary condition for any form of psychoanalysis or psychoanalytically informed psychotherapy to occur.

Let us now return to one of the major demand characteristics for psychoanalysis—the bond of trust and the establishment of a safe place to explore any and all thoughts or feelings. Cocks accepts and presents the argument by the psychoanalysts that a necessary bond of trust is required between analyst and analysand and that this situation did not exist within Germany. He then presents the Göring Institute as a distinct exception to this rule, supporting his conclusion that Nazi Germany was not a perfect totalitarian order; that conditions existed in which the practice of various modes of psychotherapy, including psychoanalysis, was allowed in the Third Reich. This seems very reasonable. It is hard to argue for a perfect totalitarian order. There must have been many gaps. Were there confidences that were kept, safe places for exploration of fantasy and free association? Undoubtedly there were. But how many? How many would it take for us to conclude that the spirit or geist of psychoanalysis was protected? How many violations would it take for us to conclude that it was destroyed?

Turning next to the evidence on the use of language within the Göring Institute, Cocks offers examples of how carefully each analyst's presentation of case material would be guided into using substitute terms. Instead of the Oedipal Complex, the term used at the Institute was "family complex" (Cocks 1985, 161). There is a real scientific question of whether one can use such diluted terms in a valid fashion without violating significant but subtle meanings. Psychoanalysis is a highly complicated theory of human behavior that requires an integrated and systematic framework. If one asks the question whether or not the terms "pre-Oedipal functioning" and "pre-family functioning" are equivalent, the answer is obvious, even to those who do not understand psychoanalysis. The simplistic nature of the concepts used during that period would have modified the meaning of behavior and the nature of procedures so that it was no longer psychoanalysis. Here we are not referring to changes in language arising from theoretical modifications such as that of the "neo-Freudians." These changes arise in a natural way among competing professionals without the imposition of an external authority. We are referring to the time-honored tendency of totalitarian systems (however imperfect) to enforce changes in language to achieve changes in thinking. In Nazi Germany these changes were to modify a "Jewish science." What was left? The medical practice of confidentiality was also to be violated by practitioners, according to M. H. Göring's command. How often was this done? Other than our own description of M. H. Göring's breaking confidentiality in court to report the thirteen-year-old youngster's rifle collection, we do not know. The fact that the treatment alternative of extermination actually existed when a patient was deemed untreatable within the Institute only leads to further questions about the kind of spirit that pervaded the facility.

In addition, Cocks reveals that Freud's collected works did exist at the Institute, but were kept under lock and key so that not even the psychoanalysts could read these works without permission. Wangh (1991) points out that the place the books were stored was called the "poison closet." Was this evidence for or against survival of psychoanalysis in the Third Reich? The relative lack of availability of these essential works by Freud would suggest the latter conclusion. It would seem that under these controlled circumstances one could hardly conceive of any long-term survival of the practice of psychoanalysis.

Regarding the fate of psychoanalysis within the Göring Institute, we believe that the "intentionalist" approach improves our understanding of what transpired. We believe that the intentionalist perspective helps not only in understanding what happened to psychoanalysis as a profession during the Third Reich, but also what happened to the individual psychoanalysts who practiced at the Göring Institute. We have concluded that the evidence from many sources yields a pattern of events that demonstrates an unbroken sequence consistent with the elimination of the Jewish analysts from the DPG to the ultimate destruction of the spirit of all of psychoanalysis, which was considered a "Jewish science." We will briefly review the most significant lines of evidence that support the intentionalist perspective that the Nazi regime, following the dictates of its ideology, destroyed psychoanalysis during the Third Reich.

After Hitler's rise to power on January 30, 1933, the only other psychoanalytic institute in Germany besides the BPI was destroyed. The Frankfurt Psychoanalytical Institute lost its facilities when the Frankfurt Institute for Social Research was closed because of tendencies hostile to the state. The SA laid waste to the former premises, and all its psychoanalytic members (Karl Landauer, Heinrich Meng, Clara Happel, S. H. Fuchs, Frieda Fromm-Reichmann, and Erich Fromm) were forced to emigrate before the end of that year.

The BPI was also facing Nazi intrusion as soon as Hitler became chancellor. Pressures from the regime led to the gentiles Boehm and Müller-Braunschweig replacing the Jewish members of the board. The Nazi regime and the Party continued to demand various kinds of changes by the BPI. Boehm and Müller-Braunschweig continued to comply. A memorandum by Müller-Braunschweig was an attempt to meet the regime's demand that a second kind of psychoanalysis was required (i.e., a more German kind). There were several threats from the police on vague charges, and in June 1933, Boehm was told that the regime would not tolerate Jewish members. In January 1934, Dr. Kurt Gauger met with members of the various schools of psychoanalysis and psychotherapy in Berlin and revealed that the government wanted to establish a new institute under the leadership of Professor M. H. Göring, cousin to Hermann Göring. All of the schools were expected to cooperate with this plan (Brecht et al. 1985, 115-24). By 1935, the continued pressures by the Nazis finally resulted in all of the Jewish members resigning from the DPG. This sequence of events appears to us to be rather systematic and purposeful. As to the question of whether psychoanalysis had perished, let us summarize the evidence.

Two years after the Nazis took power, over two-thirds of the psychoanalysts were forced to stop practicing. This is a striking bit of datum. Whenever two-thirds of any organization is forced to resign in such an arbitrary way, how can one begin to discuss whether the organization "survived"? The fact that they were Jews is irrelevant. If two-thirds of the U.S. Congress were forced to resign in such a way, could we say the Congress survived?

New evidence has come to light during the past decade suggesting that the psychoanalytic continuum had been severed. In the English language version of *The Catalog*, the addendum contains John Rickman's 1946 report on the psychological status of the three senior psychoanalysts who were at the Göring Institute and who survived the war. Rickman's psychological descriptions of those German analysts he observed and interviewed, without their being aware of the purpose of his visit, contain a multiplicity of information that is relevant to the functionalist-intentionalist dialogue. Rickman's information about the German psychoanalysts is inconsistent with Cocks's conclusion that "Göring was able to cruise safely between the Charybdis of swirling party factionalism and the Scylla of stony state resistance" (Cocks 1985, 175). The qualitative evidence of severe deterioration in the senior psychoanalysts' personalities and ethical functioning from 1933 to 1945 argues against the idea of a safe cruise and against the conclusion that psychoanalysis had survived.

In addition, important evidence exists that by the end of the war the three most senior psychoanalysts had committed serious violations of psychoanalytic principles. *The Catalog* documents how Drs. Felix Boehm, Carl Müller-Braunschweig, and Werner Kemper had changed. Felix Boehm had capitulated on his former scientific and humanistic approach to both homosexual behavior and combat fatigue. By the war's end, he had come to accept the harshest Nazi measures against such individuals, which included the death penalty. Selected portions of Werner Kemper's scientific writings about sexuality were found to be congruent with the requirements of the National Socialist government, and his guidelines on treatment of war neurosis contained what amounted to the death penalty for such sufferers of hypochondria, anxiety, and "weakened will." Müller-Braunschweig's personality had regressed to a lower level of ego functioning than had been noted before. Müller-Braunschweig had also turned over the names of the Jewish analysts to the Italian fascists without any apparent reason. The psychological functioning of all of these psychoanalysts had been adversely affected by the constant psychological stress of working in a totalitarian state and in an institute led by M. H. Göring.

The overall evidence reveals that the Göring Institute had been more Nazified than previously reported. Scientific positions were given up one after the other; the independence of Freudian psychoanalysis was gradually abandoned. It was not just that the National Socialists found the neo-analysis of Schultz-Hencke and the theories of Jung more compatible with their view of the nature of man and society, and therefore favored them over Freudian psychoanalysis. The aims of the New German Psychotherapy of both "healing" and "extermination" were accepted and integrated. The Freudian psychoanalysts were in the position of being spied upon and denounced by their patients and vice versa. With this basic trust impaired, the extreme nature of transference and countertransference issues made Freudian psychoanalysis highly problematic. The critical issue is that the Institute had been more tainted by National Socialism than had been assumed.

M. H. Göring demonstrated by word and deed the paramount importance of the National Socialist ideology. He placed the value of Nazi ideas above the autonomy and integrity of psychoanalytic theory or the lives of its practitioners. The prohibition of Freudian terms, the monitoring of meetings for ideological consistency, the adoption of *Mein Kampf* as a basic text, and the permission to suspend patient-analyst confidentiality at the Göring Institute all lead us to question whether what actually survived was psychoanalysis.

It is our opinion that the argument that psychoanalysis survived, on the basis that it had been incorporated within the institutional structure of the Göring Institute, is not compelling. It relies on the belief in the power of "institutional structures" over time automatically to preserve the essential characteristics of a profession, a science, or even a kind of government, and to safeguard it against all destructive forces. It is our contention that to evaluate the survival of psychoanalysis, the essential nature of the science and the profession must be clearly understood and identified before its survival can be ascertained. We have tried in a rudimentary way to describe the essential nature of the science and profession of psychoanalysis. We have also tried to describe the essential political conditions that are necessary for psychoanalysis to have a reasonable opportunity to be effectively practiced within a society or culture. We have come to the conclusion that while some individual psychoanalysts survived the Third Reich, it was never M. H. Göring's intent that psychoanalysis survive. We believe he was successful in transforming the profession to such a radical extent that its essential ideas and philosophy no longer existed in a form that could be considered psychoanalysis. Thus, we conclude the qualitative and quantitative evidence suggests a historical discontinuity in the practice of psychoanalysis during the Third Reich.

16

Do All Roads We Traveled Lead to Werner Kemper as a Source of Disinformation?

THERE IS ANOTHER ISSUE, related to methodology, that needs to be addressed in the various accounts of what transpired at the Göring Institute. Historians and other observers of history are dependent to some extent on written documents and also what is told to them by participants (oral history). We have already discussed in another chapter the limits inherent in interview data unsupported by other documentation. The following analysis is a specific example of where an informant's conscious or unconscious distortions in reporting may have led to inaccurate conclusions. After assembling and presenting the evidence and having come to somewhat different conclusions than Geoffrey Cocks (as well as Rose Spiegel) regarding the continuity of psychoanalysis, we pondered why these scholars reached the conclusions they did apart from issues of differences in theoretical approach and perspective. One possibility arose, growing out of the realization that much of Cocks's and Spiegel's evidence supporting the hypothesis of psychoanalysis's survival could be traced to information provided by Werner Kemper.

Kemper, one of the leading analysts at the Göring Institute, was also an informant to John Rickman, who interviewed and evaluated the surviving analysts in Berlin in October 1946. In reviewing Spiegel's article and Cocks's book, we found that Werner Kemper had a unique role as informant in each author's approach to the subject. In Cocks's work we found that he had interviewed Werner Kemper three times while each of his other informants were interviewed once (Cocks 1985, 303). In his 1997 expanded edition of his book, Cocks has reduced the number of interviews to two, leaving out the October 17, 1973, interview (Cocks 1997, 435). In the case of Spiegel, she made the point in the text that it was an honor to have interviewed Kemper (Spiegel 1985, 524). We decided that given the significant role Werner Kemper had been given in these two scholars' investigations, it was possible his input had led them astray. Add to this the observation that Regine Lockot, a German authority in this area who tends to emphasize the discontinuities and the way psychoanalysis was destroyed, never had the opportunity to use Werner Kemper as a source. The absence of his personal impact on her provided indirect support for our hunch. We then proceeded to systematically assemble and examine all the information sourced to Kemper—what he said and when he said it. As we examined the evidence from a historical and psychological perspective, we kept finding that we had significant reason to question Kemper's integrity in what he had reported over the years.

In the early 1970s, Cocks started his major project, which was an attempt to figure out what happened to psychoanalysis during the Third Reich. Obviously he had to interview those surviving analysts who were willing to talk to him. Long before the 1970s, the three most senior and powerful psychoanalysts who had practiced at the Göring Institute during the Third Reich were no longer alive. Boehm, Müller-Braunschweig, and Schultz-Hencke had died between 1952 and 1958. Of those analysts still alive, Werner Kemper was by far the most influential and senior analyst who had survived and had a very powerful position during the Third Reich. At the time Cocks started his research, in all probability there was no reported evidence that Kemper collaborated with the Nazi cause. Although unavailable to Cocks for his first book (1985), Rickman's investigation in 1946 had revealed that Boehm and Müller-Braunschweig had collaborated with the Nazis. However, Rickman's evaluation concluded Kemper to be "a serious minded reliable worker" who "would be at home in a liberal culture" (Brecht et al. 1985, 236). In fact, Rickman considered Kemper to be the "keystone" for the future development of psychoanalysis in Germany. In the immediate aftermath of the war, Kemper was able to appear as a person with integrity while evidence about both Boehm and Müller-Braunschweig had emerged revealing the serious compromises they had made with the Nazis. Kemper's capacity to engender trust in his integrity obviously influenced Rickman and also led to a very favorable impression on Spiegel. She and her colleague Gerard Chrzanowski interviewed Kemper and described it as a "privilege" (Spiegel 1985, 524). Spiegel portrays Kemper as a very competent analyst who had been able to analyze Erna Göring, wife of M. H. Göring, who she states was originally a "staunch" Nordic "Nazi" (Spiegel 1975, 491). From Kemper and another source (Baumeyer), Spiegel concludes that Kemper turned Frau Göring's hostility toward Freudian psychoanalysis into supportive friendship. (For example, she would pass along information about analysts who were in danger, therefore saving lives.) From Spiegel's point of view, Kemper seemed to be a reliable source, congenial and forthcoming. Cocks's decision to interview Kemper two times while interviewing the other surviving analysts once strongly suggests he also considered Kemper a reliable informant.

The evidence that clearly identified Kemper's Nazified outlook was only put together later by the editors of *The Catalog* in 1985. Kemper wrote on eugenics laws and population policy. It was found that the book Kemper published in 1942, *Disturbances of the Sexual Capacity of Women: Symptoms, Biology and Psychology of Sexual Function and Orgasm*, revealed "he was implicitly in agreement with National Socialist ideas" (Brecht et al. 1985, 164). The most significant evidence indicating Kemper had become Nazified were the guidelines he helped write for special treatment of the Wehrmacht troops demonstrating signs and symptoms of battle fatigue. As a representative of M. H. Göring, Kemper had participated as a member of a committee of psychiatrists to determine how to assess and treat soldiers with various kinds of psychological reactions. The purpose of this group was to prevent psychogenic reactions from becoming a mass phenomenon as had happened during World War I. The increased psychological disturbance among the Wehrmacht was considered a serious political danger that could impair the army's effectiveness, and worse yet lead to revolutionary action by an informed public. To ensure the army's effectiveness, those diagnosed as "psychopathic" were sent to a "penal company," which was tantamount to receiving the death penalty. For those individuals diagnosed as having "weakened resistance," there was temporary rest, hospital treatment, and psychotherapy. If this failed, the "special" treatment of the penal company was indicated. This "special" treatment was to ensure the troops at the front and those at home would be protected from the destructive effects

> of hypochondriacs of the apprehensive and the weak-willed persons. They tend towards purposeful conflict reactions, that is to say, toward the so-called flight into illness so as to escape more or less consciously from a situation they find intolerable and at the same time to arouse

and exploit the sympathy of those around them. This is the group which, in the first World War in particular, were said to be suffering from "shell shock" (war neurosis). (Brecht et al. 1985, 165)

Kemper was one of the eight members of the committee who made these recommendations, which were completed on May 19, 1942 (Brecht et al. 1985, 164-66). Kemper never made his participation on this committee known to Cocks.

Kemper did, however, make other claims to Cocks. Kemper indicated that since the directors of many of the military clinics around Berlin were former students of the members of the Institute, they cooperated in keeping soldiers alive by playing a "back and forth game." The medical organizations would send endangered soldiers from the hospital to the Göring Institute and back to the hospital again for further testing. They would carry out these delay tactics until the military or government lost interest in punishing the patient. Cocks cites several cases in which this apparently happened (Cocks 1985, 229). On the other hand, there is the evidence of Kemper's signature on the order mandating the death penalty recommendations (Brecht et al. 1985, 165) and Boehm's blatant admission that he sent malingerers to their deaths (Brecht et al. 1985, 237-38). We do not deny Kemper may have saved some lives in the way he described, but he was far from admitting his overall role in participating in one of the crimes of the Nazi regime. We must conclude that Cocks's reliance on Kemper's honesty was an obstacle that kept him from assessing the true nature of the degree of Nazification at the Göring Institute. It also appears that Rose Spiegel's findings were influenced primarily by her interviews with Kemper and with M. H. Göring's son Ernst. This would account for her conclusion that not only did psychoanalysis survive, but that M. H. Göring was actually a hero. On the basis of these findings, we decided to do a careful retrospective analysis of the publications by Cocks (1985), Käthe Dräger (1972), Rose Spiegel (1975 and 1985), Regine Lockot (1985), and Brecht et al. (1985), including Rickman's 1946 interviews. This led us to the conclusion that Kemper was a source of disinformation.

In reporting what happened to the building in which the Göring Institute was housed, Kemper informed Cocks and Spiegel that it was destroyed by Allied bombing (Cocks 1985, 299-300; Spiegel 1975, 488). This was clearly untrue. Müller-Braunschweig's secretary gave Regine Lockot a very detailed description of how the Göring Institute had been destroyed by Soviet troops during the final days of the Third Reich (Lockot 1985, 125-28; 1991a).

In addition, we note that Kemper had identified himself to Rickman in 1946 as a communist, and he also said "that he had so influenced Frau Göring and through her Professor Göring that the Psychoanalytical Society was enabled to keep its entity during the many changes which the Nazi regime entailed" (Rickman, cited in Brecht et al. 1985, 236). In another context Kemper indicated that he played a "hide and seek game" with M. H. Göring about becoming a member of the NSDAP. Kemper stated "we both knew that my position as head of the outpatient clinic demanded such membership especially in an Institute of the Reich." According to Kemper he was able to stall M. H. Göring's constant reminder that he needed to join (Brecht et al. 1985, 180). However, in 1973, in an interview with Cocks, Kemper admitted that had "he been political, he might have joined the Nazi Party in 1933 out of sheer enthusiasm and excitement" (Cocks 1985, 53). This is a far different version than his claim to have been a communist in 1946. Given our current understanding of the emotional climate in the 1970s, the shift from being a communist to being attracted to the Nazi Party reveals an adherence to the "politically correct" attitude of each period. In 1946, the Soviet Union was still one of the victorious allies and a cooperative member of the four powers who ruled Germany. By the 1970s, however, communism was perceived to be a major threat to western democracies.

There are other contradictions that raise questions about Kemper's truthfulness after the war. According to both Spiegel's and Cocks's interviews with Kemper, and Rickman's report in the addendum of *The Catalog*, Kemper claimed that during the war Erna Göring went from being a "staunch Nordic Nazi" to being a more relaxed person and more friendly toward psychoanalysis (Spiegel 1975, 491; Brecht et al. 1985, 236). However, according to Lockot, Erna Göring was not liked by most of the staff who worked at the Institute. An example of what led to her unpopularity was her unpredictable demands. A year-and-a-half before the end of the war, she required that staff greet her with "Heil Hitler." If a staff member would meet her demand, she would not respond with a reciprocal "Heil Hitler" but a "good morning" (Lockot 1985, 82). This description of events reveals Erna Göring to be both unstable and still an ardent Nazi at a point in time when Kemper's claim would suggest the contrary. Another factor that raises significant questions about Kemper's integrity is the fact that at the end of the war, when Erna Göring came to him almost blind and without a place to live, he turned her away when she came for help (Lockot 1985, 87; Cocks 1997, 354). Given his benevolent statements about both M. H. Göring and Erna Göring when he was interviewed after the postwar period, his behavior at a moment of truth revealed something other than a kindly attitude. With respect to Kemper's 1946 claim to Rickman that he was able to influence M. H. Göring through his analysis with Erna Göring, the present evidence suggests this is not true (Lockot 1985; Brecht et al. 1985).

The problems about Kemper's testimony continued to emerge as we looked over all aspects of the evidence that was reported and the dates involved. In trying to ascertain why Käthe Dräger incorrectly reported that only 5 percent of the members of the Göring Institute were Nazis in an otherwise very accurate and insightful article describing how psychoanalysis was destroyed (1972, 200), we decided to investigate the issue. We found that in 1972 Kemper had cited this 5 percent figure to both Feiner (1975, 543) and Chrzanowski (1975, 495). We deduced that since Dräger was still a candidate while Kemper was a senior member of the Institute in 1935, she probably learned this figure from him. We consider Kemper's estimate that 5 percent of the members of the Göring Institute were also Nazi Party members to be a likely attempt at manipulating the truth. Kemper was not only a full member of the BPI since 1933 (Eickhoff 1995, 950), his position of authority actually increased after the BPI was incorporated into the Göring Institute. Given the fact that the training at the Göring Institute was fashioned after psychoanalytic centers, it required the new candidates to participate in therapy seminars and have supervised experience in providing therapy, and traditionally gave the senior members of the Institute a great deal of intimate information about each candidate. Given that there existed such a high percentage of Nazi Party members at the Institute, and given the prevailing Nazified climate at the time, there was no reason for candidates to keep their party affiliation hidden. In fact, there was every reason to share this information. Therefore, the 5 percent figure Kemper provided both Feiner and Chrzanowski must be considered a conscious deception.

Returning to Rickman's interview with Boehm, we repeat how hostile and yet honest Boehm was during that encounter. He admitted that in evaluating members of the armed forces, if he found them malingerers they were executed (Brecht et al. 1985, 237–38). The manner in which Kemper apparently responded to Cocks's inquiry suggests that Kemper was far more evasive. He also painted a much more positive impression of the outcome of these evaluations. He indicated that if one of the military patients he saw was in danger of being punished, he would participate in bureaucratic gamesmanship until the military lost interest in the matter (Cocks 1985, 229). This was obviously not the only activity in which he participated regarding these military patients. His endorsement of the death penalty in the guidelines for evaluating the military was a gross omission on his part during the interview with Cocks.

Finally, concerning the issue of diagnosis at the Göring Institute, in 1943 Kemper put into effect a new evaluation form for the outpatient clinic that he headed. This evaluation form included the ideologically derived racial categories developed by Erich Jaensch. The diagnoses used the officially approved racial character types that designated the likely end result for individuals found not to be pure "Aryan." Kemper claimed these diagnoses were only included as a formality (Cocks 1997, 233). Given the degree of distortion already described, it is more likely that this was a rationalization rather than the truth.

What we have concluded about Kemper has to do with the facts he reported to others about what happened to psychoanalysis during the Third Reich. He provided enough information to a sufficient number of people to allow us to find significant patterns of distortion of truth. Despite the fact that he was a source of disinformation, as a person he remains an enigma. His capacity to survive was a strength, as was his ability to gain the trust of others. However, his most obvious characteristic was his interpersonal loyalty. During the Third Reich he never betrayed the Marxist activities of John Rittmeister and Edith Jacobsohn. In postwar Germany, he protected Nazi-leaning colleagues from the Allies. We learned the most about his personality in our interview with Regine Lockot in 1994. He was a compromiser, a person who wanted everyone to get along together, and he had a strong need for harmony among members of his group. Kemper tried to balance the positions of Müller-Braunschweig and Schultz-Henke. He dealt with the intense sibling rivalry among the analysts in a counterphobic way. In other words, his compromises were the result of elaborate defenses—"we all have to get along." He apparently tried to keep his marriage intact despite his wife's indiscretions with other men. He risked starting his career over in South America after having survived the worst years in postwar Berlin. When his plans did not succeed in South America, he returned to Berlin and found that the DPG had split into two groups. Characteristically, when the head of the DPV wanted a commitment of loyalty, he refused to take sides. While Kemper's propensity for slanting the truth has distinct problems, on balance his personality and motivations cannot be considered malignant (Lockot 1994c).

In sum, then, we believe that Werner Kemper was a source of disinformation to Cocks, and indeed to all others who interviewed him. In speaking to Rickman, Boehm stated about Kemper: "That man is a diplomat, he has no enemies and no friends" (Brecht et al. 1985, 237). A "diplomat" perhaps; but as part of his diplomacy he was an individual determined to gloss over his own role and that of others in the Göring Institute. He valued the well-being of his colleagues over truth, and the needs of government. In so doing, we believe he contributed to creating an incorrect impression about the continuity of psychoanalysis during and after the Third Reich.

Only Cocks can ascertain how much he was influenced by Kemper. As psychologists, however, we recognize a fundamental law of learning: that which is learned first is critical in influencing how and what we learn subsequently. It is interesting to note that Cocks is slightly more critical of Kemper in his 1997 book than previously. To his professional credit as a historian, he has significantly reorganized his account of what happened at the Göring Institute during the Third Reich.

If, in fact, we are correct in our assessment, the crucial variable might be that we never met Kemper in person. Kemper's capacity to adapt to the ever-changing political and professional realities from the 1930s to the 1970s is as close to Woody Allen's character "Zelig" as any we know. Kemper appears to be a psychological chameleon who could take on the characteristics of new groups as they changed. He was able to fit in effectively to the shifting organizational realities of the original BPI; the period of transition after the Nazis came to power; the early and late phases of the Göring Institute; the immediate unstable conditions for psychoanalysts after Germany's defeat; the initial phase of the negotiations of the DPG with the IPA; and his return to Berlin after an extended period in which he lived in Brazil. It was during this last period, in 1973, that Cocks interviewed him. Although major inconsistencies in his reports, letters, and interview data can be found (letter from Werner Kemper and Harald Schultz-Hencke to District Health Authority, Brecht et al. 1985, 193 and 262), his professional competence, his capacity to fit in, and the trust he engendered led teachers, analysts, colleagues, patients, and students to hold him in high regard.

17

Thoughts about Psychoanalysis in Germany

Perspectives and Prospectives

ONE OF OUR FINAL TASKS IS TO DESCRIBE the status of psychoanalysis in Germany today. Our study would not be complete without an assessment of the role of psychoanalysis in the reunified Federal Republic of Germany. Germany is a liberal democracy with a parliamentary system whose economic system is a social market economy. Due to the reunification, Germany has spent more than half a trillion dollars to rebuild the former East Germany. Despite this vast expenditure of funds, the government still supports the practice of psychoanalysis by including it under its health insurance coverage. Psychoanalysis became a part of the health care package of services provided all Germans under a universal health care program.

A historical perspective is needed to understand how Germany's health care system works. The path toward the present comprehensive coverage of psychological disorders by practicing psychoanalysts, including psychologists, in Germany has been a long and uneven road with some bizarre twists and turns to be sure. However, the history of German health care dates back to the thirteenth century when coal miners banded together to establish "sickness-funds" for injured workers. In the latter part of the nineteenth century, Otto von Bismark established a social welfare system in order to prevent Marxist parties in Germany from gaining more political power. Part of the welfare program was health care insurance that made use of the previously established sickness funds.

At the end of World War II, Germany was in ruins, and its population was experiencing a massive degree of suffering. In order to alleviate the suffering of the German people, the newly elected conservative chancellor, Konrad Adenauer, was committed to maintaining the benefits of Bismark's welfare programs. Ludwig Erhard became a leading figure in the postwar effort to rebuild the German economy. Trusted by both Adenauer and the victorious allied powers, Erhard was appointed the first minister of economics in 1949, a position he held until 1963. Committed to avoiding some of the graver pitfalls of the Weimar era, especially class warfare, he was determined to establish policies that promoted equality among the people. The origin of his economic programs was grounded in the theoretical work of the economist Walter Euken of the "Freiburg school," which held that labor and capital were equal partners in establishing a social market economy that was neither pure Marxism, National Socialism, laissez-faire capitalism, nor Keynesianism (Braun 1990; Hardach 1980; Radke 1995). The social market system uses the free market economy in a way that "is organized by a comprehensive framework that defines the boundaries of competition" (Krieger 1993, 840). It was developed to "produce a stable set of market policies that are implemented by coordination among public and private sector actors and improve—not impede—economic competitiveness" (Krieger 1993, 840).

One of the better features of the present German welfare program is its provision for universal health coverage. Within the development of its health care policies, the Federal Republic of Germany was to be the first and only country to meet Freud's challenge to provide psychoanalytic treatment to the "large masses of people who suffer from neurosis no less than the rich" (Jacoby 1986, 65; Thomä 1983). It is ironic that the same nation that created the horrors of the Holocaust would eventually make the "Jewish science" of psychoanalysis available to its entire population (Jacoby 1983, 65; Thomä and Kächele 1994, 203). Thus, the limited impact of Marxism in the development of the health care policies in the Federal Republic of Germany would serve to meet one of Freud's most idealistic predictions.

It is interesting to note that the initial sickness funds of the thirteenth century grew into what has been called a "corporatist system." Historically, corporatism has been a system whereby the major groups or factions in a society negotiate to solve a problem. As such, it was used in various times by rulers to limit the autonomy of the individual and to squelch democracy. However, its use in the present context appears to be limited in scope and, therefore, does not necessarily seem to us to diminish the overall democratic quality of the nation. In the present corporatist system now used in Germany there are three groups: the *workers,* the *providers,* and the *insurance companies* (if one temporarily leaves the government out), which have to negotiate with each other on how to administer the programs. The feature that makes this system work effectively is a negotiating process whereby the parties have to resolve any conflicts between themselves and be able to compromise.

How then does the present health insurance work with reference to psychoanalysis? The following information is a personal communication from German psychoanalyst Regine Lockot. From the 1970s until January 1999, all psychoanalytic fees were covered by a form of third-party payment. As of January 1999, patients may be expected to contribute something, such as a 10DM (Deutsche Mark) copay for a 100DM session. There are varieties of health insurance plans (*Krankenkassen*), including private and public (*Gesetzliche*). The public plans and most of the private plans will pay for psychoanalytic sessions. If you are licensed as an analyst, then,

> For patients that you want to treat with psychoanalysis you can start with 160 sessions—after your case study had convinced the psychoanalytical expert, who recommends the insurance to pay the session. After 160 sessions, you can ask for 80 more and then for 60 more (altogether 300 sessions). And when the patient suffers under a dramatic crisis, then it is even possible to ask for more sessions. It depends on the psychoanalytical expert if he recommends it to the insurance or not.
> (Lockot 1998)

For nonpsychoanalytic patients one also calls the insurance provider after three to five sessions. For short-term therapy, one gets twenty-five sessions. Usually, however, this is not enough, so the therapist then conducts a psychoanalytic case study in order to get fifty additional sessions. Then, if it can be demonstrated that the treatment is helping the patient, another thirty sessions are authorized with possibly twenty to forty more (Locket 1998). As in our country, there are other psychotherapeutic orientations available supported by the insurance companies, including Gestaltist, cognitive, behavioral, and Jungian.

When one considers the status of psychoanalysis in Berlin in 1945, it was obvious that the road back to integrity would not be a short or easy one. However, the combination of honest soul-searching about a compromised professional past with the enlightened health care insurance program within which psychoanalysis has been incorporated suggests that the German psychoanalytic movement has made significant progress. More time is needed to assess whether this new interaction between a quasi governmental system and the profession of psychoanalysis will enable the essential spirit or geist of psychoanalysis as Freud conceived it to flourish. Will this unique system of good faith bargaining between workers, employers, and insurance companies continue to work? Can both the government and the corporations be kept from destroying the basic integrity of psychoanalytic treatment as has happened in the United States? This would be a major accomplishment in the days of increasing global competition and a world situation in which the individual's productivity rather than well-being has become paramount. So far, the available research about the medical parts of the system appears promising, as one typical study reports. The following advantages in Germany's health care system have been clearly recognized by Wahner-Roedler, Knuth, and Juchems in the Mayo Clinic Proceedings (1997, 1061–68). They state that "Germany has met the four objectives that any health-care system should strive for: (1) universal access, (2) high-quality care, (3) ability of patients to choose their physicians, and (4) socially acceptable cost." We would like to add the factor of the existence of a system in which the integrity of the doctor-patient relationship remains fundamental. Will the German psychoanalytic community learn from what happened in the United States? Perhaps the unique nature of the social market economy will not rule out psychoanalysis as a legitimate professional endeavor as has happened in America. Sixty-six years after the BPI had set the psychoanalytic standards for the world, the world once again has a real interest in the practice of psychoanalysis in Germany.

In examining the fate of psychoanalysis during the Third Reich, what became clear was the importance of the social-political-cultural context in which psychoanalysis emerged and was practiced. The National Socialists were quite obvious in their demands that treatment affecting the behavior of their citizens needed to be compatible with their goals and their vision of man and society. They were not, however, the only group who envisioned psychoanalysis as a handmaiden to political and social change. We have shown that the efforts of the Marxist psychoanalysts extended the scope of psychoanalysis beyond the realm of treating the individual to a goal of human liberation. In today's world, we have come to take for granted the effect of context upon a given phenomenon. So Freud's caution that psychoanalysis not get involved in politics, and Jones's preference that it be politically neutral, appear naïve to us today. In fact, Bernard von Nitzschke

(1991) has convincingly argued that a neutral or nonpolitical interpretation of psychoanalysis by the IPA had the inevitable consequence of Nazifying the DPG. Prior to 1933, the IPA leadership had debated the political stance of the profession. The neutral path it selected resulted in the adjustment of the DPG to the ideological goals of National Socialism.

How then are we to look at the reciprocal relationship between psychoanalysis and the system in which it operates? Does psychoanalysis want to be "left alone?" Does it want something out of the system (government, corporation) such as financial support or the opportunity to influence the system? In return for this, are there legitimate demands a government or corporation may make upon psychoanalytic thinking and practice? And if one accepts the ever-present tension between the individual and the society, how should psychoanalysis balance the conflicting demands and concerns of the health of the individual and the health of society? A study of how psychoanalysis functions within the German health care system shows us how complex the questions are we have just raised. After psychoanalysis had been operating within the German health care system for thirty years, Joachim Danckwardt and Ekkehard Gattig (1998) conducted a historical assessment of what transpired. These authors revealed that the standards of psychoanalysis had been violated by the introduction of a new parameter — the insurance system.

The regulatory code added a third party to the classical dyadic relationship between patient and analyst. Danckwardt and Gattig also indicated that psychoanalysis was further complicated by the state's propensity to introduce both rigidity and ideological distortions that interfere with the psychoanalytic process. Between 1986 and 1992 further problems were introduced when the regulatory code limited the number of sessions to three times per week. The change was justified by the state on the grounds that the efficacy of psychoanalysis had not been scientifically justified. This in turn led to the establishment of a research commission set up by the DPV to demonstrate the need for high frequency long-term psychoanalysis. The financial support for the project was provided by the IPA and DPV. As a result of this project and other research evidence, high frequency psychoanalytic treatment has "once again come to be acknowledged as a scientifically justified technique." Analytic psychotherapy can now be conducted four times per week for no longer than eighty therapeutic hours. Danckwardt and Gattig suggest that this restriction has no scientific basis but rather is based on an irrational legalistic system developed by state authorities. The state's restrictions place significant problems on the training of psychoanalysts. However, the DPV still requires its candidates to complete two analytic treatments at sustained high frequency to the satisfaction of their training analysts. The authors indicate that the DPV could refuse to participate because of the state's interference, but conclude that this would only serve to be a self-defeating course for the future of psychoanalysis.

In addressing the relationship between psychoanalysis and political thought, we eventually veered away from distinctions between the politics of the Left and the politics of the Right. Instead, we focused upon the degree of freedom and autonomy vs. control in any given society, whether of the Left or of the Right. We asked what conditions in a society or political system nurture and support the profession and practice of psychoanalysis, and what conditions hinder it. Evidence was cited to support the proposition that psychoanalysis will thrive in, and is most suited to, liberal democracies in which the values of knowledge, freedom, and autonomy of the individual are shared by psychoanalysis. It is also possible for psychoanalysis to exist in authoritarian societies where the strict demand for behavioral compliance is limited to the public sphere and an individual is entitled to his private life and thoughts. Totalitarian systems appear to be the only ones that are incompatible with psychoanalysis. A radically intrusive state that attempts, through the use of terror, to reach into the most private spheres of the individual's mind in order to assure loyalty and control has a chilling effect on the mental processes of interpersonal relations that are involved in the psychoanalytic endeavor. Germany from 1933 to 1945 was such a state. What happens to mutual trust, confidentiality, free association, and the respect for individual rights under conditions of terror, where fear of retaliation and punishment are commonplace? Thus, despite opportunities for professional growth during the period of 1933–1945 for the analysts remaining in Germany, and despite the survival of an institutional infrastructure by the end of the war, the *geist*, or spirit, of psychoanalysis was modified in so many basic ways as to render the use of the term "survival" inappropriate. This conclusion derives from a certain way of understanding the role of individuals, institutions, and larger units of society in determining outcomes of history.

"Functionalists" have provided convincing evidence of the validity of their model in explaining much of what happened during the Third Reich. However, we have concluded that it is incomplete in explaining the Holocaust and what happened to psychoanalysis. Institutional analysis tells us much. But what have we done to our understanding if we omit individual intention (both conscious and unconscious), individual behavior, and individual choice and accountability?

Another set of questions arises as to the problems inherent in applying psychoanalytic inquiry to historical material from the past, where most, if not all, of the participants are no longer living. A live patient is able to freely associate to material and to react to the analyst's interpretation in ways that eventually validate or fail to validate that interpretation. Those conditions of validating interpretations obviously do not pertain here.

For those who were still alive and were interviewed, and for the children of those involved who were interviewed, there are other problems. The Nazi period is so emotionally charged and the participants were so universally blamed after they lost the war, it is hard to imagine anyone embarking on a journey of recollection motivated by the desire to understand, rather than the desire to justify or consciously mislead. Despite these caveats, we conclude it would be shortsighted to abandon the use of the psychoanalytic method to understand people and events from the Third Reich. Freud's theory is still capable of generating many hypotheses that can advance our understanding of a given phenomenon. What has been suggested by scholars in the field is the supplementation of interview material by archival evidence such as letters, diaries, and other records.

One needs to ask whether the conclusions we have reached about the German analysts during the Third Reich have any generalizability to other situations, other countries, and other times. Lawyers have a saying that extreme cases make bad law, and Germany during the Third Reich was indeed an extreme case. It was an unforgettable experience to read the testimony of those who spoke of the gradual nature of the changes that took place. If one's personal style was that of accommodating to authority, at what point ought it to have been obvious that this style led to morally unacceptable choices? Indeed, hindsight is relatively easy, insight much less so, and foresight is very rare.

Why was it that only two gentile psychoanalysts, Bernard Kamm and Martin Grotjahn, seemed to have understood much more than others what National Socialism was about and what implications it would eventually have for the survivability of psychoanalysis? They left Berlin with their Jewish colleagues. Unfortunately, we ask this question too late for Bernard Kamm and Martin Grotjahn to answer—both have since died. Yet, on June 3, 1980, Bernard Kamm responded to a letter from Regine Lockot. In Kamm's letter there is a key passage that illuminates the problems involved in trying to conduct psychoanalysis in Nazi Germany:

> If the environment in which analysis is to be undertaken comes too
> close to the harshness of the originally threatening environment—or
> even surpasses it—it is impossible for the poor analysand to make the

liberating discovery that the original threats have lost their power. . . .
An analyst would deceive and endanger himself and his analysand, if he
were to act as though everything could now be thought through and
freely discussed. (Brecht et al. 1985, 181)

We would have thought this kind of understanding about psychoanalysis was consistent with the state of the art in the 1930s and not so exceptional. Yet, exceptional it would prove to be.

Thoughts on the second hundred years of psychoanalysis in Germany seem to fall into two distinct but related themes. The first is working through the damage that has been done during the Third Reich, and the second is learning to anticipate possible future pitfalls. It is important to consider the relevance of the Nazi's transformation of ordinary psychoanalysts into people who would by the stroke of a pen assign a patient to death in compliance with new Nazi medical principles. During the course of the Third Reich these psychoanalysts were systematically rewarded, coerced, and intimidated by ever increasing threats of violence and/or economic deprivation, and as a result they gradually conformed. Twelve years earlier the same psychoanalysts would have considered such behavior on their part as inconceivable. This process did not happen overnight, nor were the psychoanalysts in question "willing executioners" on January 30, 1933.

The grim reality of the Third Reich will probably never be repeated in that same way again — we would know what to look for. As psychoanalysis moves into its second century, what can be remembered and what must be anticipated? More specifically, what remains to be done by the IPA, the German psychoanalytic community, and the gentile and Jewish psychoanalysts throughout the world who have been influenced by the Third Reich? It is clear that psychoanalysis does not exist in a vacuum. The Third Reich was neither the first nor will it be the last political organization to try to use psychoanalysis for its own ends. Psychoanalysis must ask which uses of its method are legitimate and consistent with its spirit, and which are not. We are in favor of Wangh's proposal regarding the need for a continued mourning process by both the German and Jewish psychoanalysts. Wangh suggested that the mourning process be carried out in meetings every several years with both the German and Jewish psychoanalysts as participants. He quotes Alexander Mitscherlich (1947) who stated, "Only when we recognize and confess what happened and why it happened, and how we were participants in the planning of it, can we, Germans, be healed." Thus, the task is one of overcoming the inability to mourn. Mitscherlich thought that the problem of mourning in Germany was avoided by the manic rebuilding of their war-destroyed Germany. The rebuilding, or "German

Economic Miracle," can be understood as a therapeutic experience of restoring depleted ego resources that was necessary for real mourning to begin. However, during the stage of Germany's recovery, there existed in Germany the view that the "Third Reich was only a dream." This phase of psychological recovery prevented the German people from falling into a melancholic state, a serious stage of depression from which recovery becomes difficult at best.

Wangh maintains that a conspiracy of silence arose between both sides of the Shoah (i.e., for the evildoers as well as for the victims). The collective silence established itself everywhere; shame and guilt for being a survivor was a frequent reaction. In discussing the German inability to mourn the loss of the Führer, there was also an intense defense against the underlying shame, guilt, and fear. By denying the death of Hitler, the German people also were unable to come to terms with the ego ideal he had been for them, as well as the promises he made. Worse yet was the fact that at his death, Hitler blamed the entire *Volk* for having failed him personally. After working through these narcissistic wounds, the German psychoanalysts who had taken upon themselves the feelings of guilt of past generations would then face their Jewish colleagues and together they would help each other complete the process of mourning that their parents or grandparents delegated to them. From June 1 to June 6, 1994, the first such meeting took place to heal the wounds and find mutual understanding. It was a "good beginning" (Wangh 1996, 300).

APPENDIX

The following report was submitted by John Rickman to Sylvia Payne, then president of the British Psycho-Analytical Society. Another, more confidential version was sent to Ernest Jones who was then president of the International Psychoanalytic Association. Those confidential passages appear here in brackets.

Report on Dr. John Rickman's Visit to Berlin
To Interview Psychoanalysts, 14 & 15 October 1946

1. Reason for visit:

(a) To find out whether among the leading members of the German Psycho-Analytic Society there were any who might be suitable as assistants to the personnel of G.P.R.B. (German Personnel Research Branch of the Control Committee).

(b) To discover what influence, if any, twelve years of the Nazi regime had on the personnel working in a special branch of the psychological field, both in respect of the development and enrichment of theoretical concepts and in respect of the capacity of cooperating with others in the same field but using different methods.

(c) To establish contact again with German citizens engaged in the same line of scientific research, in order to ascertain whether there were ideas which might be usefully imported into England.

2. Technique employed during the Investigation

(a) By personal interview on the basis of a friendly colleaguely conversation.

(b) to use the opportunity, at a scientific meeting of the German Psycho-Analytical Society, to observe what tensions, if any, existed among the members, and how those tensions were dealt with.

3. (This method of investigation, if indeed it merits the grand name of "method," arises out of the experience of War Office Selection Boards in England: though of course no tests were employed, the atmosphere was sustained of a friendly, colleaguely visit, so that whatever embarrassment arose during these visits and discussions should be so far as possible the spontaneous generation in those visited.)

4. Fräulein Käthe Dräger, Berlin-Charlottenberg, Gotha-Allee 5.

A teacher and lecturer at a training school for teachers. Aged about 45. 1 had not seen this person before, but we quickly got on to terms of friendly discussion about the development of psycho-analysis in our respective countries, and a little about our personal experiences during the war. She struck me as a person of unusual integrity of character and with fine psychological perception. During the war she was employed in teaching and part-time private psychotherapeutic practice. She felt keenly the isolation from the development of psycho-analysis in other countries, particularly England and America, and was eager to hear of the way in which the Institutes in those countries had developed.

5. Fräulein Marguerite Steinberg, Berlin-Charlottenberg, Gotha-Allee.

Also a teacher, aged about 45, lecturer at a training school for teachers. Fräulein Steinberg came in during my talk with Fräulein Dräger (they both share the same flat) and I had the same impression of her integrity of character, though perhaps she has not such a fine psychological perception. She too was most eager to hear about the way in which the Berlin Psychological Institute had flourished after its transplantation to America.

The outstanding impression is that these two, though not themselves particularly creative minds, had during the Nazi regime kept a clear picture of what psycho-analysis ought to be, that they were tolerant of other schools of thought, and that their attitude to their fellow-beings was generous. They received the presents (coffee, toilet soap, cocoa and such like things) with the modest pleasure of one receiving something from a colleague, and the many-coloured skeins of material for darning stockings with a truly feminine joy.

They asked about the bombing of London, and when I said that it was nothing like as bad as Berlin and that there had been no panic, they seemed quite relieved. They spoke with appreciation of Dr. Kemper and said that under difficult circumstances he had behaved very finely. I did not mention the name of Dr. Müller-Braunschweig nor of Dr. Boehm — nor did they.

These two were people whom I would not hesitate to accept as members of a psycho-analytical Society — if one conversation were anything to go by — in respect of their personalities. I should say that their technical equipment was, in the case of Fräulein Dräger, high; in the case of Fräulein Steinberg, of moderate quality. Neither, by reason of their shyness, seem to be suitable for employment in G.P.R.B.

6. Dr. Werner Kemper, Berlin-Charlottenberg 9, Sensburgher-Allee 6.

Aged about 45, Director of the Central Institute für Psychogene Erkrankungen, the address of which is Berlin-Schöneberg, General Paperstrasse Block 16A. Dr. Kemper gives the impression of one rather aged for his years, of great vigour and endurance, with considerable self-control. We discussed some of the difficulties which arise when people with two different schools of thought are forced to co-operate in such a joint enterprise as running a clinic. He told me that he had recently displaced Dr. Schultz-Hencke, formerly Director of the Institute of which he (Kemper) was now head, but that the difficult situation could probably be handled in a satisfactory way and that Schultz-Hencke's scientific ideas were in a stage of evolution. We had little time for talk, but my impression was that of a serious-minded, reliable worker who, like Fräulein Dräger and Fräulein Steinberg, would find themselves at home in a liberal culture.

[I was told, to a certain extent by him, more by Fräulein Steinberg and, later, Müller-Braunschweig that Kemper had analysed the wife of Professor Göring (Hermann Göring's aunt) for several years including some of the war years for a severe neurosis and he had maintained a good psycho-analytical rapport and produced good results despite the fact that he was a Communist, and that he had so influenced Frau Göring and through her Professor Göring that the Psycho-Analytical Society was enabled to keep its entity during the many changes which the Nazi regime entailed. I understand that the handling of the negative transferences in situations of this kind are unusually delicate, but he said if you don't handle them, the patient's case and your state is worse than the first, which gives I think a measure of his ability and courage.]

Although I think he might be suitable for work with G.P.R.B., as I felt that he was "white," but in any case he would require a training in the technique; I think it would be a great pity to take him away, as he is the keystone to the development of this branch of the science in Germany at the present time.

7. Dr. Müller-Braunschweig, Berlin-Schmargedorf, Sulzaerstrasse 5.

Aged about 67. I had met Dr. Müller-Braunschweig at various international congresses during the last twenty-five years. We welcomed each other cordially and he introduced me to his family. [His family consisted of his wife, a daughter aged about 18, who from things which were just not said I gathered had fared badly from the Russian soldiery, and a son about 18 or 19. Frau Müller-Braunschweig, an oppressed German hausfrau, listened eagerly to everything I had to say about England, and seemed to me desirous to make contact with foreigners again.]

A noteworthy feature of the interview was his lack of interest in the development of psycho-analysis in England and America. A second feature was the extent to which the conversation was devoted by him to the question of obtaining privileges and physical advantages, such as more coal and extra food, on which he hinted that I should assist him with the authorities, pointing out that his colleague, Dr. Boehm, was well equipped, as he had a place in the country where he could grow his food. A third point was his attitude towards receiving presents (of the kind that I have already mentioned): he became quite greedy and remarked on the frightful malnutrition that he had suffered during the war. [I know the situation is bad, but I also heard from his wife that they had presents from America. I can only give it as an impression, but it seemed to me that in some way his personality had deteriorated in this respect.]

A fourth point was the emphasis he laid on the conflict between the Russians and the English. He told me a good deal about his colleagues, most of it slightly in their disfavour, but he did not mention Dr. Boehm.

[His wife asked me how, in my opinion, German psycho-analytical colleagues would be received abroad (this was a propos of an international psychoanalytical congress). I said that I could only speak for myself as an Englishman, but that I felt sure that we, of a liberal tradition, would welcome people of whatever nationality who had throughout trials and difficulties cherished the spirit of democracy, the love of liberty and truth in their hearts. She gave a sigh of relief and looked, as I thought, in rather a frightened way at her husband. He sucked in his breath a bit, and with more hesitation looked relieved.]

Unlike Dr. Kemper I believe his personality has deteriorated during the Nazi regime. He is utterly unsuitable for employment in G.P.R.B., and I think he is "dark grey."

8. Dr. Felix Boehm, Berlin W.50, Kulmbackerstrasse 3.

Aged about 65. I met Dr. Boehm first about 24 years ago in Berlin, and have seen him on several occasions since at International Congresses. I rang him up and proposed visiting him at his flat. He hedged several times and told me that he would be seeing me at the meeting of the Society. Eventually he was persuaded to permit me to visit him.

He was obviously a very embarrassed man and found it difficult to look me in the face. He was eating his dinner at the time (for which event there were mutual apologies) but made occasion to walk all over the room looking for odd things to show me, by way as it seemed to me of interrupting the conversation. He praised the Americans, denounced the Russians, and showed his lack of tact and underlying hostility by asking me if I, as an Englishman, could explain why it was the German women despised the British troops. They were cold and frigid sexually and hadn't the spunk of the Americans, and were altogether a queer lot. He said he didn't know much about English people, but was interested in their obvious lack of sexual characteristics.

[He opened the discussion of the difficulties in the British Psycho-Analytical Society "caused by those two women, Anna Freud and Melanie Klein." Anna Freud, he said, used to be queen and wouldn't take second place. Melanie Klein had left Berlin, had gone to London, was received as a queen and wouldn't give way to Anna Freud. "And as for Anna Freud, those books (pointing to the Gesammelte Schriften of Freud) are a Bible. Freud was her Pope, and she was to be Pope. That difficulty you've got in England won't be solved until those two are gone." He then asked what I had to say about it, to which I replied that I thought distance tended to increase the apparent differences in psychological outlook, and that many of us in England thought we could see ways by which these scientific differences could be reconciled. "Scientific differences—pshaw! It isn't that, it's a personal squabble between two women." The degree of vehemence and attack in this conversation was most pronounced.]

The conversation was in German, and he professed that he understood a little English, and when I tried him at an early stage of the interview on the simplest statements in English he professed not to understand. Later on in the interview he got excited in regard to Dr. Kemper and burst out in fluent English, "That man's a diplomat: he has no enemies and no friends." I think he realised that he had made a mistake in betraying his knowledge of English, for he proceeded again to rummage in cupboards, looking for things to interest me, for example, a tin of English tobacco. Indeed I have never had an interview with a colleague in which he spent so much time with his head in a cupboard or down on his knees looking for a book which turned out not to be there, and so on. I gave him the same presents as I had given the others, and he took them in an off-hand manner and he seemed somewhat angry.

[During the war he was employed in the Army in the rank of Captain, to decide whether men were malingerers or not. If he pronounced them malingerers, they were—he drew his finger across his throat and made a noise like "esh" and chucked his thumb over his shoulder and then shrugged. He was not employed in any of the officer selection work in the German Army, but was just employed in the Yes or No answers, malingerers or not, in the case of deserters and neurotic soldiers. He also said that he had taken great risks in defying the Nazis and continuing to treat the Jews, but of course he could only do this if they didn't look Jewish.] I had the impression that he was not telling the truth about himself when he said that he had taken risks in defying the Nazis and continuing to treat Jews, or that if this part were true, it was to deflect my attention from something else.

He is utterly unsuitable for employment in G.P.R.B., and I think it likely that he is "dark grey," if not "black."

[Comparing these five persons in the order named they seem to me to represent a ranking in psychoanalytical qualities and in the integration of their personalities, or disintegration, during the stress of 12 years of the Nazi regime and war. But the first three are widely separated from the latter two, and I think Boehm is much the worse of the two deteriorated ones.]

9. I attended a lecture given by Dr. Müller-Braunschweig to students who were taking up the study of psycho-analysis and similar aspects of psychology. [This lecture course was used, as were the others according to Müller-Braunschweig, to cast the net fairly wide and then to observe the students and single out those who showed psycho-analytical interest and promise above the average. A quite independent training course for psycho-analysts had not yet been got under way.]

There were 34 students present. The light had gone out in that district that night, so we sat round a candle. I was therefore only able to make a study of the expression of about eight of the students present.

The level of the lecture was low intellectually; was exclusively devoted to sex, praising it as an activity,—and seemed to me far remote from the quality that you expect in a scientific man. [There was practically no reference to the unconscious or to conflict, his handling of the question of sex was crude, he said that Freud used the word sex in a wider sense than most people, and it was a much misunderstood subject, and he would be discussing it more at greater length later and so on.] Four of the students, I was able to observe, were in turn puzzled and incredulous;

two were disgusted, manifestly; two were wrapped in thought and I was unable to form any impression of their reactions. [Comparing this group of students with others I had occasion to observe in Germany, they were dull and unresponsive, and certainly Müller-Braunschweig's dogmatic and aggressive manner seemed to me to do little, if anything, to pave the way to these seminars which were the pride of the higher German educational institutions. I must say I was profoundly disappointed, and still more so when I had a few days later seen a group of German students handled in a way to bring out that old seminar warmth and enthusiasm.] Müller-Braunschweig came up to me afterwards and asked me what I thought of his lecture, whether I thought it was good or not, but I contented myself with saying that I was mainly concerned with the reaction of the audience, but he did not ask me what that was.

10. At the meeting of the German Psycho-Analytical Society Dr. Müller-Braunschweig was in the chair, Dr. Boehm was present, Fräulein Dräger and Steinberg, Kemper came in later, as did Schultz-Hencke still later, and there were two or three others, relatively recent members. Müller-Braunschweig began the meeting by saying that they had an English colleague present. He would not ask him to speak now but later on in the evening, at the end of the scientific session. He then opened a discussion on a paper by Frau Hanna Ries, a former pupil of his, who came to England in January 1939, and read a paper at the British Psycho-Analytical Society on the basis of which she was admitted to full membership. A copy of this paper had been sent to him and it had been circulated to about half a dozen members.

In a short time he was denouncing the paper, thumping the table with his fist, saying it was a bad paper, it wasn't psycho-analysis, "and, just think of it, the British Society actually, on the basis of this paper, made her a member!" The theme of the badness of the paper and the stupidity of the British Society recurred during his half-hour's discourse, during which time he was several times corrected, either by Fräulein Dräger or Fräulein Steinberg for misquoting the paper or obviously misinterpreting it.

He then asked Dr. Boehm to speak, but realising that something was amiss, apologised for his display of anger but said it was justified by his intolerance of a bad presentation of psycho-analysis. Dr. Boehm repeated the attacks on the paper, got muddled with the theme, and had to be corrected by Fräulein Steinberg. Dr. Boehm had not taken his eyes off the table the whole evening except to make a few glances at one or other person present, was obviously uncomfortable.

After these displays of animosity, most people present, except myself, were uncomfortable. Fräulein Steinberg made a few meditative remarks, that the paper was difficult to understand in parts, and apologised for not having circulated a better abstract of it. Fräulein Dräger made a few remarks in the same key, and then I was asked to speak.

When framing my remarks I have in mind that the person whose paper they were discussing had been an Associate Member of this Society, was a pupil of the

President, and left for England in January 1939, had been accepted by British colleagues and had been elected to full membership six months before. I knew that she had been in friendly contact with many members including the five names above, and had sent parcels of food to reach each of them through American channels, but who nevertheless might well be an object of envy and her esteem among the British an occasion of resentment.

Accordingly, after expressing pleasure at being able to join in their scientific deliberations, after the separation of the war, and though not coming officially, brought good wishes from people in England, I proceeded to remark how strange it was that they who had only seen the paper, and some of them only in abstract, should have spent so much time in condemnation of it and have paid comparatively little heed to its clinical merits. Boehm and Müller-Braunschweig were angry, Fräulein Dräger and Steinberg agreed with me. Kemper saw the point and nodded but seemed neither to agree nor disagree.

I next went on to say that the reason why she had been admitted to the Society was not on the merits or demerits of the paper (and how few people after all can write a really good scientific paper), but on the kindness and good clinical feeling of its writer, and that we appreciated her spirit and integrity in our Society. This remark, even more than the former one, produced the division which I have already mentioned, but Kemper was now warming up towards her.

The third point I made, not in respect of this paper, was in regard to the way in which the pre-Nazi Berlin Institute of Psychology, which had been anti-psychoanalytical, when transferred to America (that was because the Nazis kicked them out) and psychologists on the basis of the integration of their two research findings had proved of very great use during the war, and would continue to enrich sociological and psychological studies. Fräulein Steinberg and Dräger and Dr. Kemper now got keenly interested.

My next point related to the reorganization in the British Psycho-Analytical Society whereby the Presidency is not held for long by any single person, but the leadership revolves. In this way younger people are given an opportunity for developing constructive leadership, and a far greater number take part in the government of the Society. Kemper's response was a lively interest as was that of Fräulein Steinberg and Dräger; Boehm was so angry that he pushed his chair back from the table and Dr. Müller-Braunschweig was quite embarrassed.

I next spoke about the prospect of international congresses and of the meeting of people who had been on opposite sides during the war, and said that I was sure that a common interest, liberty of thought, scientific method, a democratic government and love of truth would overcome any obstacles which an irruption like a war inevitably places upon communications and scientific co-operation. The response to these remarks again showed differences: Boehm remained cold, Müller-Braunschweig softened his attitude a bit and took in a breath as if relieved of a strain, but continued to look about him to see how others took it. Kemper nodded in a matter of fact way, as if to say "of course," and I thought that Fräulein

Dräger and Steinberg, without any self doubt, were looking forward to a meeting of colleagues on a basis so to speak of spiritual equality. [General Comments: If one just man could save Sodom and Gomorrah, Berlin is trebly saved in Fräulein Dräger, Steinberg, and Dr. Kemper. The low morale, tactlessness, and indeed spite of Drs. Boehm and Müller-Braunschweig cannot, I think, be ascribed to under-feeding, bombing and the strain of war, nor indeed to twelve years of Nazi regime. Those two are most troubled men, and I think it likely that if they appear at Inter-national Psycho-Analytical Congresses, their presence inevitably will require excep-tionally careful handling.

There are some very fine, untroubled spirits in Germany to whom as col-leagues I think we owe every opportunity for affording them development which reasonably we can give. We must also be prepared to deal with deteriorated and objectionable personalities in the process of rendering those good ones our aid.

I have no plans for action and do not propose to take any steps in this matter (beyond the private one of arranging to have food sent to them).]

JOHN RICKMAN

REFERENCES

Aly, Götz, Peter Chroust, and Christian Pross. 1994. *Cleansing the fatherland: Nazi medicine and racial hygiene.* Trans. Belinda Cooper. Baltimore: The Johns Hopkins University Press.

Anthony, E. James, and Bertram J. Cohler, eds. 1987. *The invulnerable child.* New York: Guilford Press.

Archives of the British Psycho-Analytical Society, Institute of Psycho-Analysis, London.

Arendt, Hannah. 1973. *The origins of totalitarianism.* New York: Harcourt Brace Jovanovich.

Baruch, Lucy Rickman. 1999. Personal correspondence, April 23.

Bellak, Leopold. 1993. *Confrontation in Vienna.* Larchmount, N.Y.: C.P.S.

Berlin Document Center, Berlin. Various documents pertaining to M. H. Göring.

Bernstein, Richard J., ed. 1994. *Habermas and modernity.* Cambridge, Mass.: MIT Press.

Brainin, E., and I. J. Kaminer. 1984. Psychoanalyse und Nationalsozialismus. In *Psychoanalyse und Nationalsozialismus: Beiträge zur Bearbeitung eines unbewältigten Traumas,* ed. Hans Martin Lohman, 86-105. Frankfurt am Main: Fischer Taschenbuch Verlag.

Braun, Hans-Joachim. 1990. *The German economy in the twentieth century.* London: Routledge.

Brecht, Bertolt. 1944. *The private life of the master race: A documentary play.* Trans. Eric Russell Bentley. New York: J. Laughlin, New Directions Book.

Brecht, Karen, Volker Friedrich, Ludger M. Hermanns, Isidor J. Kaminer, and Dierk H. Juelich, eds. 1985. *Here life goes on in a most peculiar way: Psychoanalysis before and after 1933.* Trans. Christine Trollope. Hamburg: Verlag Michael Kellner. (Original work published in 1985).

Brecht, Karen, Volker Friedrich, Ludger M. Hermanns, Dierk H. Juelich, Isidor J. Kaminer, and Regine Lockot, eds. 1985. *Hier geht das Leben auf eine sehr merkwürdige Weise weiter: Zur Geschichte der Psychoanalyse in Deutschland.* Hamburg: Verlag Michael Kellner.

Breitman, Richard. 1991. *The architect of genocide: Himmler and the Final Solution.* Hanover, N.H.: University Press of New England.

Bullock, Alan. 1962. *Hitler: A study in tyranny.* Rev. ed. New York: Harper-Collins.

———. 1993. *Hitler and Stalin: Parallel lives.* New York: Random House, Vintage Books.

Burleigh, Michael. 1994. *Death and deliverance: "Euthanasia" in Germany 1900-1945.* Cambridge: Cambridge University Press.

Burleigh, Michael, and Wolfgang Wippermann. 1991. *The racial state: Germany, 1933-1945.* Cambridge: Cambridge University Press.

Caplan, Jane. 1988. *Government without administration: State and civil service in Weimar and Nazi Germany.* New York: Oxford University Press.

Childers, Haraldas, and Jane Caplan, eds. 1993. *Reevaluating the Third Reich.* New York: Holmes and Meier.

Childers, Thomas. 1998. *World War II: A military and social history.* Cassette Video Recording, no. 1, part I. Springfield, Va.: The Teaching Company.

Chrzanowski, Gerard. 1975. Psychoanalysis: Ideology and practitioners. *Journal of Contemporary Psychoanalysis* 11: 492-500.

Clay, Lucius D. 1950. *Decision in Germany.* Garden City, N.Y.: Doubleday and Company.

Cocks, Geoffrey. 1983. Psychoanalyse, Psychotherapie und Nationalsozialismus. *Psyche* 37: 1057-1106.

———. 1985. *Psychotherapy in the Third Reich: The Göring Institute.* New York: Oxford University Press.

———. 1990. The professionalization of psychotherapy in Germany, 1928-1949. In *German professions: 1800-1985,* eds. Geoffrey Cocks and K. Jarausch. New York: Oxford University Press.

———. 1992. Repressing, remembering, working through: German psychiatry, psychotherapy, psychoanalysis and the "missed resistance" in the Third Reich. In *Resistance against the Third Reich: Supplement. The Journal of Modern History* 64: 204-16.

———. 1996. The politics of psychoanalytic memory in Germany [Review of *Ein Jahrhundert Psychoanalytische Bewegung in Deutschland: Die Psychotherapie unter dem Einfluß Freuds*]. *Psychohistory Review* 24: 207-15.

———. 1997. *Psychotherapy in the Third Reich: The Göring Institute.* Second edition, revised and expanded. New Brunswick: Transaction Publishers.

———. 1998. *Treating mind and body: Essays in the history of science professions, and society under extreme conditions.* New Brunswick, Transaction Publishers.

———. 1999. Personal correspondence, August 26.

Connelly, J. 1996. The uses of Volksgemeinschaft: Letters to the NSDAP Kreisleitung Eisenach, 1939-1940. *The Journal of Modern History* 68: 899-930.

Danckwardt, J., and Gattig, E. 1998. Opinion-psychoanalysis and the health insurances in Germany. *International Psychoanalysis* 7(2) [online]. Available: http://www.ipa.org.uk/nl_1998-7-2.htm.

Dawidowicz, Lucy S. 1986. *The war against the Jews: 1933-1945*. New York: Bantam Books.

———. 1991. *From that place and time: A memoir 1938-1947*. New York: Bantam Books

———. 1993. *The holocaust and the historians*. Cambridge, Mass.: Harvard University Press.

Decker, Hannah S. 1977. Freud in Germany: Revolution and reaction in science 1893-1907. *Psychological Issues Monograph* 46. New York: International Universities Press.

———. 1998. Comments on Goggins' Paper [Psychoanalysis during the Third Reich: Its Relevance Then and Now]. November 14. Symposium conducted at the fifty-first annual convention of the Texas Psychological Association, Houston, Texas.

Deutsch, Helene. 1973. *Confrontations with myself: An epilogue*. New York: W. W. Norton.

Diller, Jerry Victor. 1991. *Freud's Jewish identity: A case study in the impact of ethnicity*. Rutherford, N.J.: Fairleigh Dickinson University Press.

Dräger, Käthe. 1972. Psychoanalysis in Hitler's Germany: 1933-1949. Trans. J. Friedberg. *American Imago* 29: 199-214.

Dührssen, Annemarie. 1994. *Ein Jahrhundert Psychoanalytische Bewegung in Deutschland: Die Psychotherapie unter dem Einfluß Freuds*. Göttingen: Vandenhoeck and Ruprecht.

Eickhoff, Friedrich-Wilhelm. 1995. The formation of the German Psychoanalytical Association (DPV): Regaining the psychoanalytical orientation lost in the Third Reich. *International Journal of Psycho-Analysis* 76: 945-56.

Erickson, John. 1983. *The road to Berlin: Continuing the history of Stalin's war with Germany*. Boulder, Colo.: Westview Press.

Erikson, Erik H. 1958. *Young man Luther*. New York: W. W. Norton.

———. 1963. *Childhood and society*. New York: W. W. Norton.

———. 1964. *Insight and responsibility: Lectures on the ethical implications of psychoanalytic insight*. New York: W. W. Norton.

———. 1975. *Life history and the historical moment*. New York: W. W. Norton.

Etkind, Alexander. 1997. *Eros of the impossible: A history of psychoanalysis in Russia.* Boulder, Colo.: Westview Press.

Feiner, Arthur H. 1975. The dilemma of integrity. *Contemporary Psychoanalysis* 11: 500–509.

———. 1985. Psychoanalysis during the Nazi regime. *Journal of the American Academy of Psychoanalysis* 13: 537–45.

Fenichel, Otto. 1945. *The psychoanalytic theory of neurosis.* New York: W. W. Norton.

———. 1967. Psychoanalysis as the nucleus of a future dialectical-materialistic psychology. *American Imago* 24: 290–311.

Fine, Reuben. 1990. *The history of psychoanalysis.* New expanded edition. New York: Continuum.

Fischer, Klaus P. 1995. *Nazi Germany: A new history.* New York: Continuum.

Fitts, Paul M. 1946. German applied psychology during World War II. *The American Psychologist* 1: 151–61.

Fleming, Gerald. 1982. *Hitler and the final solution.* Berkeley: University of California Press.

Foster, M. A. 1983. *The world at war.* Briarcliff Manor, N.Y.: Stein and Day.

Freud, Ernst, ed. 1960. *Letters of Sigmund Freud.* Trans. Tania and James Stern. New York: Basic Books.

Freud, E., L. Freud, and I. Grubrich-Simitis, eds. 1985. *Sigmund Freud: His life in pictures and words.* Trans. C. Trollope. New York: W. W. Norton.

Freud, Sigmund. 1930. *Civilization and its discontents, The standard edition, XXI.* London: Hogarth Press.

Freud, Sigmund, and William C. Bullitt. 1967. *Thomas Woodrow Wilson: Twenty-eighth president of the United States: A psychological study.* Boston: Houghton Mifflin.

Friedländer, Henry. 1995. *The origins of Nazi genocide: From euthanasia to the Final Solution.* Chapel Hill, N.C.: University of North Carolina Press.

Friedländer, Saul. 1993. *Reflections of Nazism: An essay on kitsch and death.* Trans. Thomas Weyr. Bloomington: Indiana University Press.

Friedrich, Carl J., ed. 1954. *Totalitarianism.* Cambridge, Mass.: Harvard University Press.

Friedrich, Otto. 1972. *Before the deluge: A portrait of Berlin in the 1920s.* New York: Harper and Ross.

Friedrich, Volker. 1989. From psychoanalysis to the great treatment psychoanalysis under National Socialism. *Political Psychology* 10: 3–26.

————. 1995. The internalization of Nazism and its effects on German psychoanalysts and their patients. *American Imago* 2: 261-79.

Gay, Peter. 1988. *Freud: A life for our time.* New York: W. W. Norton.

Geuter, Ulfried. 1992. *The professionalization of psychology in Nazi Germany.* Trans. Richard J. Holmes. New York: Cambridge University Press.

Gifford, Sanford. 1994. Between two wars: Psychoanalysis in Europe, 1918-1938. *History of Psychiatry* 17: 649-65.

Gleason, Abbott. 1995. *Totalitarianism: The inner history of the cold war.* New York: Oxford University Press.

Glover, Edward. 1956. *Freud or Jung?* New York: Meridian Press.

Goldhagen, Daniel J. 1996. *Hitler's willing executioners: Ordinary Germans and the Holocaust.* New York: Alfred A. Knopf.

Göring, M. H., and C. G. Jung. 1934. Geheimrat Sommer zum 70. *Zentralblatt fuer Psychotherapie* 7: 313-14.

Griffin, Roger. 1993. *The nature of Fascism.* London: Routledge.

Grotjahn, Martin. 1987. *My favorite patient: The memoirs of a psychoanalyst.* Frankfurt am Main: Verlag Peter Lang.

Hale, Nathan G. 1971. *Freud and the Americans: The beginnings of psychoanalysis in the United States, 1876-1917.* New York: Oxford University Press.

————. 1979. From Berggasse XIX to Central Park West: The Americanization of psychoanalysis, 1919-1940. *Journal of the History of the Behavioral Sciences* 34: 299-313.

————. 1995. *The rise and crisis of psychoanalysis in the United States: Freud and the Americans, 1917-1985.* New York: Oxford University Press.

Happel, Peter. 1994. Personal communication, New York City, March 23.

Hardach, Karl. 1980. *The political economy of Germany in the twentieth century.* Los Angeles: University of California Press.

Harris, B., and A. Brock. 1991. Otto Fenichel and the left opposition in psychoanalysis. *Journal of the History of the Behavioral Sciences* 27: 157-63.

Heimannsberg, Barbara, and Christoph J. Schmidt, eds. 1993. *The collective silence: German identity and the legacy of shame.* San Francisco: Jossey-Bass.

Hilberg, Raul. 1992. *Perpetrators, victims, bystanders: The Jewish catastrophe: 1933-1945.* New York: Aaron Asher Books, HarperCollins.

Hobsbawm, Eric. 1994. *The age of extremes: A history of the world, 1914-1991.* New York: Pantheon Books.

Hoffman, Peter. 1977. *The history of the German resistance, 1933-1945.* Trans. Richard Barry. Cambridge, Mass.: MIT Press.

International Films (Producer), and J. Goebbels (Director). 1933. *Hitler's first radio broadcast as chancellor: February 10, 1933.* [Film]. (Available from International Historic Films, P.O. Box 29035, Chicago, Ill. 60629).

International Journal of Psycho-Analysis. 1968. 49: 151.

Jacobsohn, E. 1971. Annie Reich (1902-1971). *The International Journal of Psychoanalysis* 52: 334-36, 355.

Jacoby, Russell. 1986. *The repression of psychoanalysis: Otto Fenichel and the political Freudians.* Chicago: University of Chicago Press.

Johnston, William M. 1972. *The Austrian mind: An intellectual and social history, 1848-1938.* Berkeley: University of California Press.

Jones, Ernest. 1962a. *The life and work of Sigmund Freud.* Volume 1: *The formative years and the great discoveries 1856-1900.* New York: Basic Books.

————. 1962b. *The life and work of Sigmund Freud.* Volume 2: *Years of maturity 1901-1919.* New York: Basic Books.

————. 1962c. *The life and work of Sigmund Freud.* Volume 3: *The last phase, 1919-1939.* New York: Basic Books.

Jung, Carl G. 1930. Your Negroid and Indian behavior. *Forum* 83: 193-99.

————. 1964. *Civilization in transition.* Collected works, volume 10. Trans. R. L. Hull. New York: Pantheon Books.

Kaes, Anton, and Jay Martin, eds. 1994. *The Weimar republic sourcebook.* Los Angeles: University of California Press.

Kenny, Anthony, ed. 1994. *The Oxford history of western philosophy.* Oxford: Oxford University Press.

Kernberg, Otto F. 1998. President's column. *International Psychoanalysis* 7(2) [on-line]. Available: http://www.ipa.org.uk/nl_1998-7-2.htm.

Kestenberg, Judith S. 1994. Personal communication, Sands Point, N.Y., December 10.

King, Pearl, and Riccardo Steiner, eds. 1992. *The Freud-Klein controversies 1941-45.* London: Tavistock/Routledge.

Knowlton, James, and Truett Cates, trans. 1993. *Forever in the shadow of Hitler? Original documents of the Historikerstreit, the controversy concerning the singularity of the Holocaust.* Atlantic Highlands, N.J.: Humanities Press International.

Krieger, J., ed. 1993. *The Oxford companion to politics of the world.* New York: Oxford University Press.

Kurzweil, Edith. 1985. Collective amnesia: A review of *Psychotherapy in the Third Reich: The Göring Institute. Partisan Review* 52: 144-49.

————. 1989. *The Freudians: A comparative perspective.* New Haven: Yale University Press.

————. 1996. Psychoanalytic science: From Oedipus to culture. In *Forced migration and scientific change: Émigré German-speaking scientists and scholars after 1933*, eds. M. G. Ash and A. Söllner. Cambridge: Cambridge University Press.

Langer, Walter C., and S. Gifford. 1978. An American analyst in Vienna during the Anschluss, 1936-1938. *Journal of the History of the Behavioral Sciences* 11: 37-54.

Lifton, Robert J. 1986. *The Nazi doctors: Medical killing and the psychology of genocide.* New York: Basic Books.

Lockot, Regine. 1985. *Erinnern und Durcharbeiten: Zur Geschichte der Psychoanalyse und Psychotherapie im Nationalsozialismus.* Frankfurt am Main: Fisher Taschenbuch Verlag.

————. 1988. Wiederholen oder Neubeginn: "Skizzen zur Geschichte der 'Deutschen Psychoanalytischen Gesellschaft' von 1945-1950." *Jahrbuch der Psychoanalyse* 22: 218-35.

————. 1991a. Personal communication, Berlin, March 21.

————. 1991b. Die Nachwirkungen des Nationalsozialismus auf Gruppenbildungen der psychoanalytischen Organisation in Deutschland (1945-1951). *Luzifer-Amor: Zeitschrift zur Geschichte der Psychoanalyse* 4: 51-77.

————. 1994a. Ein Versuch über die unbewußte Darstellung von Schuld und ihrer Abwehr—dargestellt am Beispiel der Deutschen Psychoanalytischen Gesellschaft. *Luzifer-Amor: Zeitschrift zur Geschichte der Psychoanalyse* 7: 121-35.

————. 1994b. *Die Reinigung der Psychoanalyse: Die Deutschen Psychoanalytische Gesellschaft im Spiegel von Dokumenten und Zeitzeugen (1933-1951).* Tübingen: edition diskord.

————. 1994c. Personal communication, Berlin, June 2.

————. 1998. Personal communication, Berlin, June 23.

Lohman, Hans Martin, ed. 1984. *Psychoanalyse und Nationalsozialismus: Beiträge zur Bearbeitung eines unbewältigten Traumas.* Frankfurt am Main: Fischer Taschenbuch Verlag.

Maidenbaum, Aryeh, and Stephen A. Martin, eds. 1991. *Lingering shadows: Jungians, Freudians and anti-Semitism.* Boston: Shambhala.

Mayer, Milton. 1955. *They thought they were free: The Germans 1933-45.* Chicago: University of Chicago Press.

McGuire, William, ed. 1988. *The Freud/Jung letters: The correspondence between Sigmund Freud and C. G. Jung.* Trans. Ralph Manheim and R. F. C. Hull. Cambridge, Mass.: Harvard University Press.

Micheels, Louis J. 1989. *Doctor #117641: A holocaust memoir.* New Haven: Yale University Press.

Michels, Verena. 1995. Personal correspondence, November 1.

Middlebrook, Martin. 1988. *The Berlin raids: R.A.F. bomber command winter 1943-44.* New York: Viking Penguin.

Molnar, Michael, trans. and annotator. 1992. *The diary of Sigmund Freud 1929-1939: A record of the final decade.* London: Freud Museum Publications.

Müller, Ingo. 1991. *Hitler's justice: The courts of the Third Reich.* Trans. Deborah L. Schneider. Cambridge, Mass.: Harvard University Press.

Müller-Hill, Benno. 1988. *Murderous science: Elimination by scientific selection of Jews, Gypsies, and others, Germany 1933-1945.* Trans. George R. Fraser. New York: Oxford University Press.

Nitzschke, Bernd. 1991. *Psychoanalyse als "un"—politische Wissenschaft. Zeitschrift für Psychosomatische Medizin und Psychoanalyse* 37: 31-44.

Orwell, George. 1977. *1984.* New York: New American Library.

Padfield, Peter. 1993. *Himmler: Reichsführer-SS.* New York: Henry Holt.

Payne, Stanley G. 1980. *Fascism: Comparison and definition.* Madison: University of Wisconsin Press.

Perrault, Gilles. 1969. *The Red Orchestra.* Trans. Peter Wiles. New York: Simon and Schuster.

Pollock. George H. 1994. Trauma, loss and creativity: Milton Kestenberg Holocaust memorial lecture. Stern Auditorium, Mount Sinai Hospital, New York, December 18.

Powers, Thomas. 1993. *Heisenberg's war: The secret history of the German bomb.* New York: Alfred A. Knopf.

Proctor, Robert N. 1988. *Racial hygiene: Medicine under the Nazis.* Cambridge, Mass.: Harvard University Press.

Radke, Detleff. 1995. *The German social market economy.* London: Frank Cass and Company.

Rangell, Leo. 1980. *The mind of Watergate: An exploration of the compromise of integrity.* New York: W. W. Norton.

Rangell, Leo, and Rena Moses-Hvushovski. 1996. *Psychoanalysis at the political border: Essays in honor of Rafael Moses.* Madison, Wis.: International Universities.

Read, Anthony, and David Fisher. 1992. *The fall of Berlin.* New York: W. W. Norton.

———. 1994. *Berlin rising: Biography of a city.* New York: W. W. Norton.

Rensmann, Lars. 1996. Psychoanalytic Anti-Semitism. [Review of *Ein Jahrhundert Psychoanalytische Bewegung in Deutschland: Die Psychotherapie unter dem Einfluß Freuds* by Annemarie Dührssen.] *Psychohistory Review* 24: 197-206.

Reuth, Ralf Georg. 1993. *Goebbels*. Trans. Krishna Winston. New York: Harcourt, Brace.

Roazen, Paul. 1971. *Freud and his followers*. New York: Da Capo Press.

———. 1992a. *Helene Deutsch: A psychoanalyst's life*. New Brunswick, N.J.: Transaction.

———. 1992b. *Freud and his followers*. New York: Knopf.

———. 1992c. The Freud-Klein controversies: 1941-1945. [Review of *The Freud-Klein controversies: 1941-1945,* eds. Pearl King and Riccardo Steiner]. *Psychoanalytic Books* 3: 391-98.

———. 1993. *Meeting Freud's family*. Amherst: University of Massachusetts Press.

———. 1995. Personal communication. Martha's Vineyard, Mass., August 20, 21, and 22.

Rustow, W. Margrit. 1987. Psychoanalysis and Germany: A re-encounter fifty years after Hitler. *Israel Journal of Psychiatry and Related Sciences* 24: 203-9.

Simmel, Ernst. 1932. Nationalsozialismus und Volksgesundheit. *Der Sozialistische Arzt* 8 (September-October 1932): 162-72.

———. 1994. War neuroses and 'psychic trauma.' In *The Weimar Republic source book,* eds. A. Kaes, M. Jay, and E. Dunendberg. Los Angeles: University of California Press.

Sklar, Dusty. 1977. *The Nazis and the occult*. New York: Dorset Press.

Smith, Jean Edward. 1990. *Lucius D. Clay: An American life*. New York: Henry Holt.

Snyder, Louis L. 1989. *Encyclopedia of the Third Reich*. New York: Paragon House.

Speier, Sammy. 1993. The psychoanalyst without a face: Psychoanalysis without a history. In *The collective silence: German identity and the legacy of shame,* ed. Barbara Heimannsberg and Christoph J. Schmidt; trans. Cynthia Oudejans Harris and Gordon Wheeler, 61-72. San Francisco: Jossey-Bass Publishers.

Spiegel, Rose. 1975. Survival of psychoanalysis in Nazi Germany. *Journal of Contemporary Psychoanalysis* 11: 479-92.

———. 1985. Survival, psychoanalysis and the Third Reich. *Journal of the American Academy of Psychoanalysis* 13: 521-36.

Spiegel, Rose, Gerard Chrzanowski, and Arthur H. Feiner. 1975. On psychoanalysis in the Third Reich. *Journal of Contemporary Psychoanalysis* 11: 476-79.

Steiner, Riccardo. 1988. "C'est une nouvelle forme de diaspora . . ." La politique de l'émigration des psychanalystes d'après la correspondance d'Ernest Jones avec Anna Freud. *Revue Internationale d'Historie de la Psychoanalyse* 1: 263-321.

———. 1989. "It's a new kind of Disapora . . ." *International Review of Psychoanalysis* 16: 35-78.

Strasser, Otto. 1940. *Hitler and I*. Trans. Gwenda David and Eric Mosbacher. Boston: Houghton Mifflin.

Sterba, Richard F. 1985. *Reminiscences of a Viennese psychoanalyst*. Detroit: Wayne State University Press.

Tarrant, V. E. 1995. *The red orchestra: The Soviet spy network inside Nazi Europe*. John Wiley and Sons.

Toland, John. 1976. *Adolf Hitler*. New York: Anchor Books, Doubleday.

Thomä, Helmut. 1969. Some remarks on psychoanalysis in Germany, past and present. *International Journal of Psychoanalysis* 50: 683-92.

———. 1983. The position of psychoanalysis within and outside the German University: Psychoanalysis in Europe. *Bulletin of European Psychoanalysis* 20-21: 181-99.

Thomä, Helmut, and H. Kächele. 1994. *Psychoanalytic practice*. Volume 2. London: Jason Aronson.

Trevor-Roper, H. R. 1947. *The last days of Hitler*. New York: Macmillan.

Tyson, Robert L. 1998. Secretary's column. *International Psychoanalysis* 7(2) [on-line]. Available: http://www.ipa.org.uk/nl_1998-7-2.htm.

Wahner-Roedler, D. L., P. Knuth, and R. H. Juchems. 1997. The German health care system. *Mayo Clinic Proceeding* 72: 1061-68.

Waln, Nora. 1967. *The approaching storm: One woman's story of Germany, 1934-1938*. New York: Little, Brown.

Wangh, Martin. 1991. The working through of the Nazi experience in the German psychoanalytic community: An attempt of a survey from a close distance, general and personal considerations. Paper presented at Frankfurt University, November 8.

———. 1996. The working through of the Nazi experience in the German psychoanalytic community. In *Psychoanalysis at the political border: Essays in honor of Rafael Moses*, ed. L. Rangell and Rena Moses-Hvushovski, 283-302. Madison, Wis.: International Universities.

Weinberg, Gerhard L. 1994. *A world at arms: A global history of World War II*. Cambridge: Cambridge University Press.

———. 1995. *Germany, Hitler, and World War II: Essays in modern German and world history*. Cambridge: Cambridge University Press.

Wolfenstein, E. Victor. 1993. *Psychoanalytic marxism: Groundwork*. New York: Guilford.

Wolin, Richard. 1995. Hannah and the magician. [Review of *Hannah Arendt/Martin Heidegger* by Elzbieta Ettinger]. *The New Republic,* October 9, 1995, 27-37.

Wortis, Joseph. 1954. *Fragments of an analysis of Freud.* New York: Simon and Schuster.

Wyatt, Frederick, and Hans Lukas Teuber. 1944. German psychology under the Nazi system: 1933-1940. *Psychological Review* 5: 229-47.

Zillmer, Eric A., Molly Harrower, Barry A. Ritzler, and Robert P. Archer. 1995. *The quest for the Nazi personality: A psychological investigation of Nazi war criminals.* Hillsdale, N.J.: Lawrence Erlbaum Associates.

INDEX